10641992

THE GARAGE SALE MILLIONAIRE

*Make Money in a Down Economy
with Hidden Finds from
Estate Auctions to Garage Sales
and Everything In-Between*

by
Aaron LaPedis
America's #1 Collector

With
Jeffrey D. Kern

A BEAUTIFUL MEDIA PUBLICATION
www.beautimedia.com

The information provided in this book should be used only as a guide. The detailed information and practices described in this book are in no way intended to guarantee results. Results are greatly affected by circumstances which are out of the control of the authors and publisher. Neither the authors nor the publisher assume any responsibility for losses which might be incurred as a result of consulting this book. A note of caution…always use several resources for gathering your information.

Foreword

With this book, Aaron LaPedis has proven true that the old adage, "One man's junk is another man's treasure".

As the author of a #1 best selling book and international business consultant and cash flow expert, Aaron teaches us all about the main ways that exist, for generating income from collectibles.

I have always taught that in the world of business marketing is one of the most fundamental things you must become proficient at and that still holds true, but now I am very clear in making the point that there is another way to make millions! It's simply known as "hunting"…hunting for "great deals" or "hidden treasures" and even unknown fortunes that are out there waiting in someone's garage or storage facility just waiting to be discovered by YOU!

How can you find them? Where are they? What do they look like? How can you plug into this cash generating business? What do you need to do to locate these "buried" treasures…valuable finds that can make you tens, even hundreds of thousands of dollars?

The answers are contained here in this easy, informative, fun to read book. Aaron shows you how to locate, identify and acquire treasures that can make you huge profits! He also tells you what NOT to buy so you don't waste your money on common "junk". This unique book is a fabulous resource and will assist you in your quest to make a lot of money!

Read it NOW and become a real life hunter of treasure!

Jack M. Zufelt

Mr. Zufelt is the author, of a #1 best-selling book, The DNA of Success. He is also known as the "Mentor To Millions", and a highly skilled and sought after International Business Consultant, Keynote Speaker, Trainer and Cash Flow expert.

Dedications

Aaron LaPedis

I would like to dedicate this book to my son, Logan, who inspires me every time I look at him, my wife Sandee who gives me the support I have needed to write this book, and to my Dad who recently passed away. Dad, you are a person who will never be forgotten and will always be dearly missed.

To my mom, your guidance, love, and support through the years has made me the success I am today.

Jeffrey D. Kern

I would like to dedicate this book to my beautiful wife, Mary. I could not have completed this project without her love, guidance, and support. I am truly blessed to have such a loving, caring, and supportive person in my life!

I would also like to thank my father, Lambert Kern, Jr., who helped with the editing this book. A special thanks also goes to my mother, Barbara Kern. My parent's support throughout this project has been fantastic. Thank you for being such loving and caring parents.

You are very wonderful and special people to me and I love you all very much.

Author Acknowledgements

Aaron LaPedis

I would also like to give special thanks to Cindy Dunston Quirk, Jeffrey Zimmerman, Donna Sanford, Rich Kylberg, Jack Zufelt, Eron Johnson, Don and Judy Oglevie, Katherine Phelps, Paul Suter, Dan Gibson, Masten Hamlin, Rod Reece, Brian Neville, Mark Hewlette Channel 12 "KBDI," Denver and Carolyn MacRossie.

Jeffrey D. Kern

I would like to thank Katherine Phelps from Beautiful Media Publications and Melanie Fischer from Reed Photo. Katherine, your guidance throughout this project has helped me become a better writer. Melanie, you've done a wonderful job in putting this book together and, as a result, have made it look fantastic. The hard work, patience, dedication, and professionalism you've both shown has made a tremendous difference. Thank you both very much.

About the Authors

Aaron LaPedis

Long considered one of the world's great collectors and treasure hunters, a successful television personality, fine art and memorabilia gallery owner and an expert for the FBI, author Aaron LaPedis, unlocks some of the highly guarded secrets of consistently successful and profitable treasure hunters. Aaron has been interviewed by network television, radio and cable TV. He has also been featured in numerous magazines and newspapers.

Aaron LaPedis is the host of Public Broadcasting System's (PBS) highly rated show in Denver, Colorado called "Collect This!" For the past four years the show has reached 1.5 million national viewers monthly as well as 100,000 viewers per weekend within the state of Colorado. Besides being seen in many Colorado television markets, "Collect This!" can also be seen in several Florida markets. Earlier episodes of "Collect This!" entitled "Collectibles with Aaron" and "The Collectibles Show" first began airing in May of 2001 on PBS. Aaron successfully taped more than fifty half-hour segments focusing on the diverse world of collectors and collecting. Some of the varied topics covered included coins, wine, art, animation and sports. His expertise on these subjects has made him an extremely popular and highly sought-after public speaker. Aaron's thoroughly personable and informative style entertains while educating his audiences in the many ways of becoming better collectors and treasure hunters.

LaPedis's expert credentials do not end with hosting his own TV show. The Discovery Channel has featured a half-hour program based upon on his numerous and detailed collections while Entrepreneur Magazine wrote an article based on his success as a master collector and successful entrepreneur. Aaron has also guest-hosted a collectibles show on Dish Network, written articles for The Denver Post, Denver Magazine and The Denver Business Journal. He has also hosted a weekly four minute segment on the local Denver ABC affiliate, KMGH, called "The Collectibles Guy."

Aaron LaPedis is the owner of Fascination St. Fine Art Gallery in Denver, Colorado.

My Pledge to You...

I want you to enjoy this book. So, if you ever have a collection of different items you need help with, feel free to contact me. Whether it's buying or selling, let me know and I will try to assist you. If you need a good reference for companies to insure, appraise, or even auction for you, I'm more than happy to help.

Please email me at thegaragesalemillionaire@gmail.com or visit my website at www.thegaragesalemillionaire.com. I look forward to hearing from you!

Jeffrey D. Kern

Co-author Jeffrey D. Kern has more than thirty years of serious treasure hunting experience to his credit. Like many children who begin the hunt for collectible treasures early in life, Jeffrey discovered his passion for treasure hunting by collecting coins. His love for collecting at an early age helped him develop and hone his interests and abilities in the hobby of collecting, allowing him to grow into the successful collector he is today. Jeffrey actively seeks out and collects movie and television memorabilia, autographed books, coins, art, antiques, action figures, toys, magazines, finisher medals from athletic events, as well as other sports collectibles and memorabilia.

Jeffrey has worked professionally as a writer since 2000, and has held the position of Associate Editor for Widescreen Review Magazine, a national monthly home theater magazine. Throughout his professional writing career, Jeffrey has amassed a portfolio consisting of more than 500 writing clips. In addition to co-authoring *The Garage Sale Millionaire*, Mr. Kern has written on many different subjects including consumer electronics, home theater, computers, travel, and various human interest topics.

When he isn't writing or collecting, Jeffrey is an Ironman Triathlete.

Table of Contents

CHAPTER

1

Becoming a Garage Sale Millionaire

About the Book and the Official

Start of Your Treasure Hunting Journey!

To Thos A Edison Science Club
Sunbury Pa   Thos A Edison.

An autographed photo by Thomas Edison that was given to my grandfather and then given to me. This was my very first collectible and I still treasure it.

I am a *"Garage Sale Millionaire!"*

That has a rather nice "ring" to it, wouldn't you say? Actually, there are many *Garage Sale Millionaires* out in the marketplace. You'll find them at garage sales, in second hand stores and attending auctions. As you read these very words many collectors and treasure hunters just like you are looking for and finding the next "amazing deal" that will make them a tidy profit. You too, can become a successful *"Garage Sale Millionaire."* All it takes is a little effort, along with some collecting know-how and in no time at all you'll be on your way. It really isn't as difficult as you might think. With this book you will have me to show you the ways to success as a savvy collector.

So what exactly is a "Garage Sale Millionaire?" A *Garage Sale Millionaire* is any individual who searches out those hard-to-find items, hidden gems, or "buried treasures" as I would like to call them and turns those found items into a profit. From my experience, not only do *Garage Sale Millionaires* make money reselling a few random items, they usually make very substantial residual profits over time.

Before I even begin to discuss the many ways you can become a successful *Garage Sale Millionaire*, one of the most essential elements on your new journey is the ability to have FUN. What's the point of doing something if you're not totally enjoying yourself?

In *The Garage Sale Millionaire*, I have taken all the mystery and guesswork out of this process as I show you how to turn "everyday items" into cold hard cash. Not only will you make some serious money but, you'll reap a great deal of satisfaction from the process of doing so!

Leave the boring and mundane at your 9-to-5 job (or jobs) and let's spend some quality time together as I teach you the ins-and-outs of collecting, the know-how on where to find the best collectibles to sell for the most profits and all the vital information you need to know, so that you too, can strike it rich by buying and selling collectibles to become a seasoned *Garage Sale Millionaire*. With the assistance of my co-author, Jeffrey Kern, you'll gain valuable insider knowledge based on our 60+ years of combined treasure hunting experience.

By the time you've finished reading *The Garage Sale Millionaire*, you'll have the confidence, be well-equipped in this money-making journey and will know exactly where to look for those hidden gems and buried treasures as you strike out on your own to claim your treasure hunting fortune.

A Treasure Hunter? Is That Really What I Am?

The answer to that question is a definite "Yes." One of the key characteristics of any successful *Garage Sale Millionaire* is that you must begin to consider yourself an actual treasure hunter. It takes a treasure hunter's stealth mentality, along with a healthy dose of curiosity to actively seek out and find that one hidden, never-thought-to-ever-be-seen-again item that you will be able to turn around and resell (or "flip") for much more than you paid for it.

What is this Book all About?

Within the pages of *The Garage Sale Millionaire*, collectable-savvy experts will help you navigate the many times friendly, yet sometimes quite unfriendly terrain, of treasure hunting. I will personally lead you in the right direction while guiding you along the best avenues to travel, so that you too, can turn the pursuit of finding oftentimes overlooked items into money in your pocket. Throughout the pages of *The Garage Sale Millionaire* you will gain specific knowledge and tremendous insight which can only be gleaned from seasoned collectors like me, who are willing to share decades of collecting experience.

Remember, even in a bad, down, or downright awful economy, there are definite riches to be made!

The Garage Sale Millionaire is geared specifically towards giving you the ability to gain an advantageous jump on the competition by learning how to recognize and bargain for rare, hidden items which are actually authentic, treasured finds. Although the collectibles market is highly competitive, you'll be carefully guided in your efforts to turn your newfound items into very healthy profits. I'll give you that "ultimate edge" and the advantage of the expertise and experience that the most successful treasure hunters use to make their money. Never before in the highly diverse world of collecting has one book contained so many valuable topics along with an abundance of insider secrets, tips and tricks for successful treasure hunting. This book is meant to be used as an informative, educational tool, but also as a guide that will direct you in your quest for an optimal treasure hunting and collecting experience.

Additionally, it is my goal to make this book the official "go-to-guide" and the ultimate "whenever you need it" reference that you will use for many years to come. The information presented in this book is timeless and it will never become outdated. How can that be? *The Garage Sale Millionaire* is based upon solid treasure hunting principles acquired from many decades of proven experience.

I offer the proverbial "no stone unturned" approach for you to use in your quest, giving you as much information as possible as you travel down on your personal path to becoming a seasoned treasure hunter, as well as guiding you directly to the unique areas you should seek out when searching for those hidden treasures. Throughout the years, I've experienced my own share of battles associated with getting those special pieces I just had to have. Like yourselves, I've struggled in the "trenches" common to most treasure hunters and I want to share that wealth of knowledge I've acquired with you now.

Million $ Tip

While you can't expect to become an expert overnight, you can begin becoming more knowledgeable over time by reading this book. As you gain more experience, you will become one of the more knowledgeable treasure hunters around!

Your *Garage Sale Millionaire* Journey Begins Now!

Even in difficult times, finding consistent monetary success a treasure hunter is an attainable reality. So, how do you get from

---

Point A to Point B? Point A being where you are now, to Point B, reaching a point where you're successful at generating income from your treasure hunting exploits.

Although I was never particularly talented at playing sports, I discovered at an early age how to become exceptional at collecting different items from my favorite athletes. As a kid, I loved reading comic books and in fact, I still read them today. Due to my great love for these collectibles, I have added some valuable comic books to my personal collections. Co-author Jeffrey was also really big into collecting coins as a kid and therefore he has amassed an excellent coin collection. He has had a lifelong love affair with television and the movies and as a result, has a very detailed collection of television and movie memorabilia.

> ### Million $ Tip
> After figuring out what type of collectable you want to specialize in, go to the bookstore and start reading up on that particular item or set of items. Most collectible categories have numerous books or magazine articles written about them. Even if the collectible seems rare or of very little interest, there's probably a book written on that topic.

What to collect? Start with something you really like and have a strong interest in. This will ensure that the treasure hunting process will be much more fulfilling, as well as more profitable for you. Both authors of *The Garage Sale Millionaire* found specific areas of interest to focus on…certain collectibles we really liked a great deal when we were young. This helped set us off on the path to becoming lifelong collectors.

The Necessities

Before you begin the treasure hunt, you'll need a definite plan of action to maximize the profits you're attempting to make. If you're merely collecting some items for fun, a serious plan is not important. When adding the goal of making money to the equation, a definite action plan is necessary.

There are some basic needs and necessities to consider before you can seriously begin your quest to become a *Garage Sale Millionaire*. By having all the proper tools at your immediate disposal, you can expedite the process and decrease the amount of time spent on pursuing your success. Now, let's discuss those basics and exactly what weapons you'll need to include in your moneymaking *Garage Sale Millionaire* arsenal:

Computer

An essential component for *Garage Sale Millionaire* success is having your own computer. You really need to have a good desktop computer or mobile "laptop" computer to excel in this endeavor. Accessing a computer at a library, Community Recreation Center, *Apple Store*, or some other public location really isn't a viable option.

As a *Garage Sale Millionaire*, you're going to be conducting very personal business

Million $ Tip

After setting up your email account(s), access the Internet and search out local auction listings, then subscribe to as many Auction Email Lists as possible in your area. For starters, enter "How to find local auction lists" into Google for a listing of auction websites. By taking advantage of various Internet Search Engines, you can find, sign up and be constantly notified about many auctions in your area. Another great place to find auctions, searchable by zip code and distance, is at **AuctionZip** *(www.auctionzip.com)*.

with bank accounts, credit cards and other electronic forms of commerce. Having your own computer is a necessity for keeping private matters private, especially since you'll be dealing with money. By owning your own computer, you will have complete freedom and total privacy to access the Internet, check emails and electronic correspondence and do business online where much of the treasure hunting business is conducted.

Email

Email accounts are extremely easy to establish and having your own personal email account for your *Garage Sale Millionaire* activities is another necessity. Email accounts can be acquired free of charge through your Internet Service Provider (ISP). *Windows Live, Windows Live Hotmail, GMail, Yahoo! Mail* and *Microsoft Office Outlook* are all very good email tools for PC users. *Mail* is a great email application for those individuals using *Apple Computers*. If you plan on making this endeavor a serious business venture, you may want to consider having two email accounts. That way you can better separate your business affairs from your personal affairs.

Million $ Tip

If you can't afford to pay for an antivirus and firewall program, there are some wonderful free online alternatives. Two excellent free programs to use are **AVG** *(free.avg.com)* and **Ad-Aware** *(www.lavasoft.com)*. Because I am talking about your hard-earned money, you definitely need to protect yourself online with antivirus and firewall programs.

Million $ Tip

To date, the safest computer you can buy is an Apple Computer. Rarely (if ever), have viruses been created for the Apple platform. Almost every virus that has been unleashed onto the Internet to date has been targeted at computers running on the Microsoft Operating System.

Software Packages

Having effective antivirus and firewall protection programs along with a solid financial accounting software program is another necessity for any prospective *Garage Sale*

Millionaire. Treasure hunters in the "wild" need to be protected and organized for their adventures and expeditions. Every treasure hunter requires protection from all sorts of nasty computer viruses like worms and Trojan horses, not to mention spyware, phishing scams and professional hackers who prey on innocent e-commerce buyers and sellers, hoping to steal their hard-earned cash. These thieves can only take a huge chunk out of your bottom line if you let them.

When it comes to the financial end of things, you'll need a good *Accounting Software Program* such as *Peachtree by Sage Accounting* (**www.peachtree.com**), *Quicken* (**http://quicken.intuit.com**), or *Intuit Quickbooks* (**http://quickbooks. intuit.com**). These programs will help you keep track of what you're buying, selling and any other expenses, large or small that you might incur as a result of your treasure hunting business. You need to document everything for legal and tax purposes and also so you can more effectively monitor your bottom line. Business software programs these days are quite intuitive for those of you who are not yet already accustomed to working with them.

To keep your personal identity and all your financial activities safe, you'll also need to get efficient *Antivirus and Firewall Programs* installed on your computer. Programs such as *Norton AntiVirus from Symantec* (**www.symantec.com**), *Kaspersky Lab* (**www.kaspersky.com**) and *McAfee AntiVirus* (**www.mcafee.com**) have solid reputations, excellent track records and are very effective tools in keeping you and your private information safe while you're online.

Digital Camera

You'll also need a good digital camera to take some decent pictures of your valuable finds. On websites such as *Craigslist* and *eBay,* displaying really good pictures of the items you want to sell is an essential part of helping to make great sales. A picture of an item which does not look good online or one which makes your products look cheap or inferior due to poor picture quality will be a deal breaker.

Reliable digital cameras with excellent image quality can be purchased for surprisingly low prices starting as low as $50. Your digital camera doesn't need to be an expensive professional grade model to get the job done. All you really need to make pictures of your items that look fantastic online is a solid digital camera which takes a decent, good-looking picture 300 pixels and higher. Some good choices are *Nikon* and *Sony.* Check with *Wal-Mart* (**www.walmart.com**), *Best Buy* (**www.bestbuy.com**), or *BrandsMart USA* (**www.brandsmartusa.com**) for some affordable options. If the item you're trying to sell is accompanied with pictures that look appealing to potential customers, your chances to sell that item greatly increases.

Newspapers

Local newspapers and their "Classified" sections offer a fantastic way for you to remain consistently informed about local flea markets, estate auctions, storage unit auctions, garage sales, as well as anything going on in your area that might be beneficial to your treasure hunting activities. If someone is trying to sell something in your area, the sale will usually be listed in your local newspaper. You need to subscribe all the local newspapers in your area and to newspapers from nearby major metropolitan areas. Also pick all the local "freebie" publications in your area that you'll find in racks at various locations. This is the best way to monitor what's being sold and what's going on close to where you live on a day-to-day basis

Although I've covered the basics of what is needed as you begin your journey towards becoming a successful *Garage Sale Millionaire,* there are some other important implements which will benefit you greatly as well. The following tools are also recommended to give you the best advantage possible to make a profit from the buying and selling of items:

eBay, PayPal and Craigslist
The Go-To Websites for Buying and Selling Items

eBay and PayPal

If you don't already know what *eBay* and *PayPal* are, you are about to be introduced to the most innovative and effective "1-2 combinations" on the Internet when it comes to making money from buying and selling your items and collectables. Getting registered with these two websites is an absolute necessity for any serious *Garage Sale Millionaire*. What follows are some need-to-know "basics" about eBay and PayPal. *In Chapter 6, I will discuss eBay and PayPal in much greater detail.*

ebay *(www.ebay.com)* is the #1 website to make money from your treasure hunting finds on the Internet. It is as close as you can get to a full-fledged one-stop buying and selling destination. eBay has been tagged by many as "The Biggest Garage Sale of Them All," and I really can't argue with that observation. With billions of dollars in sales every year and millions of registered users, eBay is probably the most highly recognized, most popular and most effective website that you can use in turning a profit.

When considering the best way to conduct your business on eBay, you need look no further than PayPal. *PayPal* (**www.paypal.com**) is the official electronic payment website and preferred payment method for all of eBay user's financial transactions. The signup process for both websites takes approximately twenty minutes and is free of charge.

Because you're going to be using eBay and PayPal for buying and selling items, you will need to register a credit card along with your account. Users who just want to buy items and not sell anything, only need to provide payment information when they have won an auction.

When selling items on eBay, it's very important to understand exactly what the fees are so you can price items accordingly. This allows you to gain the highest profit margin possible from any sale. On eBay, the two basic fees include an initial listing fee and a percentage paid to the website from every sale that takes place. The buyer does not pay any fees, but as a seller you can adjust the asking price to make up for any charges you may incur. When doing business with PayPal, understand that PayPal takes approximately 1.99% to 2.9 % and 30¢ of the sale price as their fee for processing each transaction. PayPal has a high level of security and protection for of all its buyers and sellers and the fees charged by the website help keep activities safe and secure. Even though the fees associated with using eBay and PayPal cost a little; the positives (profits) certainly far outweigh the negatives (nominal costs).

Craigslist

Craigslist (**www.craigslist.org**) is another online marketplace where you can buy and sell goods from toys and coins to computers, cars and art. On Craigslist, there are no registration fees or selling fees so it is a completely free website to use. Because of the tremendous profit potential Craigslist offers, this website needs to be on your short list of important places for making money. Craigslist is also a really great website full of fantastic bargains. When you're buying and selling on Craigslist, you must always be aware of the possibility of potential scams that fraudulent users enact to try and separate you from your money. Always make sure you receive certified funds, use PayPal, or accept cash for anything you sell. Always remember to get a receipt in writing.

Million $ Tip

When you take out insurance on whatever you may be shipping and something unfortunate happens to it, the USPS (United States Postal Service) has never, in my experience, paid off on any of my claims. This is sad but true.

Craigslist is in all 50 states and in over 60 countries. So, you can list your items for sale or buy items locally, nationally or internationally. I will cover Craigslist in more detail in Chapter 5.

Separate Shipping Address and Shipping Account

One of the benefits of having a *separate shipping address* for conducting your treasure hunting business is that you can more effectively separate your collectible dealings, from those of your personal dealings, from your home. Although getting a separate shipping address is optional and may cost you a nominal fee, it might be the best way to do business.

A separate shipping address involves renting a mailbox at an established business such as *The UPS Store* (www.theupsstore.com). You will also have a physical location away from your home to use for shipping your items to customers and also a place that receives and signs for all your packages. One of the best perks that come with owning a separate mailing address is that you don't have to be present to receive your packages. The store's staff will sign for any shipment and store it securely for you until you come to pick it up. There are a couple of negatives involved with having this type of arrangement. There is a semi-annual or annual rental fee for the mailbox and you have to travel back and forth to pick up items you've purchased or ship items you've sold.

> ### Million $ Tip
> Do all your own packing. Never pay people to pack items for you, as this unnecessary expense will take a big bite out of your profits.

> ### Million $ Tip
> Most vendors do not take American Express Credit Cards due to the additional fees charged to process each sale.

Another option to consider is that all of your shipping could be done directly from your home to save money on overhead. If you decide on this option, you'll need to understand that major carriers such as FedEx and UPS normally require physical signatures upon delivery for anything of value. Many times shipping companies will not deliver items if someone is not on hand to provide a signature. You will need to be present at your home every time a shipment arrives. This could become an issue for those individuals who have full-time jobs outside of their homes.

The *United States Post Office (USPS)* (www.usps.com), *Federal Express (FedEx)* (www.fedex.com) and *United Parcel Service (UPS)* (www.ups.com) are three of the best companies to consider when securing a *shipping account*. Signing up for a shipping account is free of charge and it will help you better manage and keep your records organized. All the information you'll need to get a shipping account can be found on the company websites or at any location where they conduct business.

The USPS is very reliable and is usually your most economical option. The best shipping company to choose for high dollar items is UPS. FedEx may be a very good company, but the insurance limit on collectibles, especially art, is only $1,000.

Cash

Last, but not least we come to the subject of money…cold, hard, cash. Any new venture needs some start up capital and the business of buying and selling collectibles is no different. The more cash you have access to means the more collectibles you can afford to buy. The math is quite simple…more items to sell equals more profit.

If you don't have much upfront cash set aside for getting started; no problem. There are several other ways to get some start up capital together for beginning your new venture. One option is using some of your personal savings and another is to look around your home to see if you have anything appropriate that you can easily afford to part with. Be on the lookout for items that you're not using any more such as old stereo equipment, unwanted gold or silver jewelry, baby items, used books and videos, computers, coins and furniture. All of these items can be sold to generate some immediate start up capital. Whatever you have on hand and don't need can be sold or auctioned off to help increase your bank roll.

Your journey to Garage Sale Millionaire Success is much closer than you think

In this chapter, I've introduced you to some of the basic *Garage Sale Millionaire* concepts and philosophies. As we take this journey together throughout this book, I will delve much more deeply into what is needed to become a very successful *Garage Sale Millionaire*. The necessary tools for consistent *Garage Sale Millionaire* success are out there for the taking.

The best is yet to come, so let's get to it!

CHAPTER

2

To Buy or Not to Buy

The First Big Question Answered

Civil War diary from a soldier, who was killed in battle.

There's an endless array of items to search for when you're ready to set out on your "treasure hunt". For everything that's either manufactured or found in nature, there's usually someone who has a desire to collect that particular item. Who knows what will intrigue someone to the point where they say, "I just have to have that!" On the surface what may seem like an extremely odd thing to collect for some, there is indeed someone else who is feverishly trying to collect that very item.

Of course, there are plenty of obstacles that could get in your way and possibly derail your express journey to *Garage Sale Millionaire* nirvana. For every item deemed highly collectible, there is another item which is not even close. With literally thousands collectibles available today, how does someone begin to target an item exactly? What to buy and sell? What not to buy and sell? Which collectibles will make a larger profit for you? More succinctly, how do you find what is valuable and, in turn what's not.

To give you a jump on your treasure hunting competition, I've compiled the following list of things which continue to increase in value over the years and will most likely make you the sizable profits you're seeking upon resale (What to Buy). I have also included those items which have no substantial monetary resale value whatsoever and those items you should stay away from (What Not to Buy).

As you can see, there are many areas from which to collect and many areas that

WHAT TO BUY
Animation Production Cels
Antiques
Barbie Dolls
Baseball Cards
Beatles Memorabilia
Books *(Antique or First Edition)*
Civil War Memorabilia
Coins
Comics *(Pre-1970)*
Depression Glass
Disney Collectibles
Fine Art
Firearms *(Antique)*
Maps (Pre-1700)
Military Memorabilia
(Pre-World War II)
Motorcycles *(Pre-1960, Old Harley-Davidsons, Original Indians and Military)*
Muscle Cars *(Pre-1971)*
Posters *(Pre-1977, Movie and Music)*
Presidential Memorabilia

Sports Memorabilia
(Certified Game Used)
Stamps *(Pre-1920, Not Cancelled)*
Toy Trains
Toys *(Antique or Tin)*
Toys *(Pre-1970)*
Vinyl Records *(Pre-1977)*
War Medals *(Pre-1940)*

WHAT NOT TO BUY

Beanie Babies
Bibles *(Family)*
Comics and Comic Books
(Post-1970)
Furs *(Old)*
Magazines *(Old)*
Movie Memorabilia *(Signed)*
Newspapers *(Old)*
Pokémon Cards
Rugs *(Antique)*
Silverware *(Antique)*
Sports Memorabilia *(Signed)*
Stamps *(Foreign)*
Stamps *(Post-1920)*

trust me, you should avoid. As you read through this chapter, I will highlight many of the items found on the list so you can get a leg up on your competition in maximizing the profits from your treasure hunting adventures.

What to Buy

I'll let you in on a little secret of mine, so you don't get "off track" or overly excited when you find something you believe to be of value. Don't be fooled if an item is old or looks "expensive." Just because an item is old, doesn't mean it necessarily has any real value. An item which looks "expensive" very well could be a lesser-valued reproduction or replica.

Many people see something old and they don't understand that there's a lot more to be considered than age in making an item valuable. Of course, sometimes older items are indeed worth money, but age is not the primary determining factor in assessing a collectible's level of value. For example, a newspaper from July, 1969, when American astronauts first landed on the moon, has no real value. A 200-year old family bible, although having an emotional value attached to it, also has no market value. By comparison, however, an empty liquor or "spirits," bottle which is 150 years old, could actually be worth $30,000.

Animation Production Cels

An original "animation production cel" is a transparent sheet on which objects are drawn to create an animated cartoon. Animation production cels are currently hand-painted from behind onto celluloid acetate. In the early years of animation; these cels were made out of a thin plastic or nitrate, with paint on the back or front of a cel. Each cel represents one frame of a character's movement on film. The animation production cels that have higher collectible resale value are from the 1930s to the 1960s. One of the main characteristics to observe in determining an animation production cel's value is to verify whether or not the paint is "flaking off." A pristine cel will be intact exhibiting no signs of degradation to the paint. Additionally, animation production cels can be restored with little value lost. The other main determinant in verifying if an animation production cel is worth anything is to check and see which cartoon character was painted on the cel. Animation production cels worth the most money upon resale will feature Mickey Mouse, Donald Duck, Bugs Bunny, or any other main or very famous cartoon character painted on the cel. Secondary characters such as Minnie Mouse, Daisy Duck, and Elmer Fudd will not fetch as much money upon resale as their main character counterparts. Additionally, do not let "mini-framed" prints from **Disney** *(www.disney.com)* or **Warner Bros.** *(www.warnerbros.com)* confuse you into believing that they are "authentic" animation production cels.

A fantastic resource on learning more about cels and their value is "Tomart's Value Guide to Disney Animation Art: An Easy-To-Use Compilation of over 40 Animation Art Auctions Organized by Film, Character, and Art Type" by Thomas E. Tumbusch and Bob Welbaum. This book organizes all Disney animation art sold at major auctions since 1993 by film, character, and type of art.

Antiques

Antiques are a huge business. How huge? When I "Googled" the terms "Antique Stores + Denver, Colorado" approximately 883,000 Google search results returned. The same search for "Antique Stores +" "Chicago, Illinois," "New York City," and "Los Angeles, California" resulted in 800,000; 1,200,000; and, 1,290,000 search results respectively.

When looking at any type of antique furniture, be it desks, chairs, dressers, or sofas, it is extremely important to verify exactly how that item was put together. If the item is a desk or a dresser, check the drawers. Do the drawers match the desk or a dresser, or are they additions made well after the original manufacture of that item? Also, make it a point to check the underneath and underside portions of furniture. This will tell you a great deal about the quality of the item and if it is an authentic antique, a restoration, or a newly manufactured replica. I cover all of this and more, regarding how you can tell the difference between authentic antiques, fakes, replicas, and restorations in much greater detail in Chapter 4.

> ### Million $ Tip
> Remember, just because one item is older than another like item, does not mean that there is more value associated with that older item.

Barbie Dolls

The Barbie doll was created in 1959 by inventor Ruth Handler. Since the toy's debut at the American International Toy Fair in New York City, New York in 1959, the Barbie doll has been a collectible phenomenon with tremendous staying power. Barbie doll conventions are held in every major state in the United States, but not in any one state more than once every twenty years.

Barbie dolls made prior to 1980 have the most collectible resale value of any Barbie doll. As it is with pretty much every known collectible, the main component of value in a Barbie doll is determined by its condition. Value is enhanced even more if the original packaging is included with the doll and she has not been played with very much. The most valuable among all the Barbies are the pre-1980 dolls which are still in their original packaging and have never been opened. When collecting Barbie dolls, especially, in the older pre-1980 dolls, you will want to make sure that the doll comes with all its accessories and the original box is in good condition. The box does not eliminate the value of the piece, but it plays a huge role in retaining value as well as increasing value.

There are several good price guides available to the *Garage Sale Millionaire* looking to turn a profit buying and selling "Barbies." Over the years, I have found eBay, Craigslist, and sometimes, garage sales, are all great places for looking and finding those Barbie dolls which could be bought and sold for excellent profits.

Bonus trivia: Ken, from "Barbie and Ken" fame, was created in 1961 and was named after Ruth Handler's son.

Baseball Cards

Even though baseball cards are a highly sought-after collectible item, unfortunately, many of these collectibles have little or no real value. What will increase the value for any baseball card is the condition of the card, a card's age, and the historical significance of the player featured on the baseball card. If the baseball card is a "rookie" card of a great player, that baseball card will be worth more money. Baseball cards which have increased in value over the past few years either have a player's signature included on the card, or have a piece of the player's jersey in the card. A great way to enhance and increase a card's value would be to have the baseball card professionally graded. A professional grade on a baseball card could add up to 40% to its value, and the fee for such a service costs approximately $15 to $20 per card. There are several certified companies that professionally grade cards. I talk in great detail about grading baseball and trading cards in Chapter 7.

Million $ Tip

Unfortunately, for some reason many items from The Beatles were never taken care of properly over the years. So, if you do find an authentic item from The Beatles in great shape, you will more than likely obtain very good money for the item.

Million $ Tip

Many collectibles from the 1950s through the 1970s have huge collectable value. If you have an item with its original packaging and it is in good condition, at the very least, then you will have a better than average chance to make more money off of that item.

Beatles Memorabilia

Beatles memorabilia has been a popular item to collect since the early 1960s and is a fantastic collectible area in which to do business for excellent profits! As each year passes, finding authentic Beatles items from the 1960s and 1970s is becoming increasingly difficult. Some Beatles items to look for are old concert tickets, production cels from the Beatles cartoon show Yellow Submarine, posters, figurines, lunch boxes and vinyl records. To ensure the highest value upon resale, make sure concert tickets are not ripped or torn. One of the most collectible vinyl records from The Beatles catalog includes the "Butcher Block" album cover with its accompanying vinyl record. Even small posters that promoted many of The Beatles' concerts will net you some big money. With regard to tickets and posters, always be wary and keep an eye out for fakes and replicas. You can easily find Beatles memorabilia on eBay, Craigslist, estate auctions and from time to time, at garage sales.

Books (Antique or First Edition)

Antique books and "First Edition" books are what you should look for in this collectible category to maximize your profits. **Dictionary.com** *(www.dictionary.com)*, defines the word "Antique" as "Any work of art, piece of furniture, decorative object, or the like, created or produced in a former period, or, according to U.S. customs laws, 100 years before date of purchase." A "First Edition" book refers to the first commercial publication of a work.

Why are first editions of a book so important? First of all, there may only be that one edition which was ever published. Secondly, there are normally many changes made to a book between the first and second editions. At times, corrections are made which many authors do not acknowledge in subsequent editions. Most importantly, the author may have signed the first edition when promoting the book. So, if you are able to find a first edition that has been signed, this is a huge coup. Buy it and revel in your good fortune! How valuable are signed first editions? On October 11, 2002, **Christie's** *(www.christies.com)* auctioned off first editions of the three The *Lord of the Rings* books, by J. R. R. Tolkien, which were inscribed by the author to his son, Michael. These three "First Edition" books, *The Fellowship of the Ring* (1954), *The Two Towers* (1954), and *The Return of the King* (1955) sold for $152,500 (Lot 373/Sale 1098).

> ### *Million $ Tip*
> Always buy books in the best condition that you can afford. Actually, this advice could go for any collectible.

Condition also plays a major role in determining the value of antique books. In first edition books published earlier than the 1800s, book covers were made of leather and were hand sewn. The better the sewing remains intact on the leather cover the more valuable that book has become. Many people collect antique books for years, yet still do not understand everything there is to know about this type of collectible. There are numerous reference books written on the topic, so before you jump into collecting antique books, I would strongly recommend that you read a few books on the subject. Always match the reference books you're considering purchasing with several price guides which cover the same material.

Antique books and "First Edition" books can be found at garage sales all the time. Estate sales, estate auctions, and eBay are also great places to find antique books. Luckily for you, most sellers will not know the actual or true value of the antique books they are selling. Finding an antique book is actually like finding a diamond in the rough. This is a collectible you could easily find on any given day that could easily be worth hundreds if not many thousands of dollars.

Civil War Memorabilia

I love the subject of history and I especially love historical memorabilia. Historical memorabilia does not get any better than Civil War memorabilia. There are literally hundreds and thousands of items to collect from the American Civil War. If you ever visit Gettysburg, Pennsylvania you would be amazed at how much Civil War memorabilia is on display and for sale. From this particular conflict you can collect presidential memorabilia, signed military memorabilia from the likes of Robert E. Lee, Ulysses S. Grant, George Pickett, Joshua Chamberlain, James Longstreet, and autographs from numerous well-known and not so well-known soldiers. There is also an abundance of Union and Confederate coins, currency, as well as flags, swords, canteens, knapsacks, bottles, pottery, photographs, rifles, guns, artillery, belt buckles, clothes, plates, and drums.

One of my favorite items to collect from the Civil War has been diaries. From an historical perspective, diaries are very important because each one includes the personal accounts, thoughts, and actions of that diary's owner. The diary could be from a Private, General, Sergeant, Doctor, or Nurse. If this person played a prominent role during the Civil War, the diary has increased value, as well as the added advantage of containing so much human history within its pages. These diaries will not be cheap, that is, if you can find them. Collectors are beginning to realize how highly valuable these diaries really are. Therefore, these types of items become more scarce every day. A fantastic source for determining values of Civil War collectibles is "Warman's Civil War Collectibles: Identification and Price Guide" by John F. Graf.

Nearly any item from the Civil War era is highly sought after and very collectible. Most people truly don't know what they have when they put these items up for sale. Look for these historical treasures to be found at estate sales and on eBay and Craigslist.

Coins

Coins are the number one collectible in the United States today. Collectors are always lookout for great coin finds. Condition is the most important thing to consider with this collectible. If a gold or silver coin is in poor condition, then, the coin is only worth the gold or silver which is contained in the alloys of the coin. Also, stay away from foreign coins unless they're made of gold or silver. Overall, foreign coins will not have much value. I explain in tremendous detail about coins, and their valuation in Chapter 7.

But first, there are some key resources you should seek out to gain a better understanding of coins and coin values. **The Professional Coin Grading Service**, or **PCGS,** offers up invaluable numismatic information on their main company website **(www.pcgs.com)** as well as a fantastic online reference for coins at **PCGS Coin Facts (www.pcgscoinfacts.com)**. The two best written books on coins and coin values, in my opinion are "The Official Blackbook Price Guide to US Coins 2010, 48th Edition" by Thomas E. Hudgeons, Jr. and "The Official Red Book: A Guide Book of United States Coins 2010: The Official Redbook" by R. S. Yeoman and Kenneth Bressett. Both books can be found at your local bookstore or on Amazon.com.

Depression Glass

> ### Million $ Tip
>
> A "black light" is a potent weapon for any Garage Sale Millionaire to use. So, if you are planning on being in this business for a while, a black light is a tool you should invest in sooner rather than later.

Depression glass refers to glass manufactured between the late 1920s and the early 1940s. From **About.com Antiques, hosted by Antiques Guide Pamela Wiggins** (*http://antiques. about.com*), "Manufacturers such as *Federal Glass, MacBeth-Evans Glass Co.,* and *Hocking Glass* brought a little cheer into some very dreary days by manufacturing the product we now know as Depression glass. This mass-produced molded glassware was of relatively poor quality, often exhibiting air bubbles, heavy mold marks and other flaws in the glass; yet, it came in beautiful colors and patterns to suit every taste. The most popular colors with collectors, today, are pink, cobalt blue, and green. It was made in amber, iridescent, opaque white known as Monax, and several other colors. Some of the most popular patterns buyers seek are *Cameo, Mayfair, American Sweetheart, Princess,* and *Royal Lace.* Even the pattern names alluded to better times and a longing for the glamorous lifestyles of the 1920s."

Depression glass is another important collectible for reasons you may not even be aware of. Since the 1960s, this collectible has become much scarcer the further away from the 1930s Great Depression-era times passes. When completing an eBay search on "Depression Glass," there were 33,743 search results found for this collectible with auction prices ranging from $0.99 for a "long bowl milk glass serving dish" to $2,300 for a huge set of pink Depression glass items. Some of those pink Depression glass items contained dogwood patterns and other items included cherry blossom patterns.

According to **Antique Milk Glass** (*http://antique-milk-glass.com/ category/depression-glass),* "One of the most sought after of all types of Depression glass is Jeanette Glass Company's Cherry Blossom pattern in the green color. The pattern is distinguished by having cherry blossoms and cherry clusters worked into the glass, and by having a delicate green shade. Jeanette Glass's Cherry Blossom is also extremely popular in pink."

When looking at Depression glass, always use a black light to determine authenticity. When American Depression glass is held under a black light, the piece will cast a fluorescent glow. Reproductions of Depression glass, however, will not display any fluorescent glowing properties. A "black light" or "UV light" is a lamp which emits small levels of electromagnetic radiation as well as very little visible light. Certain elements within Depression glass absorb the invisible light and then discharge that light. When this discharge occurs, the fluorescent glowing effect will be observed. Black lights can be purchased via the Internet with pricing ranging from as little as $15 up to $125.

Disney Collectibles

In 1928, Walt Disney created his iconic animated masterpiece, Mickey Mouse. From "Mickey's" humble beginnings, **The Walt Disney Company *(http://corporate. disney.go.com)*** has evolved into a multi-billion dollar company with properties ranging from theme parks and resorts located all over the world, live action and animated motion pictures, television shows, stage productions, music industry acts, video games, an amazing amount of consumer products, and a television network called *The Disney Channel*. Because of The Walt Disney Company's amazing popularity throughout the decades, anything produced by "Disney" has usually been worth some very good money. But, since the late 1980s, many items released by Disney have become less than desirable to knowledgeable collectors. Nowadays, just because an item includes the "Disney" name, there is no automatic guarantee that there will be any lasting value associated with that item. I've seen many people who think that because there is a Disney "stamp" on an item that the item is a genuine, properly licensed product from the company. Due to this common misconception, you'll need to be very careful before buying any Disney collectible.

So what are some very collectible items from Disney? Pre-1960 animation products from Disney are worth a great deal of money. Many of the "classics" Disney produced, which introduced characters beloved around the world like Mickey and Minnie Mouse, Donald Duck, Pluto, and Goofy, were introduced before 1960. Other valuable items from Disney are pieces from "The Walt Disney Classic Collection," or "WDCC." The WDCC consists of a set of porcelain sculptures which were first released in the early 1990s. These sculptures have grown in value since they were first released, but, have recently lost some value due to them being sold in mass quantities on eBay. Old Disney watches and toys, with their original boxes, from the 1940s, 1950s, and, the early 1960s also have great value. But, once again, condition is the essential factor.

Disney collectibles can easily be found at many garage sales and estate sales, and can also be found online for sale on eBay and Craigslist. When you are looking for Disney collectibles, always be aware that there are a great number of people selling these items. You need to know what these items are worth before buying anything. To get an idea of what the current values are of Walt Disney Classic Collection items, please visit *www.disneyclassics.net*. Also, there are many great books available on the subject of collecting Disney paraphernalia at your local bookstores and from sources on the Internet.

If you want to buy and sell Disney collectibles for a profit from your *Garage Sale Millionaire* endeavors, always make sure you do your research first.

Fine Art

Because I own a fine art gallery, you could say that fine art is my "true love." I have a passion for dealing in fine art, collectibles, animation cels, sports and entertainment memorabilia, as well as working closely with popular artists who consistently have "meet and greet" events at my gallery. I'm not recommending you use my gallery, *Fascination St. Fine*

Art as your fine art gallery, but if you're looking to buy art, do find a reputable gallery in your area where you can develop a rapport with the owners and feel comfortable as a customer.

I really want you to understand that art is a great investment and actually, a great collectible either to own or to resell for future profits. Most art you will find is framed. Although the frame may look very nice, that frame might be hiding many problems. Framing can hide a multitude of flaws on any piece of art. These include physical damage to the piece of art, an incorrectly trimmed piece of art, and an art piece which has colors fading near the edges. All of these defects will greatly diminish an item's value.

Before you spend money on a piece of art, you will want to separate the actual piece of art from the frame. I will guarantee you for every 30 pieces you buy and take apart; at least one of those items will have flaws that have been hidden by the frame. "Dry mounting" the art to a piece of cardboard, foam board, or foam core will eliminate the value of the piece unless it was an archival mount. An archival mount uses a dry mounting adhesive which consists of an acid-free tissue coated on both sides of the item you're getting mounted with a low temperature, acid-free adhesive. The acid-free tissue contains an alkaline buffering agent added to neutralize environmental degradation. A qualified framer can tell you if your art has been mounted using archival standards.

> ### *Million $ Tip*
> When buying art from a fine art gallery, always give the gallery a chance to earn your business. If you like something and feel the price is too high, make them an offer. It never hurts to try. All fair offers in my gallery are accepted.

When you're looking for art, whether it's on Craigslist or eBay, in an art gallery, or at a local garage sale, it's important to know the difference between "original" art, "limited edition" prints, or, simply, a poster of an original piece of art. Unless you're an expert or until you have the piece removed from the frame, it is not always easy to tell the difference. An "original" is a piece of art which was completed entirely by the artist. Nothing on the canvas or piece's surface was added by anyone other than the artist. A "limited edition" print is any work of art that has a fixed number of copies, or "examples." A limited edition item may or may not be signed. A "poster of an original piece of art" is simply a poster with the image of an art piece and has very little real value.

It is also a good idea to look at the art without any sort of barrier such as glass. Also, ask to see the original "Certificate of Authenticity" or "COA" from the publisher. A "Certificate of Authenticity" is a document a gallery or collectibles store gives to the client, which comes from the publisher who guarantees the item you want to purchase is authentic. Not a certificate originated by the gallery or collectibles store and definitely not a certificate from someone who just sold you the piece (unless they are the artist's publisher), but an original "Certificate of Authenticity" from the artist's publisher. This certificate will tell you everything you need to know about the item. Furthermore, make sure you match the number on the certificate with the number on the piece of art. If the numbers don't match, then ask the fine art gallery for the matching certificate. If they cannot provide one, you may have to rethink your purchase decision and not buy after all. When buying from a non-gallery venue such as a collectibles store, the process is still the same. Always make certain to ask for the original certificate. If the retailer does not have the original certificate (just as you would in dealing with a fine art gallery), either rethink your purchase or have your local gallery advise you on the item in question. A local fine art gallery will usually perform this service for a nominal fee or even for free if they are going to re-frame the item for you. I discuss "Certificates of Authenticity" in Chapter 4 in greater detail.

If your piece of art is damaged and the artist is still alive, there is a chance you can have your local gallery call the publisher directly, so that they can replace the piece of art for a small fee. If you picked up the piece of art for a really cheap price and it's damaged, there is a good chance you can get that piece of art replaced. What actually happens when it's replaced? The publisher takes your damaged piece of art, destroys it, reprints it, and re-numbers it with the exact number you had originally. Then he has the artist re-sign the item. This common practice is completely legitimate, totally acceptable and it's not considered fraud. What you've actually just done is purchase a brand new piece of art for one-tenth of what that same piece would have cost when it was brand new. Of course, this does not work if the item you have is an "original," as an original work of art can never be duplicated. You should always make absolutely sure there is no damage to the original which you are interested in prior to purchasing that item.

When you walk into a gallery and purchase an item, you're paying a premium to buy from that gallery. Although you're paying a premium price to purchase a piece of fine art from a gallery, there are tremendous benefits to be derived from the process of doing so. Perhaps, you only want to buy one piece from them, or you could have them do all of your framing. There's so much you can learn from a fine art gallery owner about the art business. By doing business with a gallery, no matter how small the item you purchase is, a smart owner will do whatever is necessary to keep you as a client. The gallery owner, or the staff, can also help you by answering questions and they can become a valuable resource for you in the future.

Firearms (Antique)

This is an incredible collectible to become familiar with. There is a better than average chance you will not see antique firearms being sold at your local garage sale, but there are numerous antique firearm auctions held across the country throughout the year. For firearm auctions in your area, investigate listings in your local newspaper.

Savvy collectors know when an antique firearm is not in working order its value will decrease slightly, but that particular firearm may still be a very collectible item which could net an excellent profit upon resale. Condition is another factor in determining an antique firearm's market value. Does the firearm have any rust? Is it corroded? If a gun is heavily rusted, noticeably corroded, or if the wood on the gun is seriously marred, this will take an otherwise valuable antique firearm and reduce the value substantially.

Next, it is important to know the buying and selling of firearms fall under the rules of

Bureau of Alcohol, Tobacco, Firearms and Explosives (ATF) *(www.atf.gov)*. What does this mean to you? When you purchase antique firearm or, any firearm, for that matter, it is illegal for you to transport a firearm across state lines. So, you need to be very cautious when you are buying or selling a firearm. I do need to clarify something with regard to antique firearms. If a firearm doesn't use a type of ammunition that's currently available, and instead for example, uses black powder, you will be able to transport and ship the gun yourself. It is only when a firearm takes ammunition which is currently on the market, that you cannot ship or transport these items across state lines.

If you find a modern gun that you really want to purchase, you need to find an authorized gun dealer in the area where the sale is taking place, and have them transport the piece across state lines. Whenever you're buying a firearm, there is also a better than average chance you will have to apply for either a gun permit and/or obtain clearance by the state where you legally reside allowing you to possess a gun. If you are unsure of your state's gun laws, contact the ATF or your local police department. Yes, there are certain hurdles you must overcome when you want to own a firearm, but benefits in the form of potential profits (if you want to resell an antique firearm) certainly make it worth your while.

In antique firearms, the biggest and most recognizable names are **Winchester Ammunition** *(www.winchester.com)* and **Colt Manufacturing** *(www.coltsmfg.com)*. Weapons made by "Colt" have played a part in every war involving the United States since the mid-1800s. The Colt revolver, invented by company founder Samuel Colt, is known by many historians as "the gun that won the West." The most valuable "Colts" were manufactured between the mid-1800s and the turn of the 19th century. The value of a particular Colt firearm may also be dependent upon the role it played in any given conflict. The best "Winchesters" to deal in for profit come are from the late-1800s when the Western United States was the "Wild West." These antique guns have considerable value if they are in very good to excellent condition. Once again, the "condition" of any particular collectible item plays a huge role in determining proper value. Actually, anything pre-1893 in antique firearms will have a higher value and will be easier to buy and sell. When purchasing antique firearms, always be cognizant that there are a lot of replicas which intricately resemble and copy old rifles and hand guns. If it looks like the condition of an antique firearm looks "too good to be true," this is a pretty good sign the item may be a replica or reproduction.

There are a lot of great books on this topic which are available at your local library or from your local bookstore. The Internet is also a great resource to tap into for learning more about this subject. I definitely recommend that you become as knowledgeable as possible about this collectible before you attempt to buy any antique firearm.

Military Memorabilia (Pre-WorldWar II)

Military memorabilia prior to World War II will make you the most profit in this area of collectibles. World War II, the Korean War, and Vietnam-era items have less overall value due to the fact that, from a historical perspective, these wars are considered as being "too recent." I say this solely from a monetary viewpoint. Of course, there is an unbelievable amount of emotional value and emotional currency placed on memorabilia from these conflicts, as these wars were unquestionably important to many individuals and, to the United States of America and American history.

The hierarchy of military memorabilia acquisitions, solely based on value, is The Civil War and The Revolutionary War, World War I, World War II. Any collectible dealing with the Nazi regime is difficult to address due to the psychological "wounds" and deep social resonance that still affects an amazing number of individuals worldwide. Although you may be able to find Nazi memorabilia being sold by private dealers, this type of collectible is not allowed on eBay or in the classified sections of many newspapers. If you come across any authentic Nazi items to purchase, they will indeed be collectible, but you may have a difficult time trying to make a return on your investment for the foreseeable future.

As I discussed earlier in this chapter, Civil War memorabilia is extremely collectible. A few specific items I would seek out are Civil War diaries, weapons, uniforms, and flags. All of these are items are highly sought after by collectors. If you come across good deals, you might want to purchase some pieces. With Civil War movies such as *Gettysburg, Gods and Generals, and Glory*, as well as the many Civil War reenactments which take place throughout different parts of the United States, likewise, there are many Civil War replicas available for sale. Most memorabilia dealers and individuals selling these types of items acknowledge the fact that some items are replicas, but some people are not so forthcoming with that information. Oftentimes, it is somewhat difficult to tell the real thing from the fake. Pre-1893 military weapons are also highly collectible. Guns from Winchester Ammunition, called "Winchesters," which were used during the Civil War or to tame the "Wild West" are very valuable. Muskets, as well as handguns from the Civil War and the Revolutionary War, are highly sought after as well.

You could easily overpay for some of these items so be very aware of what you're purchasing. There are a multitude of books written on this topic in addition to extensive information on the Internet. So, before you dive into this collectible, make sure you thoroughly research the topic.

Motorcycles (Pre-1960 Old Harley-Davidsons, Original Indians, and Military)

Even though I personally enjoy motorcycles, my wife does not allow me to ride them anymore. Of course, the next best thing to riding motorcycles is collecting them. Motorcycles manufactured prior to 1960, including models from historied American motorcycle manufacturing companies such as **Harley-Davidson USA (*www.harley-davidson.com*)** and **Indian Motorcycles (*www.indianmotorcycle.com*)**, as well as military motorcycles, are the most desirable for collectors to buy. The number one name in motorcycles is, "hands down," Harley-Davidson. Original Indian Motorcycles follow as a close second. The maker of Indian Motorcycles has gone bankrupt several times since their founding in 1901 but, in the late 1940s and 1950s, they were a very serious "player" in the motorcycle manufacturing business. Unfortunately, there are not many Indian Motorcycles surviving today. They were not manufactured in large quantities due to numerous financial problems and bankruptcies throughout the years. Because finding a vintage Indian Motorcycle is a rare occurrence, they are extremely valuable to collectors. Early Harley-Davidson or old military motorcycles from the 1930s and 1940s are also a very big deal. Many of these older motorcycles will be badly rusted and in poor to very poor condition when/if you come across them. If you do manage to find an old "Harley," "Indian," or military motorcycle in a deteriorated state of condition, don't worry. The condition really doesn't matter that much. The rarity of finding just one of these types of collectibles more than makes up for much of the deteriorated condition the motorcycles may exhibit. Anytime you find one of these types of motorcycles, it will be a very valuable find.

When you visit a prospective seller's home and speak with them about their collectibles, always ask about motorcycles. If people have an old barn or garage that looks like no one has gone through it in a while, make sure to inquire (politely) about what might be stored inside. You could just be the one person to find that missing original Indian Motorcycle or that one hard-to-find classic Harley-Davidson that no one has been able to discover over the decades. The worst anyone can say is, "No." If you do happen across one of these bikes, quickly think of a way to get this valuable find "off their hands" for them, negotiate a fair purchase price, buy the item, and have it moved immediately before someone else does! Congratulations…you have just put yourself in prime position to possibly make a lot of money when you resell. Believe me when I tell you that this scenario occurs every day to real *Garage Sale Millionaires* across the country. With a little curiosity and perseverance, this could also happen to you!

Muscle Cars (Pre-1971)

When searching for muscle cars during your many collectible treasure hunts, you will most likely not see these kinds of cars at your local garage sale. But, with the **Barrett-Jackson Car Auction** *(www.barrett-jackson.com)*, **Mecum Auto Auctions** *(www. mecum.com)*, and **The Speed Channel Cable Network** *(www.speedtv.com)*, acquiring muscle cars has come onto the forefront of the American collecting scene. Muscle cars are defined as American mid-size cars manufactured from 1964 to 1972 that were enhanced with large, powerful V8 engines, super chargers, and special exhaust systems. The first true "muscle car" was the 1964 Pontiac GTO, a car immortalized forever with the release of *Ronny & the Daytona's* mega hit record "Little GTO." The most valuable muscle cars to buy and sell for profit were those manufactured before 1971.

Because we're discussing the subject of cars, and more specifically, "muscle cars," I'm sure you understand that "golden oldies" like these cannot be purchased for $50, $100, or, even $1000. Muscle cars are going to cost you much more! I want you to keep an "open mind" about this type of collectible. Why? Because you can make substantial sums of money by buying and selling muscle cars. Pre-1971 muscle cars are generating huge sales and an enormous return on investment. Muscle cars, which carry an extremely high value, are *Fords*, *Buicks*, *Corvettes* (with big block engines), or *anything with a "Hemi"* (an extremely powerful internal-combustion engine).

Most people underestimate the money making potential involved with buying and selling muscle cars. For example, a 1965 Mustang Custom Convertible recently sold for $31,900 at the 2009 Barrett-Jackson Auto Auction in Las Vegas, Nevada. According to the Ford Mustang's entry on **The Henry Ford Museum Website** *(www.hfmgv.org/exhibits/showroom/1965/mustang.html)*, when the 1965 Ford Mustang was originally sold, the vehicle cost approximately $3,334. This single sale accounted for a profit of over $28,500. This is just one example. Many muscle cars sell for tens, and hundreds, of thousands of dollars at high-profile auctions held across the United States.

The overall condition of any muscle car is very important to consider if you want to resell any vehicle of this kind with the least amount of effort and for the most profit possible. Items to look for to determine a muscle car's condition include checking to see if there is rust or corrosion on the vehicle, verifying if all the parts on the car are original, and ensuring that the Vehicle Identification Numbers (VIN) on the car's engine block match with VIN on the main frame of the car. Also, try to get all the information you can from the current owners of the car. If you ever find a vehicle which has only had one owner and the owners have documentation which accompany the car, this adds huge value to what the car is worth.

When gathering information on any muscle car that you have a strong interest in purchasing, try to find out where the vehicle was primarily operated or housed geographically. If the muscle car came from the middle portion of the United States, "the Midwest," the vehicle will more than likely have greater value. This is because of salt anywhere in the environment. Salt is the "arch enemy" of muscle cars. The reason for being careful purchasing a muscle car from the states bordering the Atlantic and Pacific Oceans, as well as the Gulf of Mexico, is due to the salt in the air which originates from these expansive bodies of water. Over time, salt in the air can cause a great deal of damage to a car. This is damage you may or may not be able to see. Salt will destroy anything metallic on a car from its exterior finish to any part under the hood. Even though I have identified salt as being a prevalent problem from the states bordering massive bodies of water, there is also some possible trouble from the "use" of salt in the Midwest, because salt is widely used on roads to help melt snow. If a muscle car was driven at any time during the harsh Midwestern winters, there may also be salt corrosion and rust on the vehicle.

If a muscle car has all of its original parts intact, the original interior upholstery and original external paint, then the resale value of these vehicles will be much higher. If you find a car that has been restored and re-painted, it will not diminish the value of the car if that restoration has been done properly. Many muscle cars which sell at auto auctions such as the Barrett-Jackson Car Auctions and Mecum Auto Auctions, have been meticulously restored or have had a full "rotisserie restoration." A "rotisserie restoration" is when a car is completely disassembled, and the body is taken off the vehicle's frame. Next, the body of the vehicle is placed on a rotisserie, which can be turned to show any area on the car. From this point, the car's body can be sandblasted to bare metal, have any body work completed, be primed, painted, and reassembled in exactly the same way the vehicle was originally manufactured at the factory. Just remember, if an automobile restoration has been rendered, make sure that restoration was done properly.

Dealing in muscle cars offers any *Garage Sale Millionaire* the chance to make much more money than with many other collectibles. Always do your research; either from books, magazines, or the Internet before you make any purchase decisions and you'll be ahead of your competitors when it comes to buying and selling muscle cars for substantial profit.

Posters (Pre-1977, Movie and Music)

Million $ Tip

Signed movie and music posters are two of the most often and most easily faked items in the history of memorabilia collecting. It is extremely difficult to verify and/or document that the actual movie stars or musicians actually signed the posters. My recommendation is not to collect these items. They are fun to have, but don't pay big money for any of these items unless you have them certified as being authentic.

If you love to collect movie and music posters, don't pay extra for the "authentic" signatures unless the signatures are verified as legitimate and authentic through a regulated agency such as **James Spence Authentication** *(www.spenceloa.com)*. I talk about James Spence Authentication, or JSA, in more detail in Chapter 4. Signatures verified through JSA have already been certified as "genuine," so you're not just taking a store owner's word that the signature is authentic when you're ready to spend a sizable amount of money on that one poster you believe to be very valuable. Pre-1977 posters from the movie and music business are the most collectible.

Sports Memorabilia (Certified Game Used)

To be considered in the "game used" category, a sports memorabilia item must have been used in an actual sporting event. With "game used" sports memorabilia, this treasure needs to be properly documented with a "Certificate of Authenticity," which could come from the team, the player who used the "game used" item during the game, or from a certifying agency. This certification is very important, because without it this item is just a piece of used sports equipment with no importance attached to it. If the "game used" item does not come from a famous athlete, or was not used as part of an important game such as the Super Bowl, World Series, or Stanley Cup Finals, then the item will be worth less money. With "game used sports memorabilia," condition is not as important as the player who used the item and to have proper certification of authenticity.

Stamps (Pre-1920, Not Cancelled)

As a child, I remember collecting stamps and coins, but to me stamps were far more fun than coins. On stamps, there was always a cool color picture and every stamp seemingly had a story to tell. I've had great fun collecting stamps over the years, but I have to share with you that stamp collecting is the worst collectible you can be involved in. Why? Because there have been millions upon millions of stamps manufactured over the years, as a result, many stamps retain no collectible value. Another reason for stamps being an undesired collectible is, if stamps are "cancelled," that post office "stamp" (yes, a stamp on a stamp) eliminates any kind of value the stamp may have ever had. In addition to cancelled stamps, first day stamp covers have very little value.

I know what you're thinking…"Why, then, did you list stamps as something in the 'What to Buy' column when you believe they are 'the worst collectible you can be involved in?'" Although many stamps have no true value, as previously mentioned, the stamps which are the most collectible originated before 1920 and, have no "cancellation" stamp from the United States Post Office. The only exception to the "non-cancellation" rule is if the stamp is dated pre-1800. With these early stamps, any cancellation will not harm the value.

Some stamps are, indeed, quite valuable. Before you begin the treasure hunt for this type of collectible, you really need to thoroughly understand how to value stamps. I suggest you get a copy of "The Official Blackbook Price Guide to United States Postage Stamps 2010, 32nd Edition" by Thomas E. Hudgeons, Jr.

Toy Trains

With all of the great toy trains manufactured over the decades, many have become highly valuable to the model train and toy train collector. Although **Lionel** *(www.lionel.com)* will be the number one brand you recognize as you search for toy trains, there are many other manufacturers such as **American Flyer** *(www.americanflyertrains. com)*, **Bachmann Industries** *(www.bachmanntrains.com)*, and **Williams Electric Trains** *(www.williamstrains.com)* that have made classic and collectible toy trains over the years. Toy trains are a very entertaining collectible to become involved with. Toy trains have a very rich history and have proven to be a very profitable collectible item to buy and to sell. Individual toy train cars, complete locomotive sets, and entire toy train villages are consistently being resold for amounts ranging from just a few cents to the tens of thousands of dollars.

Condition and packaging are extremely important factors in determining the value of any collectible. Toy trains are no different. The better condition a train is in, along with its original packaging, the more money the train will generate upon resale. Additionally, some toy trains and toy train sets may have been restored. If restoration has taken place, value will drop. When you buy a toy train that's very old, examine it closely to make certain that your item hasn't been restored or is missing parts.

Vinyl Records (Pre-1977)

For vinyl records and vinyl record album covers to have any real value, they need to be packaged together. If you're looking to make any serious money from these collectibles, you simply cannot have one without the other. For example, if you have a record without its associated album cover, there will be no value attached to that vinyl record. Likewise, if you have an album cover without its associated record, little to no value will be connected with that item. Although vinyl record album covers made prior to 1977 retain the highest value, this doesn't necessarily mean that vinyl records have to be from this era to have value.

Certain pre-1977 vinyl record album covers are substantially collectible with or without any of the signatures from the band or music group who made the particular record. The condition of these items is considerably important in determining value. With regard to old album covers, it is commonly known that some of these covers have been restored. Many Beatles, Rolling Stones, and other album covers may be deemed highly collectible if they are the original album covers. Watch out for restored covers, because if an album cover has been restored, it loses some of its value, and loses ALL value if done poorly. This type of item is well worth collecting, but you must be highly observant and knowledgeable on the subject in order to make a profit.

Although compact discs and digital downloads have taken over the lion's share of today's audio market, vinyl records are slowly starting to make a bit of a comeback. According to the *New York Times* and *Nielsen SoundScan*, "Sales of vinyl albums have been climbing steadily for several years dispelling the notion that the rebound was just a fad. Through late November, more than 2.1 million vinyl records were sold in 2009…an increase of more than 35 percent in less than a year."

Vinyl records may still be considered a niche market, but those who continue to invest in turntables and stereo equipment that cost hundreds of thousands of dollars, are extremely passionate about their hobby. These impassioned collectors spare no expense in seeking out and buying the best vinyl available to play on their "tricked out" two-channel audio systems. It's a point of contention among those who enjoy listening to music in a digital format, as in digital downloads and compact discs, to those who prefer to listen to their music in analogue format via vinyl records, as to which sounds better and more authentic.

On vinyl record auction results websites, such as **Popsike** *(www.popsike.com)*, there are tens of thousands of vinyl record auction results listed. Vinyl records, from groups and individuals ranging from The Beatles, Beethoven, and Bob Dylan to Elvis Presley, Queen, and The Velvet Underground can fetch upwards of $20,000 to $25,000 (or more) per album. Although the majority of vinyl records may not have a lot of resale value, older vinyl records from important groundbreaking individuals in the music industry have great value and command substantial amounts of money upon resale.

Great places to look for vinyl records are at thrift stores, second hand stores, vinyl record stores, and of course, garage sales. When you find an old vinyl record, you need to check the condition of the record to see that no scratches are present as well as make sure the sleeve is intact and undamaged. Most importantly, check price guides to see if what you're holding is valuable. Websites like eBay and Popsike, as well as books such as "The Official Price Guide to Records, Edition #17" by Jerry Osborne and "Goldmine Record Album Price Guide: The Ultimate Guide to Valuing Your Vinyl" by Tim Neely are valuable tools in determining if the record you hold in your hands will be worth any money upon resale.

What Not to Buy

As great as the previous collectible items were with regard to resale value, we now transition to those collectibles that are not so good and should be "avoided at all costs!" Sir Isaac Newton once said, "For every action there is an equal and opposite reaction." This quote directly relates to the following section of the book. As great as the previously mentioned collectibles are with regard to money-making potential, what

> ### Million $ Tip
>
> "Fad Collectibles" are the types of collectible which are really hot one moment and really cold the next. With Fad Collectibles the excitement of a new collectible skyrockets and the price shoots up almost immediately. Then, when the collectible falls out of favor, the value plummets to levels never to be worth much again.

follows is a detailed description of the "equal and opposite" collectibles which are not worth your time. Dealing with the following collectibles will do one thing and *one thing only*, waste your time and money.

Beanie Babies

The number one "fad collectible" of all time, and an item which may be the worst collectible of all time in my opinion, is the Beanie Baby. A "fad collectible" is an item which when released for sale is extremely popular. A better description would be that most fad collectible's popularity is "off the charts" and the masses go absolutely crazy for them upon their release. Fads bring in many different types of collectors because there is an overwhelming misconception that since there is a huge interest in the item, there is a more than a reasonable possibility that money will be made when dealing in this collectible for years to come. Then, after the initial excitement subsides, this collectible eventually loses almost all of its importance and has no real value. I can't tell you the number of people, including seasoned businessmen, who hopped on the "Beanie Baby Bandwagon" and started collecting them when they were first introduced by Ty Warner Inc. in 1993, some even spending tens of thousands of dollars. Beanie Babies collectors were obsessed with amassing these pellet-filled stuffed animal toys that are virtually worthless in today's collectibles market. To this day, Beanie Babies are one collectible that had everybody fooled and, as it turned out, have little or no value.

Experience has shown me anytime there is a collectible that soars ever-so-quickly, the chances are equally good it will plummet just as fast.

Bibles (Family)

There is absolutely no opportunity for financial gain to be made buying or selling family bibles unless the bible comes from a famous family. The average family bible does not have any resale value. Although a family bible has personal importance to your own family, it will not really mean anything to someone else's. Once again, unless the item originates from a famous family, you should not invest in bibles as viable money making collectibles.

Comics and Comic Books (Post-1970)

Comic books are a lot of fun to read and, even more fun as a collectible to buy and sell for profit. As a matter of fact, I have a comic book collection myself.

Unfortunately, you'll have to search far and wide to find a comic book made after 1970 which has any resale value. Because comic books produced after 1970 were printed in such large quantities, value for these items has diminished. The large printing quantities have hurt their value and the chances of their value ever increasing. Are there comics from 1970 and later which have value? Of course, there are always exceptions. To view a detailed listing of comic book values, please look in Chapter 7 where I list the Top 100 Comic Books ranked according to value.

With pre-1970 comic books, there are a lot more that have value than those that don't. Unfortunately, the condition of most of these comic books is very poor. Because the majority of older, pre-1970 comic books are very valuable, some have been restored to enhance their quality and ultimately their potential resale value. If comics are restored properly, they will retain value quite well. Be mindful and ask about restorations when you find a comic book you want to purchase. Condition is everything, especially when dealing in buying and selling of comics.

If you find an original comic book illustrated by a famous comic book artist, that particular book will definitely be worth more money. For this very reason, there are a few comic books made in the last thirty years which have great value. For every one comic book that is valuable, I would say there are hundreds more which have no value whatsoever. A fantastic resource on the Internet to gain a better understanding for which comic book artists are the best in their field based on each artist's technique, storytelling ability, accomplishments, and longevity, visit the "The Top 100 Artists of American Comic Books," sponsored by **Atlas Comics** *(www.acomics.com)*, at *www.acomics.com/best.htm.*

When seeking comic books that have resale value, don't spend much time on comics produced after 1970. For the best possible profits, search out and acquire older comics made before 1970 that are in great condition.

Magazines (Old)

I know many people who collect old magazines. Actually, my mom saves old National Geographic magazines and she believes "with all her heart" that her stash of "Nat Geos" is going to "set me up for life" if I ever need to sell them. With old magazines like of *National Geographic, Time, Life* and, even a classic, *The New Yorker*, it's difficult to find any true value. The only collectible value would be from that magazine's premier issue. However, there are a few exceptions to the rule. *Playboy Magazine* has had a few issues, other than its first edition, that have true lasting value. The very first issue of "Playboy" published December 1953 with Marilyn Monroe on the cover is the most valuable of any Playboy Magazine and can command sales of several thousand dollars. Many issues that originated in the 1950s and 1960s are also valuable collector's items, particularly if copies are in pristine condition. With National Geographic, Time, and Life, among others, there may be something on the cover that makes an issue very rare. Looking for these magazines is like finding "a needle in the haystack." I would stay strictly away from this collectible because any upside opportunities are quite limited.

Movie Memorabilia (Signed)

Movie memorabilia is wonderful to collect, but you need to be aware that signed movie memorabilia has a great deal of fraud associated with it. Many of the signatures and autographs used to sell this kind of movie memorabilia are often verified as fakes. When you're buying a signed piece of movie memorabilia from that famous movie star you absolutely adore, you need to realize that the chances the item was actually signed by that particular person are basically slim to none. Signatures on movie memorabilia are extremely hard to verify unless you take your item to a company such as **James Spence Authentication** *(www.spenceloa.com)* to professionally certify your item as being authentic. I cover the topic of movie memorabilia in more detail in Chapter 4.

Newspapers (Old)

Whenever I speak to large audiences, small groups, or when I'm interviewed on the radio or television, people always ask about old newspapers. Unfortunately, the value of old newspapers is similar to stamps. Because there were tens of thousands, if not millions of newspapers printed over the years, many have very little value. Another strong negative component dictating a newspaper's lack of value is that they tend to "yellow" very quickly. So, finding a newspaper in good to pristine condition without any "yellowing," is difficult. Most newspapers are stored together so they tend to "yellow" much more quickly. If you want to talk about newspapers that may have considerable value, you'll need to go back to newspapers which were printed in the 1800s. Try to look for newspapers dating historically close to the time when President Abraham Lincoln was assassinated (1865). If you find a newspaper you think has value, you definitely want to take care of it right away by placing it in a protective plastic cover. Like old magazines, this collectible has very little upside.

Pokémon Cards

Pokémon cards are another example of a "fad collectible." The desire to collect this item was driven by kids between the ages of four to 18 years that got so caught up in these cards, that they made this collectible one with huge initial interest, and in turn, had a very large initial resale value. As with any "fad collectible," what goes up must come down. Eventually, the value of Pokémon cards came "crashing" down just as quickly as its interest skyrocketed. Many millions of dollars were spent on this collectible in the years which followed its 1998 introduction in the United States but, eventually, Pokémon card sales slowed. As a result, Pokémon cards currently have very little to no value at all.

Once again, always be very careful if you're interested in collecting something that could be considered a fad such as Pokémon cards or Beanie Babies.

Rugs (Antique)

Authentic antique rugs have great value, but this is another specialized collectible arena in which you have to be an absolute expert if you are to determine what's valuable and what's not. This is also a collectible item that demands that you have an expert in your corner. You need someone with experience, someone you can completely trust, and someone who will actually buy your rugs for you. Even if you work with professional, experienced rug dealers, you can still be misled on antique rugs because there are a great many replica rugs manufactured that can easily double as authentic, real and antique.

This collectible can be very expensive and if you're not an expert yourself, or you don't work with a reputable expert, I can almost guarantee you that you're going to lose a lot of money. Antique rugs are a difficult-to- learn collectible that takes a great deal time to understand.

Silverware (Antique)

Pure silver was never used in antique silverware because it is actually too soft a

---

Million $ Tip

When verifying look at the knots that hold it together. If they are uneven and the pattern is off center, this is good evidence that it is handmade. Carpets made after 1920 were usually made by machines. Take a few small pieces of that rug's fabric and light them on fire. Then, look at the color of the flame. If there is a color in the flame (that is, other than the color of a normal flame), then you know you have a newer carpet and not an "authentic" handmade. Also, if the carpet is made of real silk, when you light a small piece of it on fire, it will melt and smell like burnt hair. If it turns brittle and breaks off, it is something else. Of course, always use the utmost caution when working with fire to avoid any accidents!

---

compound unless mixed with other alloys. All antique silverware was produced with different types of metals other than just the pure silver alone. Antique silverware is collectible, but now it's mainly only desirable for the potential amount of silver these items may physically contain.

Throughout the years there were a few early manufacturers such as *Gorham Whiting, Towle, Dominick & Haff, Reed and Barton, R. Blackinton & Co., Tiffany,* and *Unger Bros. and Wallace* who created silverware which has maintained some lasting value. Finding antique silverware may pose challenges at times due to the rarity of the more valuable pieces. You really want to become very knowledgeable about this area of collectible before you buy.

Do not get overly excited when you find something at an antique store or a garage sale which you think is under-valued. Always do your homework before you make any purchase. Make sure you verify whether the piece of silverware is "sterling silver " or just "silver-plated." Many times people think just because a piece is old it's going be sterling silver. Silver-plating was actually used more commonly than most people think, so be mindful of this point before you buy. Also, look for the hallmark maker's mark stamp on the underside of the item. stamps on silver are usually on the backside of the silverware. Look for these marks on the neck where the sharp edge meets the handle of a fork, knife, or spoon. With tea sets, these marks are always on the underside of the pieces. Most of the pieces should have some markings on them. These marks will tell you who manufactured the item as well as the percentage of silver it contains. This is a good way to tell if what you have is truly silver and if it is from a well-known maker.

> ### *Million $ Tip*
> As a rule, antique silverware will always be worth no less than the amount of actual silver each piece contains. If you are only interested in an item for its silver content, you will now need to find out that information on the item before buying anything in this area of collectibles.

If you don't have the proper knowledge of what's collectible and what isn't, that antique tea set you're thinking of purchasing for a sizable amount of money, because of its potential resale value, may not be worth as much as you think.

Sports Memorabilia (Signed)

Having been in the sports memorabilia business, I still enjoy buying and selling the occasional piece of authentic sports memorabilia. Recently, I had a Yellow Jersey from The Tour de France worn by Lance Armstrong during his last "Tour" for sale in my animation art and collectibles gallery. This piece eventually sold for $10,000.

Sports memorabilia can really be as exciting and challenging as sport itself, but like anything else in the world of collectibles, you must always be cautious when verifying to make sure that an item is authentic. When you're thinking of purchasing a piece of sports memorabilia, always ascertain that the item has been certified by one of the major certification companies such as **James Spence Authentication** (*www.spenceloa.com*), **The Upper Deck** (*www.upperdeck.com*), **Steiner Sports** (*www.steinersports.com*), and **Mounted Memories** (*www.mountedmemories.com*). Also, because of the prevalence of eBay these days, there are many well done fakes which have been mass produced by an amazing cadre of sellers so they can make a quick "buck" from you. I estimate for every one authentic signature there are probably two which are forged. For any piece to truly have any value, you need to have it certified by a well-known certification company such as those mentioned in this section. This topic is covered in more detail in Chapter 4.

Stamps (Foreign)

You should stay as far away from foreign stamps as possible. Yes, like everything else in this world, there will always be a few exceptions to the rule. You could possibly find some foreign stamps with some value, but, from my experience, there aren't many out there. Even if someone is selling one hundred thousand stamps on eBay for just $100, it will take you an exponentially longer time to find that one stamp which is worth a few dollars. This collectible takes so much time and effort to discover even a few stamps that might eventually have any true value. Again, this is one collectible I recommend staying away from altogether. When you're offered a "great deal" on some foreign stamps, although the deal may be tempting, I'm telling you, by all means, trust me on this…run as fast as you can in the opposite direction!

> ### Million $ Tip
> Never buy international stamps if you're hoping to make money. Their only value is to people who are expert in this field.

"To Buy or Not to Buy, That is the Question!"

In this chapter, I want to detail some of the items you will often see on a daily basis as you foray out on your many adventurous treasure hunts. When you do come across a piece that interests you, you'll need to determine if that is an item that falls under the category of "What to Buy," or if it falls under the category of "What Not to Buy."

Eventually, you'll find one particular item that intrigues you so much that you're moved to start collecting. When you find one collectible that's right for you, and one which you want to start buying and selling, read everything you can about that item. Strive to become an expert in that collectible. Thoroughly research your interests and re-read this book. And always remember, there is much to learn and great fun to be had as well in learning about your particular collectible.

Often, when you first begin collecting one item, like antiques or fine art, you will most likely become interested in collecting other items in many different genres. You may eventually pursue something far different that interests you in an area you never imagined would ever hold your attention. When you become a *Garage Sale Millionaire*, you need to be knowledgeable in several different collectibles. Why? So, when you go to garage sales, auctions, storage unit auctions, estate sales, or buy and sell items via the Internet, you'll be prepared to purchase items to sell for a profit.

In this chapter, when I say a collectible has no value, please understand that I am generalizing. For every Beanie Baby, Pokémon card, or recently created comic book, there will be a few items which will still have a value to some buyer somewhere. Also, no matter how often I say that an item is something you should not buy; there usually exists a certain individual…a collector who will be looking feverishly to collect that exact item.

Most importantly, be careful throughout the course of your *Garage Sale Millionaire* adventures. I would rather you err on the side of caution, sometimes because the overall collectible category I referenced either has a bad reputation, or at other times, it may be that you're trying to purchase that one hard-to-find item in an entire genre of collectible which simply has no value. For all of the details I've shared in this chapter, I have merely scratched the surface with the information regarding the collectibles I recommend you buy and the also with the ones I suggest you stay away from. As always, there are many great collectibles to be bought and sold for substantial profits!

CHAPTER

3

Mastering The Art of the Deal

Negotiating Like a Pro

This is a 50 million year old fossil that was found in Wyoming. This rare fossil is called Notogoneus/Diplomystus Aspiration. The fossil took two weeks of negotiation and I saved 41% off the original price.

In the first two chapters of this book, I've suggested which items are best to look for and also those items it's really best to distance yourself from. The next step in becoming a successful *Garage Sale Millionaire* is to learn the proper way to negotiate the best deals for your treasured finds.

The "Art of the Deal"

To master the "art of the deal," you'll need to understand a few different techniques for becoming the greatest buyer you can possibly be. Even though you won't become an expert negotiator overnight, the more you "deal" on items at garage sales, second hand stores, estate auctions, storage unit auctions, on eBay and Craigslist, the closer you'll come to achieving expert *Garage Sale Millionaire* status. Being successful at negotiating is not based solely on how aggressive you are as a buyer, but more importantly, how well you can "talk somebody down" on their price in order to achieve the greatest deals possible. There are three ways to buy an item for any sale: face to face, over the phone, or by using email. Of course, there are different tricks to employ for each of these methods that will yield the highest rate of success.

Dealing with someone "Face to Face"

When dealing with someone in person, the seller will be able to look at you "real time" and make lasting judgements regarding what your financial status might be. This is accomplished largely in part by the way you're dressed. Whatever you intend to purchase, whether it be jewelry, art, cars, or pretty much anything else, a salesperson will always "size you up" by giving you the "once-over." I'm not saying this practice is fair, or that I agree with it, but it is a reality.

I know what you're thinking. You're probably thinking that sales people don't look at, or even take time to notice these types of personal details. I can guarantee you this happens all the time! Attention to detail and observations help us as sales people to better understand our buyer, meaning YOU. Three to five years ago, the probability of someone actually asking for a deal when they walked through my gallery doors was about 50/50. Due to the poor economic climate we are currently experiencing, I estimate that easily 80% of my customers will ask for some kind of a deal.

When you participate in any type of sale, be it a garage sale, antique shop, art gallery, or a collectibles store, you will want to dress appropriately. Don't get all dressed up. Don't wear an expensive watch, never wear big, gaudy rings and always leave the designer clothes and shoes at home. When you're shopping for any item which is going to require negotiation, you'll definitely want to dress appropriately for the experience. Looking "the part," especially in the way you're dressed, is one of the main considerations that will help you become a master negotiator and a *Garage Sale Millionaire* success.

Personally, I like to wear something simple like a pair of jeans and a shirt. Button down shirts are fine. A plain pair of tennis shoes will also work out fine. The only acceptable piece of jewelry to wear would be a wedding ring. If you have a big diamond ring, leave it at home and wear a simple gold band instead if you have one. Also, an inexpensive or casual watch is acceptable. When sales people see that you can easily afford the finer things, it's much harder to negotiate any kind of bargain with them. Another dead giveaway that you are too "well-off" is if you drive a high end car. If you don't have access to a "clunker" and you arrive at the store in your nice flashy vehicle, never park in front of the store where the owner can see what you're driving. Leave it down the street and walk a block.

As you walk around the store, always be cordial and pleasant. Never act aloof or be rude towards the salesperson. As soon as you're deemed to be discourteous or difficult, your chances of getting a better deal have just flown right out the window. Salespeople will literally "jump through hoops" and be more accommodating to a potential customer who is polite and affable.

When you find something you like, you don't have to pretend you didn't see the item or don't want it and then ask for a deal on the item. Of course, always examine the piece closely and make sure it's something you have a strong desire to buy. If you need to leave the store to do your research and then go back later, this is always considered an acceptable practice. Traveling back and forth to the store once or twice is fine, but if you start coming back three, four or even five times and you're always looking at the same item, you will definitely hurt your chances of making a good deal. Best case scenario, you'll only want to leave once, then come back and make the appropriate offer. Enter a store, browse to your heart's content, find the items that interest you, make some notes if necessary and then perhaps go home for a while and do some research on your computer. Then, when you feel confident that you are armed with all the knowledge you need to make an informed assessment, go back to the store one final time and make your best offer.

If you're completely certain you want to make a purchase, always make sure the item that you have in mind is in a state of condition to your liking. Ensure that the item has not been restored and it has all the original packaging. If the original packaging is not included, you'll need to make a decision as to whether or not this is something you really want to buy. I will discuss the importance of having original packaging and how this directly affects resale value in Chapter 7. If your item requires accessories such as keys, you need to make certain that what you want to buy has everything included before negotiating a price.

When you're ready to make a purchase, ask if there is an owner available so you can speak to someone in charge to start the negotiation process. When speaking to the owner, always be friendly and civil. Never be critical of the item you want to purchase. It's always amazing to me how many people will insult the very items they want to buy. What constitutes an insult? If the item is an antique, don't begin the conversation by stating that the item is heavily over-priced or in bad condition.

Never try to find fault with the item in hope of getting a better deal. Remember, the owner has been in this "game" for quite a while and for much longer than you have. The person standing in front of you fully understands that when you're trying to find the less attractive points relative to an item, you're really trying to position it at a lesser price. In simple words, this is just an obvious and blatant negotiation tool being played out poorly on your part…and in bad taste. The store owner has heard it all before and he or she will be less willing to make a deal if you employ this type of unsophisticated bargaining strategy!

Now, if you point out scratches or dents which are not so obvious, that is fantastic and considered fair game. When you do this, always acknowledge that the item in question is none the less a "nice piece." Remember, never be too negative. Begin your dialog with the store owner by saying you're looking at the piece and the item is of genuine interest to you. Also take time to make the usual small talk. There's nothing wrong with asking how long the store owner has been in business and that it's "unfortunate" that he or she has to work on the weekend or on such a nice day. You should definitely try to find some "common ground" to discuss. By finding something in common, the owner will look at you more as a "person" than a "client," and more as a "friend" than a "mark." It's very important that you have a good working relationship with the owner or whomever is in charge when you start the dealing process on an item of interest to you. If you do this, there's a better than average chance they will like you, take an interest in you and give you a much better deal.

Dealing with someone over the telephone and by email

Now that you understand some of the tricks used to negotiate a better deal when working with someone face to face, let's discuss how to handle other forms of negotiation. These types of transactions take place over the telephone or via email. Using methods other than the face to face approach to negotiate the best possible deal are a bit trickier, but with some experience, they can be easily mastered. Because you're not dealing with someone face to face, you don't have to worry about your "look," speak any differently than you normally would, or put-on-airs to make your point. You will, however, have to pay extra careful attention to what's being said. With the evolution of technology over recent years, the average person relies heavily on using the Internet and email to get the best deals on a broad range of merchandise. Prior to the current popularity and downright dependence upon the Internet, "high-speed technology" meant using the telephone to negotiate a deal. Using the phone to negotiate deals and buy items is still a potent weapon in any Garage Sale Millionaire's arsenal, but the Internet makes getting a great deal done quickly and efficiently that much easier.

Let's turn our focus to transacting business by email. Many businesses have items available for sale on the Internet. In antique stores, art galleries and second hand stores, there is usually a designated person who places items for sale on the company website. A good website operated by a proficient company is updated regularly by removing information about items that have already sold and posting new items as soon as they become available. Because the Internet is such a potent sales weapon for these stores, much of their overall business is transacted across state lines or worldwide. If you find an item you're interested in buying on a website, the best thing to do is to email the owner directly. In your message, identify and describe the item you have an interest in (be sure to include any item number associated with a posting) and make it very clear in a nice way of course, that you also have a limited budget. You are a serious buyer and want to purchase something right away, but you need the very best deal they are willing to offer. In your email, you need to emphasize that the decision to buy any item is all about price and that you are shopping around. In the current down-state of the economy, people are always looking for the best deal they can find. When you discuss price with a store owner, you'll want to let them know right away if they want your business, they'll have to offer you their best price, immediately.

The majority of shop owners, art gallery directors, or store managers prefer communicating by email because they know they'll have one or two "shots" to get you to buy. The impetus for convincing you to buy is contingent upon these individuals making you the right (best) offer. If they are unsuccessful at getting you to make a purchase in their first or second email, there's a good chance you will have obtained the item elsewhere. If you're contacting the seller from another state, you'll want to make your location known so you are recognized as being exempt from sales tax. This will make the transaction a bit easier for the seller as well. Also, let the seller know you will accept the easiest and least expensive method for shipping the item. You definitely do not want to incur costly overnight charges for shipping. Always inquire about getting insurance on your shipment to protect it while in transit to your location.

Making any kind of deal over the telephone is, in my opinion, the toughest way to negotiate. Why? There's no real sense of bonding between the seller and the customer, or vice versa, on a cold call. Many store owners don't feel as though they have a reason to give you a better deal, because they don't know you or anything about you. In the very the least, with email correspondence, there's usually a sender's name, a personal greeting and some sort of contact information listed prior to first contact between you and the store owner. Usually, a telephone number is listed in the signature portion of an email. Even with the smallest amount of information provided in an email there is some level of trust built into that first actual moment of contact.

If you're calling about an item you saw on the store's website, you will want to start a dialog with the owner immediately to find some sort of "common ground" so the seller will begin to feel comfortable with you. Once you've found your common ground, it's time to begin to negotiate.

The Art of the Deal: How to Negotiate

In this chapter, I have discussed the best way to work with people in person, remotely by telephone, or by email. I've also made you aware as to how sellers instantly "size up" buyers and what they're thinking of during every aspect of the sales process. I've given you the essential information about what goes into a sale and now it is time to discuss how to properly negotiate a sale to get the best deal possible.

When you begin discussion about any item you want to buy, you'll definitely want to ask questions specific to that item. Once again, always make sure that the item you're interested in is the exact item you want to purchase. Ask everything you want to know about the item, even if you're positive it's the "piece" for you. If you're 100% certain you know everything there is to know about the item, there's nothing wrong with asking the seller for more information. You can never perceive what additional enlightenment might be divulged in the conversation as you discuss specifics about an item. Remember, nothing is final until you spend your hard-earned money. So, why not try to find out as much information as possible?

After you've spoken for a few moments about the item you want to buy, it's time to mention the fact that although you're really interested, you have a limited budget to spend. Let the seller know how much you like the item, but also that you don't know if you can afford the asking price. Now is the time to ask if something can be done to "help you out" on the price. The owner, manager, or whomever is in charge of the store at the time will then more than likely begin to tell you about their free "layaway policy."

A "layaway" is basically a paying for items in installments. The way it works is that you put a small amount of money "down" on the item as a first payment and then continue to make small payments every month until the item is paid in full. Your purchase will remain in the store until all the "layaway" payments on the item are made. A "layaway payment plan" simply makes it much easier for you to pay for the item you want to purchase by allowing you to make smaller payments spread across a set period of time instead of having to pay for the item in full all at once. Let the owner also know that you appreciate knowing about their "layaway policy" and that you might eventually want to use this means of payment. By mentioning that you may possibly accept some sort of "layaway agreement" to purchase an item, you could get an immediate break on the price. Usually, most shop owners, gallery directors, or managers will decrease the price up to 10% knowing that the item will soon be out of the store. Store owners would rather take a percentage "hit" on the item to accelerate immediate cash flow and free up space in their store right away. Believe it or not, this is a common practice within the industry.

But, you're not looking for a meager 10% off on items that you have a serious interest in. You did not buy this book so you could find a way of getting a better deal which "only" amounts to a 10% discount.

Now you're going to say to the store owner on the other end of the line "Thanks, but 10% discount really isn't a such a great price for me. There's a store where I live that will offer more than 10% on the exact same item you have in your store. However, I do prefer conducting all of my business out of state because that way I don't have to pay any sales tax." By making this statement, not only could you get an immediate price drop on the item you want to buy, but you will also help the seller better relate to you. This lets the person you're dealing with know that you will be a serious buyer in the future.

All shop owners love to hear, "I'm starting my collection and I need many more of these kinds of collectibles." Every store owner absolutely loves finding out that they've come across someone new to deal with now and deal with in the future. This is the point where you say, "You know, right now we're at 10% and I really appreciate the discount, but, I was thinking more of a number closer to 25% or 30% off."

This is your time to shine and to "go for it" to obtain an even lower sales price.

Now's the right moment to reference whatever discount you're comfortable with discussing and asking if you can have the item you're interested in at the seller's maximum discount. If you ask for more than a 50% discount over the telephone, more than likely you're going to hear a dial tone very quickly. Furthermore, if you're asking for more than a 50% discount in person you may get the "cold shoulder," and whomever you were dealing with may shut the door on future business dealings forever.

I recommend that you go to a percentage somewhere between 15% and 45%. You should realize that whatever final sales price you agree upon, the seller is going to offer a final sales price higher than your lowest proposal. If you try to get a discount between 40% and 45%, the seller will more than likely offer a discount which is half of your offer.

If you truly love the item and you know it's a great value, be careful not to lose it no matter what the final price may end up being. You should always be ready to concede the final price and possibly accept something for much less of a deal than you originally wanted. I can't tell you how many times I wanted the best deal in the world and I ended up losing out on the deal altogether because I wouldn't accept a final sales price barely 5% over my final offer. I walked away from the sale after "standing my ground" thinking the seller would call me or email me, in turn, to accept my final offer. A day or two later, I usually find out that I wanted was sold to someone else. I could have made a huge profit from reselling the item, but I got greedy and blew the deal.

After you've agreed on a price, you should be willing to make your payment arrangements over the phone with the store owner or manager. There are two ways to

The Garage Sale Millionaire

proceed. You can offer to come in and pay cash for the item, or you can offer to pay with a credit card. If you don't live in the city or state where the business you're dealing with is located, then it's best to pay by credit card. Also, make sure the seller offers free shipping.

One of the benefits of negotiating for the best price on an item over the phone is if you're still unhappy with the price, you have the option of leaving your name and number for a call back. Tell the shop owner, "If you're interested in the price I offered, please give me a call. I'm going to consider your offer for the next few days (or a week…whatever time frame you are comfortable in using) and then I'll make up my mind." The reason you have to give the seller a set number of days is that you don't want this "cat and mouse game" to continue on for an indefinite period of time. Your decisiveness and commitment in offering a set time limit will entice and motivate the shop owner to make the deal, or forever hold his peace by not making you a better deal. There's always a very good chance if the counter price you offered is fair, the store owner will call you back to make the sale. If you're impatient (try not to be), if you need this piece as a gift, or if you're afraid of losing the item then you need to make the deal right then and there on the phone.

If time is on your side and it's acceptable to lose out on the item, try to "bluff" the store owner by offering a very deep discount with the hope he or she

will call you back to accept your "lowball" offer. It never hurts to try a bluff with the owner as long as you're prepared to lose out in the end. I have a 70% success rate when I bluff. Sometimes, the store owner will call you back to apologize and that they won't be able to make the deal at the low price you offered. They may ask once again, if there's any way you might still want to buy the item at a higher price than your final offer. Depending on what you really wanted to spend, you can discuss another final price and see if the store owner is intent on working with you to move that item into your possession and out of their store.

Expert negotiating strategies by example, personally from "America's #1 Collector," Aaron LaPedis

I would love to give you a detailed look at and talk you through, the negotiation process based on my decades of professional and personal experience. I've worked in the art gallery business over 25 years, I've also been a memorabilia and art collector for most of my life as well. The following example perfectly illustrates what the negotiation process is all about. Let's take an item which is originally marked at $500 and let us negotiate this treasure down to something a "bit" more affordable!"

If an item is marked at $500, you'll want to start by offering the seller almost half the original sales price. That means a little less than a 50% discount. If you go under $250, you'll basically insult the seller. This is not a very good strategy to use, but if you have no problem losing your chances of getting a good deal, you can always try it. Remember our "bluff" example earlier in this chapter! Of course, if you're serious in acquiring an item, I strongly do not recommend this strategy! When people offer me less than half the price on any item I'm selling, I am personally insulted. I never price items in my own gallery too high, but rather at a fair price where I can make an honest living. So, be forewarned, if you were to use that tactic on me, maybe one time in 50, I would "bite" and make the deal. If it's worth it to you to try to get the "best deal in the world" and you believe this sort of tactic works, then by all means give it your best shot. Don't be surprised if you're asked to leave from many stores if you choose to employ this tactic. When you really like the store, shop, or gallery and want to come back in the future, the goal is not to insult people. Remember, store owners need to earn a living as well!

I do recommend offering a little bit above half of the original sales price, perhaps using $275 to $300 (based on a $500 price tag), as an appropriate starting point. The store or gallery owner will always counter higher and they will never say okay to your first offer. So, whatever you do, you don't want to give your best dollar offer knowing that the counter offer will be much higher. You could start by offering $450, which is quite high for a first offer, but I guarantee the counter offer will come back at $475. By starting off your negotiations with the sales person by making a lower initial offer, you'll leave room for both of you to "meet in the middle" and eventually come to an acceptable final sales price.

For fun, let's go bare bones and offer a very low starting price of $275 (this first offer is to buy the item, at a 45% discount. Good for you!). The store owner will probably counter your offer at $400. Pay careful attention here. At this point during the negotiation, you will want to be holding the item in your hands if it's not too large...an old clock, an antique or collectible toy, a coin, a vase, etc. This action shows the seller a seemingly sincere and emotional attachment to the item. You are actually sending a signal that you have marked the item as your own and are making a statement by literally holding onto it. Now, as you stand with the item in your hands, having offered the store owner $275, the salesperson or owner counter-offers $425. This is $25 more than you expected at $400. If the salesperson does this, look the salesperson straight in the eye, then glance at the item in your hands and shake your head back and forth. Put on your best "sad face" and place the item back on the shelf.

You may not think this is going to accomplish anything, but right there that salesperson, manager, or store owner just got really scared! They may have just felt a little twinge or a funny feeling and are thinking they have just lost you as a customer. It has also just occurred to the person you're dealing with that their commission on the item you were holding is about to leave the store right along with you. While placing the item back where you found it, you should be shaking your head and muttering under your breath, "Yeah, that price is more than I can spend…it's too much," using a very disheartened tone. At this moment, it's almost a guarantee that the person who was assisting you, is going to come after you, "magically" dropping their price. Let the tried and true psychological maneuver known as the "put back" work for you.

Let's go back to the salesperson's $425 counter offer. Usually, after a counter offer of $425 is made, the next best offer by the salesperson will be somewhere near $375. When you make your counter to their counter offer and come up a little bit in your new price, do not touch that item again. Never touch the item again until you both are a little closer to agreeing on a final sales price. If the salesperson offers $375 and they usually will, you counter their offer with $325. The goal will be to stand "pat" at $325, which is a 35% discount off of the original $500 price!

If you are so sure the salesperson is not going to budge any lower than the $375 he or she offers you, at this point you have two options. The first is holding firm at $325, saying, "I'm sorry, but I just can't accept that price. Thanks anyway for your time." Always wish the salesperson a good day and then leave the store. There's a very good chance this will rattle the salesperson's cage and he or she may agree to your $325 price. I have to tell you that this strategy works like a charm…seven out of ten times for me.

OK now, if this course of action hasn't work for you and you get to the door without making the deal, you may want to turn around and nicely say, "Is it okay to leave my name and telephone number with you? If you change your mind on my offer and I hope you do, please call me right away." At this point in the negotiation process, write down your name and telephone number and leave the information with the proprietor. Another option is to counter offer once again with a final acceptable price of $350. This "final" price is $25 more than your $325 offer, but still $25 below their top offer of $375. Tell the proprietor "you will take it at $350 and that is the best you can do." You still have a good chance that the salesperson will accept your final offer, because it is very close to the middle point of your negotiations. There is always a middle point in all negotiations and usually people will accept the middle ground. The owner might "hem and haw" a bit, but they will usually accept.

This is the best example I can give to you, my future Garage Sale Millionaire, to show you how proper negotiation is performed in any situation during the course of any sales venue. This kind of negotiation should be employed at art galleries, garage sales, antique shops, collectibles stores, or any place where a customer, salesperson and merchandise are involved. I have had a 80% success rate when I enact this negotiation strategy and I have made some good money over the years by implementing these tactics. Good luck!

As an art gallery owner, if I'm given contact information during the negotiation process, I will start thinking about accepting the lowest price the customer has offered. Then, I think, "Well, maybe the price the customer offered was not bad at all and their offer was not all that low." If I've had a week when sales were a little lower than expected and I don't really have anyone else interested in the piece, I'll call every one of my customers to see who might be interested in this item. If I still don't have any takers after making all my calls, there's a good chance I will call back the person whom I originally bargained with and accept their offer.

Another negotiating ploy, or strategy that works in saving 2% to 3% on items is offering to pay for an item with cash. Now that you have the item you want at a price you can live with, it's time to inform the store owner you'll be paying by credit card. The store owner is going to say, "Okay," because you already know they take credit cards, but not American Express (Remember what I said in the first chapter: that American Express charges the store owner a per transaction percentage higher than all the other credit card companies). Once the store owner accepts the idea that you'll be paying by credit card, you have one final way you might be able to get an additional 2% to 3% more off the price of the item. After you make it known that you will be paying by credit card, simply ask, "I can use my credit card, but I also have cash. If I pay with cash, will you be willing to take off another 3%?" *Not many shop owners will say no to that.* Why? The first and most important reason is that they're going to have to pay the credit card companies for processing each credit card transaction. If the merchant accepts "cold, hard cash," there will be no additional processing fees. Secondly, when you pay with a credit card, the merchant doesn't receive their money at the time the transaction takes place. On average, it takes from two to five days to have the money from each credit card sale deposited into their store's bank account from the respective credit card company. So, with every deal, you will want to have cash as a backup whenever possible. Cash will always leverage the deal. When you agree on a price, always ask for 3% less than the final sale price if you pay for the item entirely in cash. If the store owner offers only 2%, you should immediately counter with, "No, then it's not worth it." Usually, that's enough to get the merchant to let you have the item at the full 3% discount. *Cash really is and always will be, "King!"*

Once your offer has been accepted, you've paid for your purchase in cash and the item is all wrapped up and ready to go, make sure the store owner has your complete contact information. By having your name, telephone number and email address on file, store personnel can call you if anything interesting arrives which may be on your wish list or pique your interest. By leaving your contact information with the store, you've made an informal "announcement" to the store that you want to continue to do business with them. As a result of your actions, you've made a valuable ally who will go to battle for you in the collectibles business and be there to give you a heads up regarding great finds that come through their vast information pipeline or databases. Store personnel will search out new items for you. They'll be available to answer any questions you may have about items that may be of special interest to you and they'll be happy to do so. Additionally, now you will have someone to share announcements and provide expert recommendations concerning expos, events and gatherings you should attend to further your knowledge. By establishing an on going relationship with established collectibles businesses, you'll be privy to any future store sales, VIP and "invite-only" events and over time, if you continue to spend more money with them, you will start getting deals on items you may want to buy in the future.

Once you've made your best deal deal and you were able to negotiate a perfect sales price, be kind. Don't ever gloat, or do an "I got the best deal" dance in front of the store owner. The merchant already understands your good deal, so be nice and cordial. Leave on a good note so you can comfortably visit the store again in the future. Remember, when you come back the store owner "has your number" and he will already have a feel for how you do business. The second visit and during any subsequent visits, should also be a bit easier than your initial visit. When you want to visit a store or gallery again, don't call ahead and say you're dropping by to look at certain items. If you do this and store personnel know what you usually buy, believe it or not some unscrupulous establishments (a small minority within the industry) will raise prices on specific items knowing full well that you have an interest, before you arrive at the store! Then they will lower prices on those same items when you leave the store.

Million $ Tip

Never send checks or money orders in the mail. Don't wire money to any store if you haven't previously worked with the seller. Furthermore, using checks, money orders, or wire transfers is not the optimal way to get the best deals on the items you want to purchase. Once you send money in any of the aforementioned methods, you have no recourse if events don't go well and there is a dispute with your transaction. Also, never use a debit card. With a VISA or MasterCard debit card, money is taken directly out of your account and recourse of any kind is almost impossible.

Million $ Tip

I always recommend that you leave the store and do the proper research on any item if you cannot get the exact deal you wanted. Visit **eBay** *(www.ebay.com)* to make sure the price the store owner is offering on an item is a fair deal. eBay is a great starting point for any value-based collectibles research. Nothing is worse than buying a collectible then finding out you overpaid for it.

To get even deeper discounts, try the following strategy. When a seller offers you a discount of 10% or 15%, this is where you want to counter with 10% more than what they offer. If they offer 15%, you should counter offer a discount of 25%. There is a better than average chance they will say they can't go that "deep," but once again, you're going to agree on an amount in the middle of both your offers. If the salesperson is at a 15% discount on an item and you've offered 25%, try to come to an agreement on a final discount of 20% (once again, right in the middle of their 15% and your 25%). Once you've secured a 20% discount, this is a fantastic time to consider whether or not you'd like to purchase a second piece from the store. Perhaps it could be another chair, or a decorative vase, to place along side your antique dining room table. Be sure to ask the seller, what sort of discount they are able to offer if you purchase two, or even, three pieces?

This is where your discount is going to grow exponentially. Never put all your "cards on the table" by telling the shop owner you want to buy more than one piece at the beginning of your negotiations. If you do, you will have lost any leverage you might have had. The key to negotiating this way is to bring the salesperson into your negotiations at a very gradual pace at a time when you have the optimal vantage point. Start to "reel in" the seller with the initial concept that you are only going to buy one item. Once you agree on a price for that one item, you then drop "the hammer" and let the sales associate know you are actually thinking about two or three additional pieces. The seller should instantly give you the original discount, plus maybe a little bit more. You want the best deal possible and from my experience they're more than likely going to give it to you!

Are you a Garage Sale Millionaire?

Mastering the "art of the deal" takes a little practice, but if you follow the personal strategies I've outlined in this chapter, you should move to the head of the class very quickly. Any successful *Garage Sale Millionaire* will eventually master and consistently be proficient in, the "art of the deal." One of your main objectives, in trying to achieve *Garage Sale Millionaire* status, is to become a "Donald Trump" in the fine art of negotiating. Take your time, be knowledgeable, understand the process, remember to have fun, be cordial and respectful and know that by implementing what you've learned in this chapter, you're going to have a better opportunity for purchasing the item you want at the price you want.

By following these few simple steps, you'll become a master of the "art of the deal" in no time!

CHAPTER

4

Fakes, Replicas, and Restorations

How Not To Get "Taken"

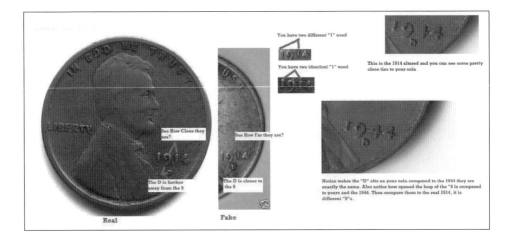

You have two different "1" used

You have two identical "1" used

This is the 1914 altered and you can see some pretty close ties to your coin

See How Close they are?

See How Far they are?

The D is farther away from the 9

The D is closer to the 9

Notice where the "D" sits on your coin compared to the 1944 they are exactly the same. Also notice how opened the loop of the "9 is compared to yours and the 1944. Then compare them to the real 1914, it is different "9"s.

Real

Fake

This is a good example of what can happen
if a coin is not looked at carefully.

For every great collectible item there's also a fake or replica made of that item. If you have a collectible you love and it's worth money, someone, somewhere, has already realized how they can make more money from that same collectible by creating an authentic-looking fake. Whether that item is an autographed piece of sports memorabilia, a Civil War-era item, a piece of American presidential memorabilia, a movie poster signed by the cast and crew of your favorite film, or a 125-year old antique, there's always someone working diligently to forge and replicate authentic items to make them look like the real deal so they can make a quick "buck" from you. *That, dear reader, is a guarantee.*

When you finish reading this chapter, you'll have a thorough understanding of how to keep one step ahead of the people who create the frauds, fakes and restorations so when you place your hard-earned money down to purchase that special item, you won't be bilked or "ripped off." The way to protect yourself from being "taken" by these nefarious individuals is to acquire as much information as possible about the collecting process. In the following pages I will personally share my secret tips that have protected me throughout my 30-plus years of collecting.

How To Protect Yourself

With all of our rules, regulations, and laws we have in place, just how can people "get away" so easily as they blatantly continue to produce products that mimic and replicate authentic items? More importantly, how in the world can these individuals make such consistently good money and evade the law time after time? I know the idea may come as a shock to you, but the practice of perpetrating this type of fraud is common place. This is one of the main reasons why I decided to write *The Garage Sale Millionaire*. I wanted to provide a means of showing you how to protect yourself from these unscrupulous individuals and to provide you with knowledge that will prevent you from becoming another "rip off" statistic.

The practice of creating and passing off fakes, replicas and restorations was far more difficult to accomplish in the past when people dealt with others in a more personal, "one on one" manner. With the emergence of eBay, Craigslist, email and the Internet, this sort of criminal activity has become ever increasingly easier to pull off.

Protecting yourself against fraud, like many other processes detailed in this book, is easy enough to accomplish. All it takes is understanding some basic information, using that information and implementing that information so you can proceed with your Garage Sale Millionaire activities fortified with the utmost confidence and armed with the peace of mind that comes from believing that you won't get cheated on your purchases. In 1537 Francis Bacon said "Knowledge is Power," but, today, it's what you do with your knowledge, that is power. This is what chapter 4 is all about…getting you the understanding and awareness about fakes, replicas and restorations, so you don't get cheated while attempting to acquire what you believe to be an authentic item which turn out to be unauthentic.

As stated in earlier remarks, any item manufactured today can be duplicated. My goal here, is specifically to discuss with you what collectibles are the most lucrative for and most often dealt with by crooks and where you are most likely to encounter fraudulent documentation, fakes, replicas and restorations.

Presidential Memorabilia

Collecting presidential memorabilia is one of the most problematic areas collectors encounter. Why? As far back as 1789, when President George Washington was in office, there were certain individuals who were authorized to sign the President's name for him. Yes, you read that correctly! Often times, a signature from a President is actually signed by a secretary, other staff members, even friends and family members, rather than the President himself. If the signature you have on your document is not signed directly by a particular President, the value of that item just decreased by 75% or more. There are also other items used by the Presidents for example, clothes, blotters, even dentures that are very collectible, but these items must have a verifiable certificate and/or auction record where the item sold.

> ### Million $ Tip
> Autographs from Presidents are very valuable and are among some of the most often forged items among all collectibles.

Unless you're an expert in the art of collecting signed presidential memorabilia, it's very difficult to determine which presidential signatures are authentic and which "presidential signatures" are not. This is one collectible you don't want to venture a guess on, because even the experts get fooled. You need to be very careful when buying "authentic" signed historical documents, especially when it involves presidential signatures.

Sports and Entertainment Memorabilia

People are buying and selling fake autographs 24/7. The only way you can fully protect yourself is by verifying the authenticity or "source" of the autograph. It's a known fact that for every actor, director and professional athlete who lends their signature to an item, there are probably two signatures from the same celebrity verified as "fakes." The Emmy award-winning CBS news program *60 Minutes* recently broadcast a segment about the potential pitfalls of collecting signed sports memorabilia. After speaking with numerous experts in the field of collecting, *60 Minutes* concluded that roughly half of all signatures on the market are fakes.

Many people selling what they consider to be "authentic autographs" will note they were actually present with the person who signed an item and personally saw them attach their signature to whatever they were signing. One of my very good friends, who is a well-known professional in the autograph and collectibles business has always told me, "It doesn't matter how good the seller's story is, if buyer can't personally back it up." Basically, what he meant was, if the signature is not real, then, whatever story is being told for the purpose of proving the authenticity of that autograph doesn't even remotely matter.

It's astonishing to me and *I am actually in the art and collectibles business*, just how many times over the years I've heard similar stories from almost every autograph seller. They proudly say, "I was there and watched (fill in the famous person's name) actually sign it."

Then, I'll take that signature to the back room of my gallery and match the seller's "original and authentic" signature with a real signature from the real person I know to be verifiably authentic. Almost always I find that this promised "authentic" signature is not even close to being a match. When I advise them that the signature isn't authentic, only then do they admit, "We actually didn't watch him sign it. A secretary took the paper to another room, came back and handed it to us.

Regardless of various stories coming from the person selling you the autograph, you definitely want to have a "Certificate of Authenticity" or "COA" to accompany the item you want to purchase. As I mentioned in Chapter 2, a "Certificate of Authenticity" is a document that a seller issues which guarantees that the item being purchased is authentic. Of course, a "COA" can always be faked by any seller and many people will tell you a certificate of authenticity is usually not worth the paper it's printed on. Actually, almost anyone can print out a "COA." It's as easy as printing

> ### *Million $ Tip*
> If you want to make money dealing in the buying and selling signatures, you'd better "know your signature." Astronauts, movie stars, entertainment moguls, Presidents, athletes, business leaders...anyone who is, or was famous, as well as infamous may very likely have had a secretary or assistant signing for them.

out a generic certificate generated from any number of inexpensive computer desktop publishing software programs. To make sure your "COA" will be recognized as representing an authentic item, always do business with a reputable art and collectibles dealer and always ask for a money-back guarantee on the item you want to buy. For example, over the last decade, co-author Jeffrey has done business with several art and collectibles companies including *Antiquities International* (Las Vegas, Nevada) and *Fascination Street Gallery* (Denver, Colorado). Both companies have stellar reputations and have been in the art and collectibles business over 25 years. Jeffrey knows when he buys art and collectibles from these two companies the "COA" they include with each purchase is going to be authentic and will be recognized as such in the future by professionals the art and collectibles business or individuals who will buy his items upon resale.

> ### *Million $ Tip*
> eBay is one of the easiest places to get "ripped off" on any type of autographed or signed memorabilia. So when you use eBay for this type of collectible, be extremely careful.

"Page Signatures" are obtained when stores or agents contract with an athlete or famous person to autograph multiple memorabilia pieces in exchange for a set fee. This type of arrangement usually occurs with sports figures, movie stars, former presidents, or anyone else whose signature has an assigned value. When this is the case, there should be a contract for the page signature signing that can be produced upon request for your examination, as well as actual photos of the celebrity signing the item(s). If the store where you're shopping is a reputable establishment, there's a good chance that the signature is legitimate.

Stores such as *The Upper Deck*, *Mounted Memories*, *Latitude Sports*, as well as many other memorabilia businesses, contract for these types of signings many times throughout the year. But, if your "COA" just states the location where the signing took place without an address, phone number, or working website, then the "Certificate of Authenticity" is most likely junk and you should steer clear of that particular item. Know that signatures from individuals in the entertainment industry, both film and television, are usually acquired at public events, on the set, through private meetings, or from autograph companies or individuals who have direct access to these types of celebrities. When collectible merchandise and memorabilia is professionally graded, the agency verifying an item's authenticity will affix a sticker that displays a one-of-a-kind image in the form of a hologram, proving the item is deemed to be authentic.

Before you buy any item with a "verified as authentic" signature, you should always know what the signature you're attempting to collect really looks like.

There are many resources available to the autograph and memorabilia collector which include photographs of authentic signatures of famous individuals so you can look and compare what may be real and authentic to what actually is real and authentic.

One fantastic company for self-verifying and self-authenticating celebrity signatures, from both the sports and entertainment industries, is **StarTiger** *(www.startiger.com)*. As of February 2010, StarTiger has an exhaustive database of over 290,000+ scanned celebrity autographs, 300,000+ celebrities listed (with addresses and contact information) and 470,000+ test results from members who have sent out their items to be signed by a particular celebrity. There are multiple scans and numerous examples of each celebrity's signature on the website so you can compare the variations in a personal signature every time a celebrity has signed an item. Although you can do a basic website search free-of-charge, a membership fee is required to enjoy full access to the website.

Million $ Tip

Money can only be made on a signature or autograph if it is verified to be authentic. The only way to officially verify that a signature is legitimate is through a professional authentication service. Self-authenticating a signature through **StarTiger** *(www.startiger.com)*, or if you have several books so you are able to match the signatures, will be a big help in determining if a signature is authentic before you pay the necessary fee to get a signature professionally verified.

Million $ Tip

When you are serious about getting into the business of buying and selling autographs, you should buy "Collecting Autographs and Manuscripts" by Charles Hamilton and "The Standard Guide to Collecting Autographs: A Reference & Value Guide" by Mark Allen Baker. Because this is such a diverse topic, you can never read enough on this subject.

Antiques

A whole generation of furniture has entered the marketplace and was created to look just exactly like true antiques. There are companies located in every part of the world whose sole purpose is to replicate antiques. What do I mean by "replicate?" This type of "antique" furniture is built from newly-sourced raw materials and then roughed up, distressed and placed in the weather to fade or to rust. Basically, these manufacturing companies will do and try anything they possibly can to make their product look "old" and "worn." To the untrained eye, these newly made "antiques" look convincingly like "authentic" antiques. Of course, the result of this unscrupulous business practice is that good people often wind up paying good money for a fraudulent products.

Fortunately, most conscientious shops know the difference between a genuine antique and a replica. A few less than honest stores won't tell you the difference and will charge you as if the item were an authentic antique. They will even go so far as to say it's an antique! But, the good news is that there are ways you can look at any piece to determine if what you're seeing is genuine or not.

The first thing you need to do is to flip the item over and look at its underside. If the piece you're looking at is a table, get down on your hands and knees and examine the underside of the table. Look at the way this item is put together. Were any screws used? Did they use nails? What specific kind of screws and nails were used? Certain types of nails are dead giveaways for determining if an item is newly manufactured. For example, the flathead nails we use today in manufacturing furniture is a dead give away for knowing that you're looking at a newly made item. In fact, nails utilized over 100 years ago in building furniture were very long, skinny, sort of "lumpy," and had heads which were not perfectly round. This was due to the fact that blacksmiths of that era personally hand made every single nail.

When you see what you believe to be a "genuine" or "authentic" antique, please take your time and study that piece. Look very carefully at the item and see what kind of nails and screws were used when it was built. If glue or staples were used, you need to stay away from that piece. If glue or staples are present on any "antique," you are most likely looking at a "restoration or a fake." Many times antiques are restored incorrectly. If restorations are completed properly, they can be performed without damaging the item and this process will usually bring the piece back to its original state. Many collectors agree that the cleaning and restoration of antique items is an acceptable practice. I will cover restoration items in more detail later on in this chapter.

The easiest way to find out if there is any glue present on any item and if a restoration was done properly, is to use a "black light." Whether the item is furniture or pottery, if glue

Million $ Tip

Antiques are a great collectible to make money on. To gain an advantage in your Garage Sale Millionaire competition, proactively search out and make friends with some of your local antique dealers and store owners. Not only will these individuals help advise you about the antique business, but they will make you some great deals when they know you are in the business of buying and selling antiques.

has been used incorrectly in the restoration process the added glue marks will stand out visibly with the use of a black light. What makes these marks so obvious are the compounds used in making the glue. When glue is present, the object in question will emit a "glowing" characteristic when held under the black light.

If possible, go into a room where you can control the lighting and use a hand-held black light device. Certain colors and pigments, such as those found in glue compounds, absorb the invisible light and then discharge that light. When this discharge occurs, a glowing

---

Million $ Tip

A "black light" will determine if a piece of art has been restored and even identify a "missing" signature. What do I mean by a "missing" signature? When some pieces of art were originally created, the item's artist may never have placed their signature on that particular piece. A "black light" will properly identify if a signature was added after the fact by a collector. If this has occurred, then the piece that you coveted for its resale money-making potential has lost almost all its value.

---

effect will be observed. While the room is darkened, turn on your black light and carefully inspect the item in question. Hopefully, you won't encounter any tell tale traces of glue and nothing else you observe will have any glowing properties. The "antique" item you believe to be authentic will indeed be an antique.

Black lights are extremely helpful in determining if an item has been "restored," or if it truly is a genuine antique. The difference between a "restored" item and an "unrestored" antique item is big money.

Jewelry

When purchasing jewelry, I want to warn you strongly that counterfeiting diamonds is big business. Additionally, when someone is trying to sell a fake diamond, more than likely they will present you with a counterfeit grading report to support their "authentic" claim that the diamond they want to sell you is verifiably authentic. To make matters worse, even authentic diamonds are not always "thoroughly and carefully examined during the grading process." What exactly do I mean by this? If a jeweler personally examines and grades the diamond or "stone," he or she could be "off," or misjudge the diamond by several different grades or colors. These discrepancies directly affect the value of the jewel and the retail sales price. To protect yourself, you'll always want to have a diamond graded by the **Gemological Institute of America (GIA)** *(www.gia.edu)*. The diamond grading set by the GIA is the preferred nationally accepted standard. In a quote taken directly from the GIA website, "Because diamonds are so valuable, it is essential to have a universal grading system for comparing their quality. In the 1940s and '50s, GIA developed the 4Cs and the GIA International Diamond Grading System™ to objectively compare and evaluate diamonds."

If a diamond has been graded by the GIA, the seller will have GIA-certified papers which accompany the stone. If the diamond does not come with certified grading papers from GIA and a jeweler grades the diamond, the chances are good that an error in grading will occur. By buying a diamond which has been mis-graded, you may very well pay a substantial amount of money for a diamond of a lesser quality and value.

The 4Cs include:

Carat - Diamonds and other gemstones are weighed and categorized in what is called "metric carats." One metric carat is equal to 0.2 grams.

Color - Diamonds are valued by how closely they approach what is referred to as "colorlessness." The less color a diamond has, the higher its value.

Clarity - An indication of a diamond's purity. Diamonds without faults, or "inclusions," or "blemishes," are rare. Of course, the more rare a diamond is, the higher it will be valued. Diamonds are assigned a "clarity grade" which ranges from "Flawless" (FL) on the top end of the grade range, to diamonds with "Obvious Inclusions" (I3) on the lowest end of the grade range.

Cut -The verifiable level of craftsmanship applied in cutting the symmetry, shape, proportions and polish into a stone. The better the "cut" of a diamond the higher its value.

This grading methodology also applies to Gold. Just because gold is stamped "14K," or "18K," does not mean the carat grading is correct. If you buy gold or silver outside of the United States, even if it's marked with an authentic-looking stamp, chances are good you're not purchasing the real thing. If you don't trust your seller...buyer beware! Always know your grader and always, make sure any piece of jewelry you purchase is certified by a respected organization, the same way GIA is respected throughout the gemological industry.

Also, make sure you receive a money-back guarantee and always use your credit card to make any jewelry purchase. By using a credit card, you will have the most recourse regarding any transaction, just in case you need to exchange or return an item for a refund. Jewelry is one of the areas where most people get taken because they never realize they've been duped until it's too late. Again, when buying jewelry, always remember to be extremely careful.

Restorations and Replicas...Not As Advertised!

I have talked a bit in this chapter regarding restoration and I haven't had a lot of good things to say about the practice. Believe it or not, "Restorations" are not all bad. If you know you're buying something that has been restored and the item is exactly what you want at a price point you find reasonable, then good for you! By all means, enjoy your purchase! When I speak badly about "Restorations," I'm referring to the term from the viewpoint of a *Garage Sale Millionaire*. I can't tell you how many times I've talked to individuals from across the United States who have been "taken" by buying from someone selling what they thought to be an "authentic antique," only to discover later that what they've actually purchased is a newly manufactured and badly done restoration or replica.

As I stated at the beginning of this chapter, "For every great collectible item available today, there is also a fake or replica made of that item." If you have a collectible you love and it's worth money, someone, somewhere, has realized how they can make more money from that same collectible by creating an authentic-looking fake." As a savvy *Garage Sale Millionaire*, you always need to be aware of this duplicitous practice and that at any time you could be mislead into buying something that is not "as advertised." You not only have to be aware of restorations, but you also have to be aware of the way in which an item is restored. If the restoration is completed incorrectly, this can also hurt the value of any piece.

Consider comic books, for instance. There are so many comic books available today in poor to extremely poor condition and in need of proper restoration. If you are a comic book collector and have an extensive collection, chances are that one or two of your comic "treasures" have probably been restored at some time in the past. Restorations are not entirely bad when they involve comic books. It's only when a comic book restoration is completed improperly that the book's value is diminished. A restoration, when rendered properly, will decrease the value of your comic a little, but the subsequent value of your comic may be improved more than had it not had been restored in the first place.

Many antiques are also improperly and properly cleaned and restored. As I suggested earlier in the chapter, if the restoration process on antiques is completed in a proper manner without hurting the original item, then that item will be brought back to its original vibrancy.

The restoration of antiques and comic books is acceptable, but cleaning coins is not. Period! If you clean coins, ever so slightly you will be wearing away the sides of the coins and causing very fine scratch marks. These scratch marks degrade the coin's overall quality and inevitably lowers the collectable value of the coin. Because of this, I never recommend cleaning coins. In my professional opinion, you will always do more harm than any good. There is a whole contingency of learned collectors and individuals who will argue both sides of this "to clean or not to clean" theory, but once again, you will probably want to leave your coins alone. By letting coins sit in their current state, even if they are a little "rough" and a bit dirty, you will always retain the value of the coin and will avoid permanently damaging the coin in any manner.

If the Deal Sounds Too Good to be True, it Usually is

Whether you're looking to buy an item on eBay, Craigslist, at a thrift store, or in a secondhand store, you'll need to do more investigation prior to making any purchase. As the saying goes, "If the deal sounds too good to be true, it usually is."

On eBay, you have to ask detailed questions and ask for better pictures, request specifics about the seller's return policy and you must always pay by credit card. Remember that using credit cards gives you better recourse if your purchase is not as it was represented in the seller's auction. With eBay, in particular, it's a huge plus if the seller will refund your money if you're not completely satisfied with the item you won at auction and eventually bought. Learn to live by these words on eBay..."Money Back Guarantee." Usually, you'll only have up to seven days to return an item. This seven day return policy is the "norm" on eBay, so be aware of that policy. If you go beyond the seven days, the seller will most likely not honor your merchandise return and you will be left keeping something you really don't want because you didn't keep better track of time.

Million $ Tip

Always get a "Money-Back Guarantee" in writing. When this guarantee is listed in an auction on eBay and even though it will be saved on eBay's corporate servers, print out a copy of the auction with the "Money-Back Guarantee" listed on your printout for your records. This "paper trail" will help you prove your case in the eventuality that you need to contact eBay's Security Department if you have a dispute with the seller about merchandise you bought from that seller's auction.

Items obtained through Craigslist are handled in much the same way as items acquired on eBay, albeit with some minor differences. If you're buying an item from someone on Craigslist who's not in your area, implement the same strategies you do on eBay to more accurately verify items. Ask detailed questions, ask for better pictures, ask about the seller's return policy and always pay by credit card (usually through PayPal, which I cover in Chapter 6 in greater detail). As far as I know, rarely is there ever a seven day return policy, or any return policy for that matter for sales transacted on Craigslist. This is very important to know before buying something from someone on this website. One of the reasons why there is no return policy enacted on the site is because much of the buying and selling on Craigslist is completed in person or "face to face," and almost every transaction is completed with cash. This is very similar to the way sales are transacted at garage sales which I discuss in Chapter 5. When you buy an item from someone locally on Craigslist, the transaction usually goes like this...people meet at a designated location, the item is presented for the buyer to determine if the item is worth buying, money is exchanged and both parties go their separate ways.

In secondhand stores, antique shops and thrift stores, once you leave the premises you own the item you just purchased. When you buy something and walk out the door; you immediately become the official owner of that item. In these stores, the owner is counting on you to know what you're buying. If fakes are sold, or if items are misrepresented in an antique store, the owner will usually return your money. The proprietors of these stores don't want the bad publicity generated by doing something unethical, or in a worst case scenario, doing something illegal. Once again for your financial protection, always pay with a credit card if you have a worry as to whether an item is real, or if there is something that worries you about the item's authenticity. The best way to continue in situations like this don't make the purchase until you do your research.

A Penny Saved

The most important element of this chapter and the point I want to emphasize most is, that not everyone who sells memorabilia, antiques, or collectibles is honest. There a few people in the "business" on another level who genuinely may not know "exactly" what they have to sell or know what the true worth of their items are when they place them in their stores, garage sales, or estate sales. However, there is a third group of people selling collectibles who prove to be very honest and their items are represented as verifiably authentic or properly deemed as replicas and/or reproductions. When you shop with the last type of individual listed here, you can comfortably transact your dealings and have the utmost confidence that you'll know exactly what you're buying.

Unfortunately, it's always up to you to be at a heightened state of awareness regarding everything you're purchasing. You always need to make sure what you think you are buying and what you're actually buying are exactly the same thing. If you make a hasty decision, don't do the proper research into verifying and authenticating the validity of an item and cover all your "bases," the chances are good you may buy something which has very little value or no value whatsoever. You know... the usual "Buyer, Beware" stuff applies as always!

When Ben Franklin said, "A penny saved is a penny earned," he very well could have been referring to future *Garage Sale Millionaires*. As *Garage Sale Millionaires*, we fervently strive not to get taken because we know the subtle and not so subtle differences between what is truly authentic and what is fraudulent. We cut through the purposeful lies of unethical and unscrupulous shopkeepers and always complete the necessary research before even thinking about putting down our hard-earned money to purchase any item. By avoiding illegitimate or unauthentic items, we save our collective pennies and then use that money to purchase those "hidden gems" and "buried treasures" which will make us much more money in the future.

Remember at all times, be aware, be ready and have all your bases covered! We are informed *Garage Sale Millionaires* and we will not get taken by those individuals trying to sell us fakes, replicas and restorations!

CHAPTER

5

Launching Your Own Treasure Hunt

Searching Out, Finding, and Making a

Serious Profit on Items From Craigslist

to Estate Auctions to Garage Sales

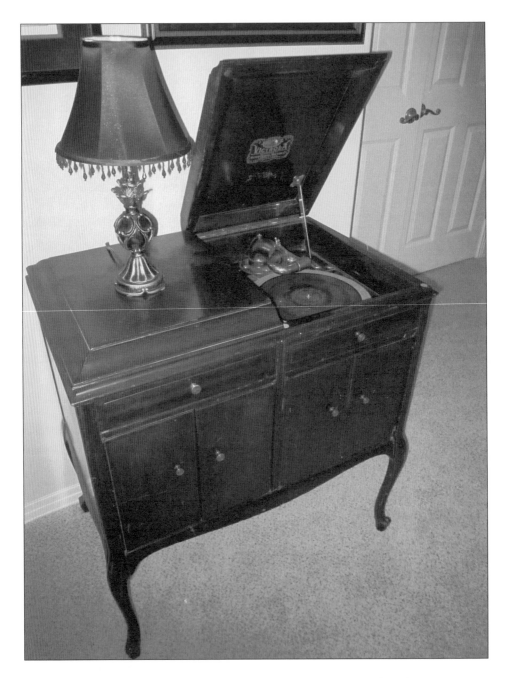

This Victrola is circa 1910. It has not been restored and sits beautifully in my President's Room. I bought this in an auction that was on live TV for $125.

Now it's time to launch your great treasure hunting adventure. In this chapter you'll learn where to find those hidden gems, one-of-a-kind pieces and extremely valuable treasures. Take your chance at attaining fame and fortune and become the next "Indiana Jones" of urban tombs. Your adventures will lead you to Goodwill stores, Salvation Army thrift stores, estate sales, second hand stores, antiques stores, auctions, storage units and the online marketplace. So, without further adieu, let's get started!

Tools of the Trade

Before your quest for treasure hunting immortality can begin, there are certain tools you'll need, as an aspiring treasure hunter and to insure you the best chances for success. By supplying yourself with the proper treasure hunting tools from the start, you've given yourself the best opportunity to achieve financial success in all of your treasure hunting activities.

Acquiring the right tools for all your treasure hunting adventures is simple. Let me start with a list of what you will need to have in your possession before you venture off to make some great finds:

- **A fanny pack**
- **A good magnifying glass (With at least 5X magnification)**
- **Sturdy gloves (Strong work-type)**
- **White cotton gloves**
- **Pen**
- **Small note pad**
- **A large, high-powered flashlight**
- **Extending pole (That you can put a mirror on the end of)**
- **Calculator**
- **Padlock (Combination or keyed)**
- **Black Light Flashlight**
- **Box Cutter or Sturdy Knife**

Along with these tools, there are a few more items which could really help you out a lot in certain situations. The following treasure hunting tools go above and beyond the scope of basic items listed above and are very beneficial to have.

A trailer or any vehicle large enough to carry big loads - Having a larger-sized vehicle available is a huge asset, especially when you're looking to bid on contents held in storage units. I will cover storage units a little later in the chapter, but know that when you buy the contents of a storage unit you'll need to move all the items usually within 24 hours after the purchase. Having a means of moving all those potential treasures without having to rent a truck will add to your efficiency and ability to get some great deals.

Sales tax license - An excellent tool to have if you're planning on eventually reselling any of the items you purchase. A license also could save you thousands of dollars over time. Your sales tax license allows you to avoid directly paying tax on items you've acquired from estate sales, auctions and storage unit sales, since you'll charging sales tax upon resale of your items. In most states, sales tax ranges from 6% to 9%, so for every $1,000 dollars you spend your savings will range from $60 to $90. This amount can add up substantially throughout the course of a year. Additionally, if you sell the items you buy in your own state, you must charge sales tax. As of the publication of this book, if you sell your items across state lines you're not required to charge sales tax. Of course, there are different tax zones for every city and county, so seek your accountant's advice on what to charge. A sales tax license will usually cost you approximately $25 to $100.

These two treasure hunting tools will streamline your business activities and in the end will save you time and money. Now that you have all the necessary tools at your disposal, it's time to start hunting for goodies.

Where to Treasure Hunt

Second Hand Stores

When I talk about "second hand stores," I mean places such as Salvation Army thrift stores, Goodwill Industry stores, AMVETS (American Veterans) Thrift Stores, "Mom and Pop" second hand stores and consignment stores. These are all excellent locations to find some very valuable items.

People ask me regularly, "How can there possibly be treasures at second hand stores?" Believe me; people are making huge finds at these locations every day. In February 2009, a person found a piece of art at a second hand store which was verified to be 150 years old. An appraiser friend of mine valued it and wouldn't you know it, that "buried treasure" ended up being auctioned at Sotheby's for an eventual $450,000!

That particular treasure was found at a Goodwill Industry store. The item was "waiting" in the store for what could have been days to weeks to months. One day, because someone knew what to look for, they found a treasure worth close to half a million dollars. It's an amazing story, and it's true!

Whether you're cleaning up your home or someone else's, you're bound to find items which could eventually be worth good money. Opportunities lie in wait in places you might never imagine. You could be helping a relative or neighbor with spring cleaning. Your parents unfortunately may have just passed away and you could find items that are no longer needed and must disposed of. A family friend might need help cleaning out their attic or garage. Always be alert! You never know what "buried treasure" you could come across and make a substantial amount of money from it.

After everything is gathered and finally cleaned up, people usually stick all their found items in a truck and try to help out their community by taking the items to a local community thrift store. Unwanted belongings are usually taken to Goodwill Industry stores, the Salvation Army thrift stores, or the AMVETS Thrift Stores. If it's not possible to personally deliver the items you've collected, these organizations will gladly come and pick them up for you. By choosing this easy way out as your first option and not taking into consideration the money that could be made from what you collected, you've made a huge mistake. This is how items like the 150 year old piece of art, previously mentioned, get discarded. *It happens every day in second hand stores.*

I recommend that you go to these types of second hand stores on a weekly basis and usually at the beginning of the week. I find that Mondays or Tuesdays are the best days to visit and do your treasure hunting. These are the days of the week when shelves are completely restocked with new merchandise. Stores receive most of their goods over the weekend and the employees will work very hard to price everything for placement on their shelves early in the week. If you really want to be thorough and

persistent, check back more often if you have the time. The more often you visit these businesses, the better chance you have to find that one item worth hundreds to thousands of dollars.

Second hand stores usually accept credit cards and a few of them even accept checks for payment. Unfortunately, the practice of accepting checks is becoming the exception to the rule because so many people have tried to pass bad checks. Many of the second hand stores have limited budgets and closely monitor operating costs just to survive, so the practice of not accepting personal checks is becoming the norm. I suggest that all of my customers bring credit cards or cash. As far as credit cards go, bring your Visa or MasterCard, but not your American Express. You can leave that card at home. Why? The reason is that credit card companies charge the retailer transaction fees. Every time a credit card is used, it costs the retailer from 2.5% up to 5% of the purchase price on every sale. American Express is the most expensive with regard to fees.

When can you negotiate prices? If the second hand stores are more Mom and Poptype stores, you can always try to negotiate the sales price. The worst thing they can say is "no." The smaller the store, the more negotiating leeway seems to be allowed. If the store is a Goodwill Industry store or a Salvation Army-type store, from my experience these larger second hand stores hardly ever negotiate. If you become friends with the manager and they see you all the time, then maybe something can happen. However, it is their explicit corporate policy not to negotiate.

Almost every major city has these types of second hand stores…stores packed with great items, valuable finds and hidden treasures. They're yours for the taking. To locate the closest Mom and Pop second hand stores, check local listings either via your telephone book, your local newspaper's classifieds section, or searching the Internet. To find some of the major second hand stores located near your community visit:

- Goodwill Industry stores (www.locator.goodwill.org)
- Salvation Army thrift stores (www.salvationarmyusa.org)
- AMVETS Thrift Stores (www.amvetsnsf.org/stores.html)

Some of the main things you'll want to look for in second hand stores are art, books and china. Also look around for whatever treasures you believe could be considered valuable in someone else's home. For art items, check the walls, the back room, or anywhere else art could possibly be placed in the store. Small sized items such as books and china are usually scattered throughout the store. Many items considered valuable by the store owner are kept close to the store front in glass cases. Actually, most of the items displayed in the cases have little value. Don't be fooled by their conspicuous placement!

Many times, individuals will go into their parent's homes when they've recently passed away or moved into an assisted living facility, taking anything and everything they can lay hands on. Then it's off to the second hand stores with the concept that what they're bringing will be very valuable. Although the majority of

items carry no value whatsoever, there are ordinarily some items of value to be found. I constantly hear stories of people finding items worth a great deal of money this way.

Estate Auctions

Estate auctions might seem a bit intimidating to you initially since you're bidding against other people, but this fear is totally unfounded. Not only are estate auctions a great deal of fun to attend, but you can find some real treasures that can possibly net you some serious cash.

When a crowd of very excited individuals sets the price for all the items being auctioned in a room, you can bet your bottom dollar that it's going to be an exciting day. Whether you're in a bidding war against a group of people, or just with one other person, it's important to know why people bid-up an item so you can make sure you don't get caught up in the middle of an unnecessary bidding frenzy and wind up paying too much for an item. Consider the following:

- **These individuals know the real value of the item and they're willing to pay whatever they think the actual value is on that item.**
- **They may have some sort of sentimental attachment to the item they're bidding on. Money is a secondary concern in these cases.**
- **They think there's big value for the item in question but they truly have no clue whatsoever about what the proper value is.**

Once you understand why people bid-up on an item, knowing as much as possible about the item you're bidding on is also extremely important. If you truly do not understand what you're bidding on, you will get caught up in a bidding war with one of these people and pay much more money than you should.

Knowing the way estate auctions work is key, too. One of the best ways to understand how the process works is to attend as many estate auctions as possible before you start bidding on anything. A major benefit of attending multiple estate auctions is that you'll be able to pick out those "professional" bidders, (the elite group that you'll become a part of soon), once you know how the system works. These bidders are experienced in

knowing exactly how to place the right bid at the right time and work the system, so the final auction price stays as low as possible while they get the best deal possible. Also, by attending many of these estate auctions, you can also see what these "pros" are bidding on so you can get an idea of what may be valuable and what may not be.

When you attend an auction, you'll need to be ready with the right method of payment and know in advance what the preferred method of payment is at that particular auction. Cash is fantastic for items up to a few thousand dollars. If you're going to be buying something in the ten thousand dollar range and up, it's probably best to make good use of your credit cards for payment. By paying cash for auction items, you'll save on credit card fees. (Some places may charge you more if you use a credit card.) Auction houses usually do not take American Express and many places do not accept Discover Cards either. If you stick with Visa or MasterCard you'll be just fine. As mentioned earlier, many auction houses are not taking personal checks due to fraud issues associated with them. Again, it is imperative to call ahead to make sure what payment options are accepted because every auction house is different.

Estate auctions can last from a couple of hours to an all-day event. Set your schedule to afford yourself enough time in case the auction runs late. If the auction takes all day, make sure you bring extra food, snacks and water. This may sound funny and may feel awkward at first, but many auctions don't have any type of concession stand available for their customers. If they do have one, prices are exorbitant and can cost double what you might normally expect to pay. Also, check to see what the weather will be like on the day of the auction. Some estate auctions are held outside or in warehouses that could be wither very hot or cold depending on the time of year. Dress accordingly.

Storage Unit Auctions

When I talk about the most exciting treasure hunting out there, I'm talking about going to storage unit auctions. You may be asking, "Storage unit auctions? Are you serious? How can they be exciting? They're just storage units, right?" Well, they really are great fun as I will explain.

In every city, in every county and every state in the country, millions upon millions of people use storage units to hold many of their belongings due to a variety of circumstances. When people move, many times they need some place to store items. When people can't fit everything in their home, or simply don't want to have their homes filled with clutter and unused items, they will store their extra items at an external location.

Storage unit operators usually charge a monthly rental fee for the use of their space and many times offer discounts if you sign up for rental on an annual basis. If a storage unit customer fails to remain current on rental payments, lapses for a period of 90 days and doesn't respond to repeated calls or letters from the storage unit operator or company, by

---

Million $ Tip

A quick warning about participating in storage unit auctions. Many of these units have never been "gone through" before the auction begins. From my experience, there could and probably will be almost anything in there including knives, guns, drugs, or even (used) needles. It is safe to say there are going to be items which could really injure you, so wear very thick, sturdy gloves and be mindful of how you are sifting through and opening all the items.

---

law the contents of the unit may be auctioned off. Usually the owner or manager of that specific location will place auction advertisements in the local paper, list the auction on their website and continue making minor attempts to let the storage unit renter know that their contents are subject to a potential auction. Once a storage unit customer has reached the

90-day delinquent mark, an auction date is set, the auctioneer is called to the storage unit and the bidding commences.

Once the bidding starts, it's up to you to take a look at the contents to see if you want to bid on the items contained in that storage unit. You will only have one to three minutes to take that "look." There could be only you and a few other people bidding on the contents, or there could be dozens of other individuals trying to bid on whatever is in that unit. It's a "crap shoot" with regard to what you may end up buying and you really need to be prepared for any situation. Everyone at a storage unit auction is thinking the same thing…they'll find that big treasure and huge payday. This is the point where the excitement begins. You really are going to have to put that excitement in check if you want to focus and score big at the auction.

> ### Million $ Tip
>
> When you're ready to bid at a storage unit auction, don't get caught up in the excitement of the bidding. Stay calm. Because you can't see everything in the unit and most items you may never be able to see at all, you have to be extra careful when you're bidding. Make mental notes about what you can see, try to figure out what the value is based on what you're seeing and then make the best educated guess on what the remaining contents of the unit may be worth.

Let's backtrack a bit, to give you better insight into the storage unit auction process. As I mentioned before, you'll be given a short time to look at the contents. This is where the "Tools of the Trade" items I listed at the beginning of the chapter come into play. Remember to bring your large, high-powered flashlight with you so you can get a good look at the contents tucked in the back of the unit. Of course, there's a catch to viewing the contents. You can't "break the door jam." What does that mean? Your head cannot cross the threshold of the door to the storage unit. As I've already implied, this process is a real "crap shoot!" If your head crosses this line, the auctioneer will shout at you. Truth be told, I've been yelled at on more than one occasion!

This is where the extending pole with a mirror enters the fray. I like to rig a mirror on a long pole so I can get a good look at what is wedged way in the back of the storage unit. Have this pole-mirror arrangement set up in advance and practice with it so you can get a good look quickly.

When it comes to bidding on the contents, only about 10% of the crowd will make a bid. Usually, after the first couple of bids, most bidders will drop out. When it comes to the end of the bidding, usually it will be you and one other person. This is really when you have to put your emotions in check. If you don't, you could wind up paying much more than the contents are actually worth.

Additionally, you will need to calculate the time it will take to clear out the unit if you are the person with the winning bid. You not only need to consider the money you spend to win the auction, but also the total amount of time you'll need to spend throughout the entire process. It's really beneficial and a huge time saver if you can find someone to help you empty out the unit. Family members or good friends are the best helpers. Plus, they usually work cheap! For the price of a trip to *Starbucks* or *McDonald's* whatever your helper chooses, you'll usually get all the help you need. Along with your helper(s), you need to have a trailer or large vehicle available so you can get all the goods you've just bought removed quickly within the allotted time.

If everything goes well and you've won the bid, now what? Usually, you'll have 24 to 48 hours to remove everything in the unit and leave it completely empty. If you feel you're unable to clean out the unit within this time span, then you'll need to rent the space for a month. I strongly recommend this course of action. By renting the space for just a month, you will save on having to pay the deposit money which is usually between $50 and $75. There's nothing worse than knowing you are "under the gun" and cannot get the storage unit cleaned out in time. Now you'll have more time to find a place to permanently put all the new found treasures you've just acquired.

> ## Million $ Tip
>
> Antiques are HUGE money-makers! When people see antiques, they're going to start bidding the price up immediately. You have to consider your ability to sell what's in the unit for more than the other person. People will bid and push their bids high. Ultimately, you have to place a ceiling on what you're willing to spend.

Don't buy the contents of the storage unit and then go home and think about it. You'll want to clean out the contents from the storage unit immediately. Get it done ASAP, as time could be of the essence if there are treasures that need to be resold promptly. You certainly don't want to miss your window of opportunity if a potential buyer for whatever you have goes elsewhere because you procrastinated.

It's also handy to bring large plastic bags to dump trash and to have a wheel barrow, dolly, cart, or something you can load items on and move them to your vehicle. Most times, you won't be able to back up to the storage unit. Many franchise storage facilities are located indoors. Obstacles may include elevators or stairs used to get to and from the unit. The easier you make it on yourself the faster you can remove all your new found cache out of the unit.

When you're looking at items in storage units, you're going to see almost everything. In my many years of buying and selling storage unit auction items, I've seen items ranging from furniture and antiques to kitchenware, personal items such as clothing or personal paperwork, even food items. You name it; I've seen it all! Quite a few storage unit operators recommend that if you find something of a very personal nature such as a birth certificate,

> ## Million $ Tip
>
> If you don't have enough cash to pay for your storage unit auction winnings approximately thirty minutes after the auction closes, the storage unit operator will re-auction the unit and you will lose your claim on all the items in the unit.

you should attempt to return it to the unit operator and ask that he get it to the rightful owner. I think this is a great idea because some of the personal items discovered in these units are of no value to you and irreplaceable to the person who lost them.

Also, be prepared to find metal objects in a storage unit. There may be items you can sell for the metal weight such as copper, silver, or even gold. You'll find many tools as well. Tools have a huge amount of resale value and many people will bid on the unit if they see tools as part of the contents. Additional items to seek out in this type of auction are televisions and computers. There's a catch here, as these items could be obsolete and have little to no resale value. You should never place much value on older computers and televisions. These items may not work, or newer versions have been produced at much cheaper prices. Don't let obsolete electronics distract you when you're looking through a unit.

Many times what you might find will most likely be trash, so always be prepared for that instance. You'll find that many items in a storage unit have no real market value and can be easily donated to Goodwill or the Salvation Army. If you don't have any need for an item, make a donation. You'll be helping families in need and in addition you might be able to use your donations as a tax write-off.

Make sure when you buy at these storage unit auctions, you bring cash. Credit cards and personal checks are almost never accepted. What happens when you run out of cash and you just bought something but don't have the money to cover your purchase? Hopefully you can leave for a few moments and run to an ATM, your bank, or call a friend or relative to bring you more cash.

> ### *Million $ Tip*
> If you discover anything you believe is illegal, call the police right away. You do not want to be a part of any crime so call the police and advise them you just bought the contents of the unit. They will completely understand and you will not be charged with anything criminal.

Storage unit auctions move very quickly. I'll bet you anything, if you put a stopwatch to it, the time a unit is originally shown to the time the auction for that unit ends, is less than eight minutes. Storage unit operators want to move quickly to get the unit's contents sold so they can make money from the next renter of that space. Individual auctions can include a single unit to fifteen units being auctioned off all at once. You'll want to make sure you have the bankroll to bid on all of them because you never know what's in the next unit while only one is shown and auctioned at a time. You'll never get to look through all the units and then bid on the one or ones you want; it's all or nothing.

> ### *Million $ Tip*
> To get the best deals at garage sales, go early and go often. Hit garage sales when they start and go to as many sales as possible.

For information on where the storage unit auctions are in your area, look to the Internet and search for storage unit auctions in your city. You can also find these auctions listed in the free newspapers in your town. Daily newspapers will have these sales in the classifieds. When you locate the auctions you want to do business with, get on their email list so they can send you an alert when their auctions will take place. This is the easiest way to get advanced notice of the auction time and dates as well as locations and number of units to be auctioned. In case the emails are not sent or your Internet connection is down, always double check your local newspapers as suggested above.

Garage Sales

Attending garage and yard sales as a buyer and seller is how I got started in the collecting business a long time ago. With garage sales and yard sales being similar in nature; I will just refer to them from this point forward as "garage sales."

Way back when, I was putting on garage sales with my mother and got to better know the kind of goodies we were putting out to sell. Frequent garage sale goers would tell us we should raise our prices on this or lower our prices on certain items. It was kind of those people to tell us those very helpful pieces of information. If people were telling us that our prices were too low, imagine how many garage sales there are where people who not only do not know what they are selling, but do not also know the best price to charge for their sale items? It happens all the time.

> ### Million $ Tip
> When you are at a garage sale, just because an item is not out does not mean it is not for sale. You need to ask the seller about items you are specifically looking for - antique chairs, old photographs, old baseball cards, pretty much anything in which you are interested. Ask them very politely and with courtesy! You never know what you may be able to get!

The main component of any garage sales besides the buying and selling of selling items, of course, is to negotiate every sale. As a buyer, you never want to pay the asking price. If you are not negotiating every sale, you are wasting your money.

I've had garage sales in the past where I put the sale sign up and someone was at my front door waiting for me before I got back from putting up the sign. People absolutely love going to garage sales because they usually go to find things they may need or want to own. As a *Garage Sale Millionaire*, you're going hunting with the express intent of finding items you believe to have a high resale value…items that will make lots of money!

If your garage sale begins at 9:00 a.m., you want to be there and be ready to go at 8:30 a.m. Don't be at all surprised if people, wanting to get a jump on the crowd, arrive at your sale before it's scheduled to begin.

When people hold a garage sale, there is a great deal of time involved and stress expended in the preparation. You have to make certain everything is laid out and displayed the way you like. Items need to be labeled and prices need to be set correctly to guarantee you're getting the maximum sale value possible. People often forget they have items they want sold and forget to put them out. One of the keys to a successful garage sale is to take your time in the days before your sale and make sure everything is accounted for with regard to what you want to sell.

The old adage of "the early bird gets the worm" applies perfectly to garage sales.

By arriving early for any garage sale, as a buyer the savvy garage sale customer gets the jump on their competition by being able to see everything laid out and ready to be sold before others arrive. The only reason you would show up at the end of a garage sale is if the seller had something that was really good for sale at the onset of the sale; but the item was priced way too high. If you show up during the last moments of any sale, make a "low ball" offer on the items you're looking to buy. They may take your offer knowing they won't get any other offers. If you don't want to drive back to the garage sale as it nears completion, you could try and get the name and telephone number of the seller before you take off and call back at the end of the sale to see if they still have the item you were interested in. Most sellers will gladly give out their name and telephone number.

Newspapers are a huge asset in finding local garage sales. Most newspapers have a separate garage sale section in the classifieds. Another way of locating garage sales is to drive around to as many neighborhoods as you can on a Friday night or a Saturday. People will begin putting out signs for their sales during this time. Another great way to view garage sales around your area is to use the Internet. By using specific search terms, there's a great chance a website will pop up listing sales in your area. A quick Google search for "Garage Sales + Denver, Colorado" netted 1,300,000 results. Another Google search of "Garage Sales + Los Angeles, California" yielded 3,350,000 results. It's truly amazing how popular garage sales really are!

Whenever you attend a garage sale, always be prepared so you don't pay more for an item than you should. If you have a smart telephone such as an iPhone or Blackberry, you can search the Internet and track down any item's value. As I will discuss in detail later in the book, a good place for determining value is eBay.

When you're trying to track down and research items very quickly, be very certain to take the extra few moments needed to match "apples to apples." For example, if you just found an original Star Wars Kenner Darth Vader action figure in near mint condition from the 1970s at a neighborhood garage sale and it was being sold on eBay for $2,495, make sure you search out the exact item on eBay. You would hate to find out when you got home that the $375 cash you just spent on what you thought was valued at about $2,500 ended up being a "Star Wars ROTJ Darth Vader figure MOC KENNER" action figure from 1983 valued on eBay at only $55.

When buying at a garage sale, it's definitely "caveat emptor," buyer beware. You need to make sure you're very happy with whatever item you buy. Try to do your due diligence, research on the spot and of course, if you're not happy with the item at all, don't buy it. There is a "no return, no refund" policy at almost every garage sale. This is true even if you walk to your car, turn right back around and try to return your purchase immediately. You're stuck because "all sales are final." That's one of the main reasons why garage sales are operated on a cash-only basis. The Salvation Army thrift stores, Goodwill Industry stores and second hand stores will not take items back either, but they may give you a store credit. Store policies may differ from location to location, so be sure to check those policies prior to making your purchase. You always have to buy things with the understanding that you are not going to be able to get your money back even if you decide to return an item.

There is no harm in bringing collectibles resource books along to help you make your decision at a garage sale. No one will say anything negative if you have a coin book in one hand and an antique book in the other. This is just what a smart and savvy *Garage Sale Millionaire* does; they arrive prepared.

Auctions

Auctions used to occur maybe a few times per month depending on the size of the auction house. Now that the current economic conditions have worsened, auctions occur more much more frequently. Auction houses now hold multiple auctions on a weekly basis. Auctions are very easy to find once again by looking in your local newspaper or searching online. In the business section of your newspaper classified section, you'll find a section just for auctions.

Don't confuse regular auctions with estate auctions, as they are completely different. An *auction* is a public sale of property which is sold to whoever is the highest bidder. With an *estate auction*, all merchandise is valued by an appraiser, priced accordingly and sold on a "first come, first serve" basis. At auctions or estate auctions anything and everything could be auctioned off to a lucky high bidder. Items at any auction may include entire inventories from an auto parts store, valuable (and not so valuable) coins, used cooking equipment from a restaurant, television or movie memorabilia, old tractors, antiques, guns, or home theater equipment. You personally need to determine what auction may be interesting to you as someone who wants to buy items to make an eventual profit.

Besides the crowd that sets the auction prices, the really interesting facet of the auction process is that an auction can be held anywhere. They can be held in the capital of your state or in the smallest rural towns. The auctions held in small remote areas are the ones you definitely want to frequent. If it's difficult for you to get there, likewise it's equally difficult for everyone else. The fewer people attending an auction means the better chance there is for you to get a fantastic deal.

For every auction, there's usually an online listing for what's going to be auctioned off. Some auctions also hold "preview days" where you can show up at the auction location to look at everything that will be going up for sale. Preview days usually take place 48 to 72 hours before the start of the auction. Taking advantage of preview days and asking questions about the items on the auction block are very important components of the auction process. Why? Because you can get an in-depth idea and understanding of what is up for sale at an auction, make detailed notes about what's going to be auctioned and do some research before the auction begins to find out the actual values on the items being offered at auction. By taking advantage of the preview days, you can also view any item, make sure it hasn't been damaged or restored and make sure it has all the parts, packaging, or whatever it takes to make the item worth the highest amount of money possible. If you can't attend the auction preview days in person, give the company holding the auction (usually an auction house), a call if you have any questions about their auction items.

Now is the time you need to set your top end price on items. If you do not complete your due diligence and research on the items you're interested in owning, you can easily overpay for them. I've seen so many people overpay for auction items over the years that I lost count decades ago. It doesn't happen once or twice; it happens at every single auction. I've seen people pay many times over the retail price for items being auctioned. However, the way to become a *Garage Sale Millionaire* is being able to find those hidden treasures which will eventually turn a profit.

If you are bidding against someone, or against a group of bidders, there are usually two reasons why people bid on an item:

1. People think the item is more valuable than the current bid.

At some point during every auction, people believe they are way ahead of the curve and believe the current auction bid price on an item or set of items is undervalued. This usually occurs when proper research is not done prior to the beginning of an auction. You would be surprised at how many people believe they know what an item is really worth, when in reality, they have no clue. This happens all the time. These are the moments when you can really clean up as a Garage Sale Millionaire. If the bidding doesn't reach the actual value of an item you can win the bid and make a fantastic profit upon resale. If the bidding goes way above the actual value of an item, by not bidding too high because you have done the proper research on the item, you won't overpay for something.

2. The item has some kind of personal meaning to the bidder.

When you're bidding against someone who has an emotional attachment to an item, it's definitely not about the money. These are the types of individuals who want to have the item at any cost. These individuals usually have the means and bankroll to buy any item they desire. You need to be very cautious and watch out carefully for this kind of bidder because it will cost you big if you're not ready. You're thinking they know something about the item, when in reality, they know nothing about the item and just want it because it has some degree of personal meaning or importance to them. When you get caught up in the bidding war against this type of bidder, this is where you can go way upside down on an item and pay too much. How can you spot this type of person? Before an auction begins, people linger around the items they are interested in and are very chatty about what's going to be up for auction. Listen closely to what seems to be innocuous and innocent banter, as it could give you great insight and save you money when the bidding begins! During the bidding, also pay careful attention as to the how people are bidding and how emotionally attached they seem to be with regard to certain items. Are they excited? Are their eyes wider than usual? Are they unusually attentive and does their posture-- the way they carry themselves appear as though they're excited about something that's happening? All these signs mean there's more than a passing interest is involved in what is up for sale at the auction.

If you do your research before the auction and place a mental ceiling on what you are willing to pay, that will always protect you.

I was at an auction a few years ago and I wanted to win a particular item very badly. It was an old vase I saw with some very interesting markings. I found out about the auction at the last minute so unfortunately I did not have time to research the item, but I did place a ceiling on what I was willing to pay for it. A woman began bidding against me and the bidding quickly escalated. Everyone else but the two of us dropped out of the bidding for the vase. I made an exception to my own rule as I kept making bids above my ceiling. As I said, I really wanted this item! As a result, I got unnecessarily caught up in the heightened level of excitement! Unfortunately for me, she kept on making higher and higher bids. By this time, I was way above my ceiling and eventually I had to end my bidding and bow out. To my chagrin, she eventually ended up buying the item.

After the auction, I approached her and asked her what she thought was so "important" about this vase. She told me that she actually knew nothing about the vase, but she had described it to her mother over the telephone and her mother was extremely interested in acquiring this piece. I further inquired as to why her mother was so interested in this particular item. It was because her mom had a similar vase at home which was irreparably damaged. Her mother thought quite simply, that this vase could easily replace the broken one. She had no idea what the vase was worth and she didn't care. She just had to have the vase.

I guarantee you that once you begin attending auctions you'll start seeing the same faces at almost every auction. Many people do this for a living and they attend auctions every week like clockwork. These are the people who will also drop out of the bidding quickly when the bidding goes too high. If you want an item more than they do, they see this and they will stop bidding when the bidding rises past their ceiling.

When I talk to my customers, I find out all the time that people are intimidated and afraid of the "magical" and "mystical" bidding process at an auction. Some people think like they see in the movies, that they have to do something very elaborate like tweak their nose or pull their ear to even take part in an auction. This couldn't be further from the truth. All you have to do is to take your bid number, which is provided to you at the start of the auction and raise it in the air. This is always the acceptable sign that you are bidding on an item. It's that simple.

Bidding and buying an item correctly at an auction separates the successful *Garage Sale Millionaires* from the "wannabes;" and the money-earners from the money-losers.

Along with completing your due diligence and research in finding out what items are the ones you want to bid on and deciding what to buy based on what kind of profits you eventually want to make, you also need to consider your costs. Costs throughout this process include three factors:

Time - Time is money. The time it takes you to research an item, determine how much to charge for an item, sell the item and collect payment all factor into the time equation. The more time you spend on something diminishes the actual profit you will make. If you made $4,500 on something which cost you $4,000 and it took you nearly 40 hours to sell it, that to me does not sound like it was a "win-win." It sounds more like a "lose-lose" situation. You need to figure time into your bottom line because it directly affects profits.

Auction House Premiums - Whenever you win something at an auction, you're going to be charged a "Buyer's Premium" by the auction house. This "Buyer's Premium" is a fee which is charged in addition to your winning bid amount. In the higher-end auction houses such as Sotheby's and Christie's, there's a better than average chance you will be charged a fee ranging anywhere between 12% and 24%. In smaller auction houses, the premiums are a little less than what is charged in the high-end auction houses. Unfortunately for the buyer, all auction houses have this "Buyer's Premium" as this is how these houses make their money and stay in business. Sellers also pay the same type of premium or fee called "The Seller's Premium." These premiums are also steep and can range from 10% to 25%. If you ever wondered how auction houses stay profitable, now you know.

Sales Tax License - Earlier in the chapter I discussed the benefits of having a sales tax license. Sales tax licenses can are easily obtained and will potentially save you money. Again, the cost of acquiring a sales tax license is approximately $25 to $100.

Every auction house has slightly different rules regarding what is considered acceptable payment. As mentioned earlier, credit cards and cash are usually universally accepted forms of payment; whereas the practice of accepting personal checks is becoming rarer over time. Some auction houses take checks but some do not. I recommend calling ahead and inquiring what the rules are for your particular auction house concerning payment options.

Almost every auction house takes credit cards as a form of payment. By using a credit card to pay for your auction wins, you can keep track of financial activities in much more detail than by solely using cash to make your purchases. Credit cards also have some level of theft protection, so if your card gets stolen you're usually going to be protected. Please check with your credit card issuer to determine and verify what level of protection you have as every card is different. Many credit cards have some type of mileage rewards programs attached to the card, so after a long week of buying at auctions you will get reward points as well. Visa and MasterCard are usually accepted. Sometimes Discover Card is not, so it pays to check out what is accepted in advance. Carrying a lot of cash on your person presents problems. I'm not talking about $50 or $60 in your wallet, but many hundreds or thousands of dollars in cash. Cash can be lost, or it can be stolen and once it's gone, it's gone. If you don't have to carry cash, don't. Use your credit card.

For an exhaustive list of auctions, by category, visit **The Internet Auction List** *(www.internetauctionlist.com)*. Please keep in mind that many times auction houses hold auctions covering many categories. For example, **Heritage Auction Galleries** holds auctions in the areas of art, comics, currency, entertainment memorabilia, historical items, movie posters, natural history items, rare books and sports collectibles. Some of the major companies in the auction business are:

Type	Auctioneer	Internet Address
Art	G. B. Tate & Sons Fine Art	www.gbtate.com
	Lunds	www.lunds.com
	Phillips de Pury Company	www.phillipsdepury.com
	Swann Galleries	www.swanngalleries.com
Automotive	Barrett-Jackson	www.goodingco.com
	Kruse International	www.kruse.com
	Mecum Auto Auctions	www.mecum.com
	RM Auctions	www.rmauctions.com
	Russo and Steele	www.russoandsteele.com
Baseball / Trading Cards	Baseball-Cards.com	www.baseball-cards.com
	Legacy Sports Rarities	www.legacyrarities.com
	Memory Lane Inc.	www.memorylaneinc.com
Books	Americana Exchange	www.americanaexchange.com
	PBA Galleries	www.pbagalleries.com
	Quinn's Auction Galleries	www.quinnsauction.com
Coins	Bowers and Merena Auctions	www.bowersandmerena.com
	Spink	www.spink.com
	Stack's	www.stacks.com
Comics	Comic Book Auctions Ltd.	www.compalcomics.com
	Mile High Comics	www.milehighcomics.com
Consumer Electronics	AudiogoN	www.audiogon.com
	VideogoN	www.videogon.com
Entertainment Memorabilia	Heritage Auction Galleries	www.entertainment.ha.com
	Premiere Props	www.premiereprops.com
	Profiles In History	www.profilesinhistory.com
Firearms	GunBroker.com	www.gunbroker.com
	International Bonhams	www.bonhams.com / us
	Christie's	www.christies.com
	Freeman's Auctioneers	www.freemansauction.com
	Heritage Auction Galleries	www.ha.com

Firearms-con't	Neal Auction Company	www.nealauction.com
	Regency-Superior	www.regencystamps.com
	Sotheby's	www.sothebys.com
Online	eBay	www.ebay.com
	eBid	www.ebid.net
	Overstock.com	www.auctions.overstock.com
	uBid	www.ubid.com
Sports Memorabilia	Lelands	www.lelands.com
	Rob.Edward Auctions	www.robertedwardauctions.com
	SCP Auctions	www.scpauctions.com
Toys	Smith House Toy & Auction Co.	www.smithhousetoys.com
	Theriault's	www.theriaults.com
	Toyzine	www.toyzine.com/sale.htm
Wine and Cigar	Acker Merrall & Condit	www.ackerwines.com
	Chicago Wine Company	www.tcwc.com
	Cigar Auctioneer	www.cigarauctioneer.com
	Hart Davis Hart Wine Co.	www.hdhwine.com
	Wine Bid	www.winebid.com
	Wine Commune	www.winecommune.com
	Zachys Wine Auctions	www.zachys.com/auctions

Antique Stores

Antique stores are very interesting to visit and there are thousands of these shops across the country. In some locations, there are also huge conglomerates housing antique stores and antique booths in the same location. Each booth and/or store is usually owned or rented by a different individual or company.

I like to go to antique stores in small towns and big cities because there are wonderful treasures to be found in both. Even where you think there aren't many antique stores, like in the tourist cities of Santa Barbara, California or Gettysburg, Pennsylvania, there actually are many of these shops available for you to browse in and buy to your heart's content. When visiting any antique store, don't think just because there are seemingly knowledgeable people behind the front desk that proper research has been done on every item on the floor. People make mistakes all the time. Sometimes, big mistakes work in your favor. It's up to you to search out which items are priced incorrectly. When you find those mistakes and hopefully it will be a big mistake in your favor, make an immediate offer on the item. You might go home with a gem of a find

> ### Million $ Tip
> When you offer a credit card for payment and they give you a price, ask what happens if you were to pay in cash. There is a better than average chance they will drop the price down a minimum of 2.5% to 3.0% immediately.

which will net you big money upon resale.

I've gone to some wonderful antique stores in my time and have seen some really tantalizing items being sold. Some of the antiques are priced well; others not so much. If I befriend the manager or store owner while I'm in their store, I'll usually learn more from them (not to mention there's a better chance I can make a deal on any item I find.) I've seen almost anything you can imagine in these antique shops. It doesn't ever hurt to ask questions. In fact, I highly recommend it.

Always make an offer on anything you're interested in buying. In these harder economic times, I've not seen a reasonable offer rejected at an antique store. People need to make the sale "right now" so their business will survive. When you go into an antique store, look around and take your time. If you find an item you like, then, negotiate. Quite a few antique stores will take credit cards. If you pay in cash, you might be able to get a better deal. Antique stores prefer taking cash for a sale because it saves them money by not having to pay any credit card transaction fees.

The Online Marketplace

There are many places online where you can find new or used items. The Internet is full with websites where people can buy and resell personal items for a profit. Since attending garage sales continues to be an increasingly popular activity, it's only natural that this garage sale-type of activity has evolved onto the Internet.

With so many places to sell buy and sell goods it's an essential business strategy to choose the most successful from among all of the websites listed in this chapter. You have the best chance for success, making the most money possible as a seller, and saving as much money as possible as a buyer by doing business online.

There are a couple of websites which have not only stood the test of time and survived an ever-changing economy, but ones that are also still thriving in a very down economy. These two websites have been in business for many years and are considered the heavy-hitters of the online marketplace: Craigslist and eBay.

Craigslist

The one website which first comes to my mind when discussing superior online marketplaces is **Craigslist** *(www.craigslist.com)*. Craigslist is the most amazing online shopping experience I could ever imagine. Craigslist, began operations in 1995 and originated as a bulletin board-type message service to help people around San Francisco, California find things to do. Today the company has grown into a global marketplace reaching all 50 United States (including Washington D.C.), as well as having a presence in over 60 countries.

The items offered on Craigslist change every minute of every day. The most recent listing is on the top of the webpage. In as short a time as 30 seconds, listings will dramatically change and brand new listings will be posted. If you want to find some great items to make you money, it's very important to check the website often throughout the day. If you see something you want to purchase, email the seller immediately. Business transactions on Craigslist happen extremely quickly. If you don't act in a very timely matter, which could be from minutes to hours, there's a strong possibility you'll lose out on an item because there are other individuals trying to make money just like you are on this website.

As with anything online today, don't let your guard down when it comes to conducting business. Always be on guard whenever you're thinking of parting with your money by making a purchase or when you're ready to accept payment on an item you're going to sell.

As a buyer, there are several ways to protect yourself when doing business on Craigslist. If you're conducting business with someone locally, don't send any money to the seller until you actually see the item of interest and arrange to meet the seller in a public place such as a local coffee shop to look at that item whenever possible. In my experience, a local coffee shop seems to be the best place to meet the seller.

If you do business with someone from another state or country, try to get as much background information (i.e. a detailed description of the item, multiple pictures of the item and references of past business dealings). It is not that buying on Craigslist from a different part of the world is a bad thing and deals can be had, but it's just a bit trickier. If you are the seller of an item, the ways to protect yourself when doing business on Craigslist are pretty much the same as they are for a buyer. This means to do business locally, always verify the item in question and personally meet the buyer in a public place (preferably) to get payment on the item.

The best payment option is cash when doing business on Craigslist. Almost every time I've sold items on the website, the buyer pays in cash. Because people usually sell their items to someone else locally, people expect to pay cash for whatever they buy. Be wary of accepting Cashier's Checks or Certified Checks. They can be easily be counterfeited. Since there can be fraud associated with these kinds of payments, I don't recommend going that route. It's better to meet the person face to face and ask for cash for your item. If you sell to someone outside of your area, such as another state or country, make sure the payment you receive clears the bank and funds are verified before sending the merchandise. If you can't meet someone in person to exchange funds, use a merchandise payment service called **PayPal** *(www.paypal.com)*. I will discuss PayPal in much more detail in Chapter 6.

Remember, when looking for items on Craigslist, items change very rapidly and there will always be something for everyone to buy. Also, do not limit your search to the state you live in. As previously mentioned, there are Craigslists for areas from all over the world. If you live in California, take a look at what's being sold in New York. Searching these lists can consume hours each day, but when you find that rare hidden treasure all your efforts will be worth it.

Many of my friends who buy items at second hand stores, thrift stores, storage unit sales, estate auctions and garage sales will put those items on Craigslist to move them quickly, so they can get cash back along with a profit as soon as possible. My friends also note that they'll sell items for less on Craigslist because they want to move their sale items quickly. Don't ever be afraid to make a counter offer on items you're interested in buying on the website. Talk to the seller, make the counter offer and you never know what you might get for less money than you ever expected to spend!

eBay

Everyone who has a computer and even those who do not own a computer, seems to know about eBay. Over the years, **eBay** *(www.ebay.com)* has managed its way into the popular vernacular as the default expression and term for selling and buying anything on the Internet. eBay is where more items are bought and sold than any other single location in the world with a reach spanning over 30 countries. I've dedicated an entire chapter on eBay in Chapter 6 to explore this website in greater detail.

I sell a lot of items each month on eBay. As a businessperson, eBay has opened up avenues I could never have even imagined for my art and collectibles gallery. The same opportunities I have as a gallery owner and private collector to sell my "stuff" globally is also easily afforded to you. With a simple and straightforward user interface, tens of millions of users with hundreds of millions of items listed for sale and a support community that helps buyers and sellers alike, eBay is the best place to get your items noticed and to make a handsome profit.

> ### Million $ Tip
> Use websites which allow you to conduct a more thorough search by searching many states at once for the treasure in which you are interested in purchasing. **CraigsPal** *(www.craigspal.com)*.

With the information provided to you in this chapter, you now have the necessary tools to launch your own grand treasure hunt. The rewards are too numerous to mention and the riches you can make are only limited to your desire to succeed. Think big and in no time at all, you will be on your way to becoming a *Garage Sale Millionaire!*

CHAPTER

6

eBay

Virtually Limitless Potential to Buy and

Sell Collectables for Great Money

An Officer's sword from the Civil War bought on eBay.

For any potential *Garage Sale Millionaire*, one realm rises above all others for making amazing amounts of money. It's an arena where almost any object...baseball cards, toys, action figures, sports memorabilia, art, antiques, watches, DVDs, magazines and books, sporting goods, home and garden items, movie memorabilia, electronics and even cars can easily be sought out, acquired, then flipped and sold for sizable profits. That province, conveniently located on the Internet, is known as **eBay** *(www.ebay.com)*.

By the time you've finished this chapter, you'll see that eBay is a dynamic, multifaceted online community where almost anything can and is auctioned or sold to an enormously active and extremely loyal customer base. Endless streams of people continuously support eBay with their prodigious purchasing demand to buy items for amazing amounts of money. Never before in the long, illustrious history of collecting and treasure hunting, has there been one singular resource that brings together so many people from around the world... people with diverse interests, the way that eBay does. eBay has been described at times as the "World's largest garage sale." The reason that eBay has continued its momentous growth in popularity lies in the website's simple format...an environment that makes it extremely easy to conduct business. When you want to become a *Garage Sale Millionaire*, time is money. Selling items on eBay offers maximum simplicity. We all know that time saved equals substantial profit making.

In this chapter, you'll learn many valuable insider tips gleaned from my own years of experience working on eBay that will allow you amplify your quest to make money more quickly. These are personal tips which you will absolutely not be able to find anywhere else. My main goal within this chapter is to show you how to make your eBay experience not only more gratifying and fulfilling, but exponentially more profitable.

The eBay Homepage - A Starting Point for Your Garage Sale Millionaire Treasure Hunt

As it is with most every corporate homepage on the Internet, the eBay homepage is the launching point for the entire website. eBay's homepage is divided into ten primary sections:

- **The Top Header -** This is the uppermost section of the eBay Homepage which includes access to Sign-In to your account or Register for a new (and of course, free) account. Also included on the top header section are links to buying and selling items, a link to your personal "My eBay" page where you will be able to monitor all the auctions you're involved in, a "Contact Us" link to approach eBay directly, a drop down menu for over 30 different auctions categories, links to their "Motors and Stores" sections, as well as a link to eBay's "Security and Resolution Center."

- **eBay Website Advertising -** eBay lists promotional advertising in this space. Sometimes. Here will be links to the "Daily Deal," "great items to buy" and items with "deep discounts."

- **Daily Deal / Cool Stuff** - This section of the homepage includes items eBay highlights for its bidders.
- **Welcome To eBay** - An additional area on the eBay homepage where you can either sign-in to your account or register for a new eBay account.
- **Great Buys** - Links to items listed as "the coolest, wildest and most watched."
- **My Recent Activities** - Whatever you have searched for recently on eBay is listed here.
- **Favorite Categories** - Links to over 35 categories of goods and services within the eBay website, as well as a "Visit All Categories" link.
- **More Fun Finds** - This section highlights additional areas to visit. Some of the items here can include promotional items from television show-sponsored auctions (Ellen / Oprah) or items for upcoming holidays (Mother's Day).
- **From Our Sellers** - This section highlights featured items up for auction on some areas throughout the website.
- **The Lower Tier** - The bottom of eBay's homepage contains links to many websites within the eBay system. This last section at the bottom of the eBay homepage includes: links to all 30 international eBay websites from eBay Australia to eBay Vietnam; links to partner websites such as Half.com, PayPal, StubHub, Shopping.com; and links to more than 15 additional eBay services such as Feedback Forum, Security Center, Resolution Center, Gift Cards & Gift Certificates and Announcements.

A note from Aaron: *eBay's website content and organization change frequently. The eBay homepage may be altered due to seasonal changes, such as the advertising for American holidays of Christmas, Chanukah, Kwanzaa, etc., or to promote a special addition to the website.*

eBay and PayPal: Registration, Bidding and Buying

Registration

To take advantage of all the potential that eBay has to offer; you must first register with eBay and PayPal. You might be asking yourself why in the world would you have to register with PayPal to attain success on eBay? Not only is **PayPal** *(www.paypal.com)* the official payment website for all of eBay's transactions, but it's the easiest, most secure way to do business with the auction website as well.

The process of registration on both eBay and PayPal is a very simple and straightforward "fill in

> ### *Million $ Tip*
> When setting up your PayPal Account, use a credit card and not a bank account. This will add an extra layer of protection to all of your eBay transactions.

the blanks" kind of exercise. Almost all the data fields which need to be filled out to register on eBay and PayPal are many of the usual data fields you would find on almost every other website. Examples would include name, current address, email address and date of birth. After filling out the proper forms, all you have to do is to create a "unique user ID," password and agree to the terms and conditions of each website. Once this is completed, you are now officially registered with both eBay and PayPal.

Searching the Website

Searching for those buried treasures is a simple and easy process on eBay. All you have to do is to enter what you're searching for in the *Search criteria dialog box*, click on the *Search button* to the right of the search criteria dialog box and then the results of your search are listed on your computer screen. The best way to get more hits when you search for items on eBay is to be as detailed as possible. If you use a set of more generic search terms, your search may not yield as many results as you would like.

After your basic search results are displayed and you want to further refine your search criteria, you can do so by finding the *Refine search box* on the left side of the page. In this area of the page, more categories and empty data fields will be listed if you need to use them to help you find your search goal. Another way to refine your search is to check the *Include title and description box* and, then, retype your original search terms. Hopefully, what will be displayed will be the exact item you're looking for. Information such as *featured items* (the actual auction item and description), *price* (the current high bid in the auction) and *time left* (time remaining in the auction) will be displayed next to a picture of the item for auction. Sometimes, *Free Shipping* or a label of *Top Rated Seller* (for those sellers who meet certain successful sales criteria) will be listed for each sales entry to try to entice you to further investigate a particular auction.

All the pertinent auction information will be displayed for you on this page. Now it's up to you to either investigate a particular auction further or to keep on searching for that exact item you're interested in.

Before You Bid: Understanding the Auction Page

After finding an item you'd like to bid on, you'll need to click on the picture or description to select that item. The auction page you see displayed will have everything you need to make a proper decision regarding whether or not to bid. It's on this page where decisions to either bid on an item or to look for other items will be made.

The auction page is split into two sections. The top half of the page gives bidders exact data about the current auction as well as the seller; and the bottom half of the page gives more detailed information about the auction item and details regarding the auction process.

The top half of the eBay auction page displays for the bidder:

>*Item Condition* - Is the item you are interested in new, used, never opened, refurbished, or mint-in-box? You'll find that information here.

>*Time Left* - The time remaining in the auction. If the auction is getting close to ending, the time left will countdown second-by-second directly on your screen.

>*Bid History* - Shows how many bids have been made in this particular auction.

>*Current Bid* - Shows the current price, or what the high bid is so far in this auction.

>*Max Bid Field* - If the auction is still open, then you can place your bid here.

>*Sale Info* - Shipping, payment and return information will be located under this heading.

>*Seller Info* - Seller ID, link to feedback profile, feedback percentage and links to ask the seller a question are listed in this section of the auction page.

>*Miscellaneous* - Item number, location and where the seller ships to are listed here.

The bottom half of the eBay auction page contains more information including:

>*Description* - More specific details of the auction item are listed in this section.

>*Shipping and Payment Info* - This section lists the terms and conditions of the sale such as shipping costs, estimated delivery time and any return policies.

>*Related Items* - Many times a seller will have multiple auctions on eBay. This section gives you specific hyperlinks to access the auctions of those items.

You might see something on the auction page where the current bid price of the auction is listed with an option known as *Buy It Now*. When this option is available, any bidder can pay the current price of the auction and immediately "win" the auction

---

Million $ Tip

Not all auctions have a "Buy It Now" option. It is up to the seller to list this option on an auction item. You can still contact the buyer to see if they would take your offer on the item they are selling to end the auction early.

---

item without having to go through the sometimes lengthy auction process. The "Buy It Now" option, when it's offered, is always available if no one has yet placed a bid on an auction. The "Buy It Now" option disappears when the first bid is made.

Extra caution needs to be taken when deciding which items to place bids on. Because a bidder is not personally familiar with the seller, care must be taken to make sure the item you want to bid on is exactly what you are interested in buying. Never bid early on an item. The best time to bid on an item is the final two minutes of any auction. The best and most efficient way to do this is in the use of *Sniperware*. I will discuss Sniperware in much more detail later in the chapter.

Getting to Know the Seller

There are some great tidbits of information which will clue the bidder into whether or not the seller can be trusted and if they are legitimate. The *Seller Info* section is one of those areas you need to examine carefully and study before you bid on any item. The "Seller Info" section is located on the right side of every eBay auction page. This section details valuable information regarding the legitimacy of the seller, including:

The Seller's Name - This is the eBay User ID for the seller.

The eBay Seller's Star Rating - This rating denotes positive feedback for the seller participating in this auction. Obviously, the higher the star rating the more you will trust and will want to do business with this person.

Positive Feedback Percentage - This section shows positive feedback from all bidders, listed as a percentage. There is also a hyperlink included which will direct you to the seller's detailed "Feedback Profile."

Ask A Question - Click this hyperlink if you need to ask the seller anything about the auction.

Save This Seller - You can add this seller to the list of your "Favorite Sellers and Stores" on your personal eBay homepage, for quick reference.

See Other Items or Visit Store - If this seller has other items up for auction on eBay, those auctions will be linked to from here.

Other Item Info - Included here is the item number, the originating location where the item was shipped from and the destination location where the item will be shipped to.

Million $ Tip

Read the "Item Description" very carefully on any eBay auction. If you have questions about any part of that description, or any part of the seller's auction, always email the seller for clarification. If they don't answer your email to your liking, do not bid on the item.

Protecting Yourself as a Bidder

Properly evaluating the legitimacy of a seller is one of the foremost ways you can protect yourself as a bidder on eBay. There are a few things you can look for when examining the authenticity of a seller:

Study the Seller's Feedback Score and Feedback Percentage - The higher the number score and percentage; the better the chance any transaction from this seller will be legitimate. You can view this data by clicking on the seller's name directly under the "Seller Info" header.

Go to the *Ask A Question* link to ask the seller a question about the item or to request more information about the item up for auction. See how quickly they answer your questions and note the completeness of their answers. See if they offer extra useful information about an item.

View all the detailed pictures of the item if they are listed on the auction page. Every seller is different and may list this feature in different areas of their eBay auction website. If you don't see a picture listed on the seller's page, or the pictures posted to the auction website are not to your liking, email the seller and ask to see additional photos and/or more evidence to show that the item is legitimate and to your liking before you make a bid.

In the *Latest Feedback section*, click on the "See All" hyperlink to the far right to see what other users think of this seller's business dealings and practices. A better breakdown of the seller's score will be listed here as well. This area of the eBay website is located on the webpage when viewing the *"Seller's Feedback Score and Feedback Percentage"* as outlined above.

The higher the numbers for a seller in both total number of positive responses and percentage the better. It's much easier to trust someone with a high number tally of 3,500 positive responses than it is if someone had only a score of 12. The same is true of feedback in percentage form. If someone rates 99.0% TO 100.0% in positive feedback, they will have proven to all potential buyers that they are a

---

Million $ Tip

Be wary of "Spoof" emails from what seems like legitimate sources such as eBay and PayPal that ask for your financial information. The act of "Spoofing" involves an email that is sent to trick the email recipient into thinking the email is coming from a legitimate email address. Instead, the email comes from a criminal source in an attempt to trick the recipient into unknowingly releasing sensitive personal information. The result opens potential identity theft issues.

trustworthy member and seller. Also, by clicking on the actual score the seller has received, you get a 12-month breakdown in "1 month," "6 month," and "12 month" increments, of all sales activity rated as "positive," "negative," or "neutral." This hyperlink will be listed as "(the seller's score and a star icon)" directly to the right of the "eBay User's ID." Personal feedback from auction winners is another major plus in verifying how reliable the seller is. Of course, anyone on eBay can claim that what they're selling is the most beautiful item of its kind in the world, but a seller's less than stellar reputation will make you think twice about bidding on that person's item.

eBay's Buyer Protection Programs

After the auction is concluded and you've sent your money to the seller, if you don't get what you paid for, there are certain avenues you can take with the assistance of eBay to help get some if not all of your money back. eBay's Buyer Protection Programs help you with what eBay calls "transactional problems with a seller." eBay prefers that you do most of the work yourself before you file a claim if you feel you've been cheated by a seller. eBay wants you to be pro-active and try to solve these types of auction disputes on your own. If eBay handled every claim from millions of users around the world, it would be quite costly and, as a result, website and company costs would rise exponentially.

> ### *Million $ Tip*
> Never feel badly about asking for more photos and information of the item you are interested in bidding on if you are unsure about the quality, authenticity, or legitimacy of that item. It is better to know all the facts upfront before bidding on something. The last thing you want is to do is to pay for something which is not exactly as advertised.

A few of the steps you can take before contacting eBay about any problem include emailing the seller with questions about the situation, contacting the seller directly by telephone to try to solve a dispute (if the telephone number was given after the auction ends), filing a grievance with PayPal and contacting your credit card company. Only after the proper steps are followed can you file any protection claim with eBay and access their buyer protection programs. Any claim of this type may take up to 60 days or more after an auction ends before there is a

Million $ Tip
If the price seems too good to be true, be very careful.

Million $ Tip
You are limited in the number of negative reviews before you get your eBay bidding rights suspended.

decision made about your dispute. Detailed information on this topic can be found on **eBay's Help Pages** *(http://pages.ebay.com/help/tp/isgw-buyer-protection-steps.html).*

You'll need to keep detailed documentation of your efforts if there's a dispute because eBay will require documentation proving what you've already done before filing a claim with them. It's not instant gratification, but by following the rules you will eventually get some help. The eBay Buyer Protection Programs range from assistance in "facilitating a communication process between the buyer and seller," to getting reimbursed up to $20,000 with a buyer co-payment of $500 when a vehicle is involved.

> ### *Million $ Tip*
> When an item is first offered on eBay, always see if the seller will take less than the asking price. You will have a better chance to get a great deal if this item is from a person who maintains an eBay store and not one individual selling one item of something.

Bidding on eBay

Bidding for items and auctioning items on eBay follow many of the practices and procedures found at a traditional auction house. The usual acts of bidding and re-bidding are the same and they are essential parts of the online auction process.

> ### *Million $ Tip*
> Sign up to have eBay text your mobile telephone on the auction status of every auction in which you are involved, if there is activity, if you do not check your email on a regular basis.

One major word of caution about bidding for any item on eBay and I cannot stress this strongly enough, *every bid on eBay is a legally binding contract between the buyer and seller which cannot be retracted.* You must be very sure you want to bid on something before finally clicking that "Enter" button. Of course, with some rules there are exceptions.

The only exception to the "legally binding bid" rule is when a bidder mistakenly adds a zero or multiple zeroes to the end of a bid. For example, a bidder incorrectly makes a bid of $2,000 or $20,000 instead of a proper bid of $200. (eBay will allow you to make a few retractions per annum without consequence.) If you do renege on a bid, your user rating will be affected in a negative way. User ratings are similar to popularity contests. When you have a higher user rating as a buyer or seller, more people want to do business with you and in turn, you become much more popular. As a bidder, being more popular means more sellers will sell to you with fewer

> ### *Million $ Tip*
> If you buy more than one item from a seller ask them to combine shipments to save on the shipping costs.

or no restrictions. As a seller, being more popular on eBay means more bidders will be attracted to your auctions because you're considered a more legitimate and trustworthy user rating is low. As a seller, not many people will take your auctions seriously. They will view your business dealings as untrustworthy because of your low rating. As a bidder, many sellers won't vend with you because you have proven yourself to be unreliable.

Being Outbid aka Let the Bidding Wars Begin!

After you've placed your bid on an item, you might be outbid. That is usually the rule and not the exception. When you're outbid, eBay issues an automated email reminder stating that in fact, you've been outbid. In the email, eBay will also provide a link back to the exact auction item website page so you may place another bid to outbid the higher bidder, or as I like to say, "Your competition." If you're like me, you really hate to be outbid in any auction.

Losing an auction that you know you could have won and turned that item around and selling it for a handsome profit, is a very bitter pill to swallow!

Being outbid is not really a problem in the early stages of an auction because of auto-generated outbid notices. The only time being outbid becomes a serious problem is if you don't check your email often enough. If you can't check your email frequently, you may come to the realization that you're reading an outbid notice for the first time after the auction you're interested in has really ended. Not good. When this happens, the sting you feel knowing that an eventual profit was lost, lasts for a little while.

After bids have been placed and you're lucky enough to be the high bidder when an auction ends, it's now time to pay for the item.

Payment on an Item

After you've won an item, eBay will contact you by email to let you know you were the high bidder. The email will contain a link to click on to go directly to the payment page for that auction. If you consistently monitor the page where the auction is being held, you can pay for the item from a direct link on the auction page.

The way you pay for an item is dependent upon how the seller originally setup payment instructions for their auction. Even though PayPal is the usual method of payment on eBay, there are other electronic transfer options which I will discuss later in the chapter when I talk about avoiding fraud. For now, I will focus on paying for auction wins through PayPal.

Once you click on the PayPal link either from the email sent to you by eBay or directly from the auction website, you will be redirected to the seller's PayPal website for the opportunity to transfer funds from either your credit card or bank account. Once you've put your data entry skills to work by filling out all the pertinent payment information, all you have left to do is to wait until you receive the item.

When you finally receive the item you've won on eBay, make sure you open and inspect it thoroughly within 48 hours so you can report any problems. After a certain amount of time has transpired, the seller will not feel liable for any problems and you will be stuck with something defective and non-returnable.

Sniping and Sniperware: Never Get Outbid on eBay Again

This brings me to Snipers and Sniperware; and the bidding process. These terms might seem somewhat scary or mysterious, but they describe the ways individuals with little or no effort can swoop in at the very last moment of an online auction and steal the deal you thought you had easily won. This is ever-the-more painful when you realize that the item you just lost out on would have made you a substantial profit upon resale.

So, what then, is "Sniping?" With just moments left to go in an auction or, in many cases, with just one second remaining, someone enters the auction with just barely enough of a bid to outbid you and becomes the winning bidder. Because of the precise timing of that single strategically placed bid…so close to the end of the auction, you have no opportunity to counter-bid to save your bid. You are stuck and you have just lost the auction. You have now been relegated to dreaming of what could have been.

Congratulations, or rather, my condolences…you have just been "sniped" by someone using Sniperware.

The term "Sniping" can also be used for someone manually outbidding you at the last moment without the use of a computer program. The term is more common with computers because electronic sniping is almost always used today.

In more "civilized" times, it used to be that the person sniping you to win an auction would do it manually. This was accomplished by physically waiting until the last moment to outbid you. This drawn-out process usually meant staying awake until midnight or later to try to win the auction by waiting until the last possible moment to (hopefully) enter and make a winning bid. As a result, you'd become sleep deprived despite the fact of knowing you had to wake up early the next morning to go to work. However, you waited patiently until the last conceivable moment in your attempt to try and win the auction item. Today, these snipers use technology in the form of computer-aided programs called "Sniperware" to do all their dirty bidding work to out maneuver the non-sniperware using public.

Sniperware can be found and downloaded, from the Internet as "Shareware."

Shareware programs are software programs that cost the user a fee after a short trial period. Just perform a Google search and you'll eventually find capable Sniperware programs to incorporate into your bidding activities.

To better understand just how easily Snipers using Sniperware on eBay can really ruin your day, please see below.

How co-author Jeffrey received an assiduous snipe he won't soon forget...

Jeffrey and his wife Mary absolutely love movie replicas, movie collectibles, and almost everything else regarding the movies that look like a really cool to own collectible. This time, the item in question that Jeffrey was aching for was a 1:1 scale movie replica of the "Samaritan Gun" from the first Hellboy movie. The main character, "Hellboy," actually uses this gun throughout the film to 'get' the bad guys. This collectible was much more valuable since it was no longer being manufactured and acquiring this particular item was becoming increasingly rare as the weeks and months passed by. A "1:1 movie scale replica," for those not familiar with these sorts of things, is a replica produced in the exact measurements and specifications as those that were actually used and seen on-screen. Jeffrey described it to me as, "An awesomely wicked cool piece that had to be mine!" To see someone actually selling this item from their movie memorabilia collection was a very rare occurrence indeed. To top it all off, the item was unopened. This meant the collectible was in perfect, or mint, condition.

Jeffrey was high bidder on the eBay auction for over a week. He really wanted this piece to add to his collection. He was also building a brand new custom home theater where this collectible would be prominently housed and displayed along with items from his prized movie and television memorabilia collection. Jeffrey had amassed a very substantial collection over the last ten years of collecting and this gun would become one of the crown jewels in his overall collection. It goes without saying that the Samaritan Gun was going to have a very special place in the lobby area of his custom home theater.

The auction, like many eBay auctions, ended at midnight. On the night the auction concluded, Jeffrey was tired and exhausted and knew he had to get up early to go to work the next morning. As you may have already guessed, despite the situation, Jeffrey remained intensely focused and determined to win this item regardless.

11:00 p.m. rolled by and Jeffrey was still the high bidder. Then it was 11:15 p.m., 11:25 p.m. and 11:30 p.m. passed with no change. Jeffrey was still high bidder! About 11:40 p.m., someone got into a minor bidding war with him and the price went up a bit, so Jeffrey matched his competitor each time and eventually rose to the position of high bidder once more. By 11:45 p.m. there was no more bidding activity. He thought he was in the clear and was surely going to win. He continued reloading his web browser every few seconds to verify that no one was slipping in any last second bids as the time quickly approached midnight. Depending on your Internet connection, it takes six to seven seconds from the time you are outbid to the time you get your next bid in to eBay to have it registered as a valid bid.

No more bids. 11:55 p.m., 11:56 p.m., 11:57 p.m., tick, tick, tick; Jeffrey was "golden" for the Hellboy gun. He could smell the sweet smell of victory as it drew closer with the passing of every second. The clock continued to tick away, rapidly approaching the stroke of midnight and the end of the auction.

Then, with just two seconds remaining, someone stepped in with just barely enough of a bid to win, OK, steal the auction (yes, Jeffrey is still bitter about his loss after all these years). By the time Jeffrey had reloaded his web browser, frantically putting in a counter bid, the auction had officially ended. Unfortunately his last bid didn't register in time; and all was lost. What a SNIPE! That evening there was no thrill of victory, but certainly the bitter agony of defeat loomed in the midnight air.

Don't feel too badly for Jeffrey though. His fellow collectors all enjoy swapping similar war stories from time to time.

Luckily, a few months later Jeffrey was finally able to purchase his Samaritan Gun from a respected movie and television memorabilia collectibles dealer. It did cost him a bit more than the eBay auction would have, but he finally had his treasured collectible.

As I mentioned earlier in the chapter, there are two avenues you can navigate when using eBay. One is buying and the other is selling.

Creating a Seller's Account and Understanding How to Sell Your Items for a Profit on eBay

Creating Your Account

One of the first steps you must take for becoming an eBay seller is to **Create a Seller's Account**. You do this of course, by filling out yet another online form. Although there are differences in registering as a seller as compared to a buyer, these differences are minor. Some of the additional information you'll need to provide when registering as a seller includes a Credit or Debit Card number. The rest of what needs to be filled out is the usual name and address information. Now that you have registered as a "seller" on eBay, you can begin the process of listing your items on the website.

Understanding the Different Types of Auctions on eBay and What These Levels Mean to Your Costs and Eventual Profits

Before you get ready to list you items for sale on eBay, or even begin considering how you're going to describe your items to get the best response, first you must understand the different types of auctions eBay offers. There are three different types of auctions on eBay…Store Auctions, Fixed Auctions and Current Auctions. Each different category offers distinct positives and negatives to the seller depending on which one the seller chooses.

The basic and most inexpensive type of auction eBay offers is the ***store auction***. The benefits of a store auction are lower listing fees, less commission taken by eBay from your sales and the ability to have your auction automatically restart after 30 days if what you're trying to sell has no bidders. Because of the lower upfront costs in a store auction, there are some negatives to consider. A store auction has the least amount of exposure of the three types of auctions and there is a monthly fee. For a potential bidder and treasure hunter to find what you are trying to auction under the store auction heading, they would have to enter the description of the item exactly to bring up an auction match. For a bidder to find that Green Lantern #10 Comic Book you are trying sell, the term "Green Lantern" will not bring up a match to your item. Only by entering the exact search term will your item pop up in any user search.

The middle classification of eBay auction is the *fixed auction*. With a fixed auction, you will be paying higher listing fees and more of a commission to eBay than someone selling in a store auction. The major benefit in comparison to store auctions is that you will also get better placement on search results that potential bidders for your auction items will have access to. This translates into better opportunity to make more substantial profits. By choosing to sell your items in a fixed auction, you also get to use the "Buy It Now" and "Make an Offer" options to enhance your selling chances. As previously discussed in this chapter, the "Buy It Now" option gives bidders a chance to pay for an item outright, forgoing the auction process completely and the "Make An Offer" option gives buyers a chance to approach the seller with a direct offer to buy an auction item.

The *current auction* is the final type of auction on eBay. The two major drawbacks of a current auction are that you will be paying the highest commission to eBay on every sale

Auction	Costs	Positives	Negatives
Store	• Cheapest Option • Lowest Commissions. • Lowest Listing Fees.	• Auto restart of auctions after 30 days. • Make an offer • Able to "Buy it Now"	• Bidders must enter exact search term to get match. • Least amount of exposure of your auctions. • Monthly fee.
Fixed	• Not as much as the Current Auction fees and more than the Store Auction fees.	• Auto restart of auctions after 30 days. • Able to use the "Buy It Now" and "Make An Offer" options.	• Higher costs than lower priced option.
Auction 1-3-5-7- 10 days	• Most Expensive Option. • Highest Commissions. • Highest Listing Fees.	• Auto Restart of auctions after 30 days. • Able to use the "Buy It Now" and "Make An Offer" options. • Can use the $100 minimum bid option on all auctions.	• Highest cost of the three options.

as well as paying the highest level of listing fees. The main benefits of a current auction are access to the product enhancements which the other two types of auctions don't have (such as the "Buy It Now" and "Make An Offer" options), the ability to have your auction rollover after 30 days if no one makes a bid on your auction and the best placement from search results eBay has to offer. The best benefit to listing your items under the current auction format is that you can set starting bids of $100 on every auction you hold.

Other Need-To-Know Criteria before You Start Thinking about Selling Items on eBay

In speaking with representatives from eBay while researching this book, there was some essential information given that all sellers need to know. Some of this information may seem very strict or somewhat inflexible, but these caveats are put in place to help make eBay run like the well-oiled machine that it is.

Before eBay puts an end to their scrutiny of you and your selling activities, you will need to obtain a score of a one hundred. To score "100," you must have one hundred sales on the website with positive feedback. Before reaching a score of 100, eBay will hold back all proceeds from every sale until the buyer receives the item they have purchased from you. eBay does this in order to make sure that you have acted properly and ethically in all your financial dealings.

Another important piece of information concerns name brand items. Until you reach a score of "50," which includes 50 positive feedback sales, you cannot sell any name brand items. You are absolutely forbidden to sell items from name brand companies such as Sony, Nike, Rolex and Samsung until you reach that 50 mark. If you do list something with a name brand item before reaching that mark, eBay will immediately pull the item from the website. In the past, some unscrupulous individuals have signed up for selling accounts and immediately tried to move what was thought to be authentic name brand merchandise, only to take the money and run without shipping anything to their customers. eBay believes, from these sorts of negative experiences, that if you try to sell these things before a certain experience level is reached, then you are a potentially fraudulent dealer with intentions of scamming people.

I

Million $ Tip

One key aspect of your research needs to include finding similar items already listed on eBay. By studying how others price and describe similar items you can price and describe your items accordingly for profitable auctions.

Million $ Tip

When selling an item, make sure your auction ends at a proper time during the day. The optimal time to end an auction is between 10:00 a.m. and 7:00 p.m. Monday thru Friday. This will insure more bidders can bid on your items.

have said it before in this chapter and I need to stress again that your feedback score is very important to your success and livelihood on eBay. Because eBay cannot work personally with every seller due to the overwhelming number of sellers participating on the website, they rely heavily on feedback information to make judgments on how well eBay vendors are conducting business.

Whenever you sell something on eBay, the buyer will usually fill out a feedback form with five topics on it to report how the sales experience went. Even though all five items are important, there are two main ratings you need to get right to do well consistently as a seller. First, *communication is the key to a good transaction*. The way to guarantee that no problems occur during the selling process means that you have to be very professional and open in all your communications with your customers. You need to answer all emails quickly, monitor your auctions closely in case people have questions for you, send buyers the tracking numbers when you ship items and make sure they always feel taken care of until they are satisfied with the item they just won and purchased from you. When sending an invoice, put your email on the invoice as well as a telephone number if you want to take customer service to the highest level. Second, *give free shipping*. Buyers love free shipping and offering this relatively low cost option goes a long way towards ensuring that your customers remain happy customers.

If these two factors are properly taken care of, there is a great chance you will get a perfect score on buyer feedback. Making sure the customer comes first and taking care of your customers from the start of any auction, will eventually help you in securing lower fees charged by eBay on your future auctions.

Researching eBay for Better Profits

For the knowledgeable and successful Garage Sale Millionaire, doing proper research on how to better market and sell your items on eBay means the difference between incremental profits and substantial profits. Along with spending quality time on eBay looking at what kind of items are being listed, how they are being listed, who may be buying items and for what amounts, take a few moments to look at and study the **eBay University Learning Center** *(http://pages.ebay.com/education/index.html)*. This section of the eBay website offers invaluable tips and strategies on how to properly use this auction website to your ultimate advantage. The topics at the eBay University Learning Center, listed in detailed tutorial form, include:

New To eBay - How eBay works, how to register and how to buy with confidence are just some of the topics discussed.

How To Buy - Buying items on eBay, searching for auction items and paying for items are discussed in this section.

How To Sell - This section details everything you need to know about selling items on eBay.

Increase Your Sales - Tips about growing your business, opening an eBay Store, growth strategies and Seller Best Practices are available in this section.

The Benefits of Becoming an eBay Power Seller

There are "sellers" on eBay and then there are "PowerSellers" on eBay. As the name would seem to imply, a "PowerSeller" is a much better designation .

According to eBay, "PowerSellers rank among the most successful sellers on eBay for sales and customer satisfaction. The PowerSellers' "icon" is placed next to each PowerSellers' member ID which means that the seller meets the criteria for being a PowerSeller. The proper criteria includes consistent sales volume, a rating of 98% or above for total positive Feedback, eBay marketplace policy compliance, an account in good financial standing and a "Detailed Seller Rating" (DSRs) of 4.5 or higher in all four DSRs. You will also need to sell a minimum of 100 items with feedback in order to apply. If a seller no longer complies with any one of the above requirements, they are removed from the program."

When a bidder sees the PowerSeller icon in any auction, the bidder can be assured that they will be dealing with someone who has earned a stellar reputation on the website. From eBay's website, PowerSeller program benefits include:

Prioritized Customer Service - Depending on a seller's level of sales, PowerSellers receive prioritized support by email or telephone.

PowerSeller Fee Discounts - As a reward for excellent customer service, PowerSellers with high DSRs over the past 30 days will receive discounts on "Final Value Fees" for their prior month's sales.

Unpaid Item Protection - PowerSellers receive a credit for any "Feature Fees" when a buyer doesn't pay for an item and the seller closes an unpaid item dispute. This program covers auction-style listings (excluding Dutch and Live Auctions) and single item fixed price listings on eBay.com, eBay.ca and eBay Motors.

Expanded Seller Protection from PayPal - Items sold by PowerSellers on eBay and paid for with PayPal accounts, will be covered against claims, charge backs, reversals for unauthorized payments and merchandise not received. Transactions must meet the terms of coverage. This protection is free to PowerSellers and eliminates the need for confirmed addresses.

Increased Visibility in Best Match Searches - To reward excellent customer service, eBay gives an advantage in the listings for those sellers rated in the upper half for buyer satisfaction. This advantage also applies to sellers outside of the PowerSeller program.

UPS Rate Discounts - PowerSellers can receive up to a 23% discount on UPS Ground

Daily Rates.

Exclusive Networking - PowerSellers share selling strategies on an exclusive discussion board open only to Powerseller members.

Special Offers - eBay works with many companies that offer products, services and discounts available only to PowerSellers.

PowerSeller Business Templates - Access to eBay approved templates to use in better marketing your business.

Powerful Giving Program - The eBay Foundation regularly donates to charities supported by PowerSellers.

Understanding and Determining Value of an Item - The eBay Way

Monetary Cost Versus Emotional Value

There are two ways to view any transaction for items being sold on eBay: ***monetary cost and emotional value***. Many times emotional value, or the "emotional currency" someone places on an item, far outweighs the actual cost of an item, or the "monetary cost." In these instances, the idea of getting the best value or price for an item falls somewhat by the wayside. In an emotional value purchase, the buyer "must have" that item no matter what - no ifs ands, or buts!

For example, when co-author Jeffrey bought his 1:1 scale, #288 of 500, life-size Star Wars' Darth Vader action figure, he spent approximately $6,100 for it (give or take a few cents). In referencing The 4th Edition of the Star Wars Super Collectors Wish Book by Geoffrey T. Carlton, Collectors Books, (A Division of Schroeder Publishing Co., Inc.) to verify the piece's value and ascertain that this

> ### *Million $ Tip*
> As a buyer and even as a seller on eBay, it is extremely important to find out how to judge the value of an item so you have the best chance to either get a bargain (as a bidder) or make more money on an item (as a seller).

was a wise "investment," he discovered the estimated value of the piece to be only $4,500. The difference in cost of the item versus estimated value of the collectible was $1,600. This

> ### *Million $ Tip*
> You certainly can use the emotional value of an item to your advantage as a seller on eBay. You could earn larger profits knowing that the item you have up for auction on eBay will elicit an emotional response from your bidders. Many times bidders will easily pay above market value for an item if that item means something personal to them. Also, if you have an item which would provoke this reaction amongst your bidders, you can set the starting price of your auction much higher.

difference was a substantial amount of money. Was that a bad investment? When considering the numbers…maybe. As it turns out, it was a great investment on several different levels.

The first question Jeffrey had to ask is what if the piece rises in value over time? The answer is it probably will. Why? The value of the piece will probably increase due to

the lower issue number. This piece is also a limited edition item with high overall quality and the fact that the company that made this collectible is not making the Darth Vader 1:1 scale replicas anymore, influenced Jeffrey's decision to purchase this rare, hard-to-find item. What also had to be taken in consideration was that this particular item was something that Jeffrey had been feverishly trying to get his hands on for over a decade.

The emotional value, compared to the monetary cost, was very high and the thought of getting the piece solely for any monetary gain became secondary. Emotion completely won out over saving some money. Would Jeffrey have spent any more money than he eventually paid to acquire this collectible? The answer is probably "yes." He happily accepted the offer and gladly paid the $6,100 because of the more important "emotional currency" associated in the act of acquiring this item.

Estimating Value on eBay

So, how does one go about estimating the monetary value of an item on eBay? **There are a several methods to use.**

One proven method on eBay is to search for duplicate items or items very similar to your items of interest. By understanding how much others are bidding for similar items, you can see the real market value or at least the "eBay market value" which others are willing to pay for these similar items. You can also do an advanced search on closed auction items and see how much these items may have sold for in previous auctions.

If the article you're interested in is a one-of-a-kind piece or an item where you can't compare what similar items sold for on eBay, then you need to use other resources on the Internet to your advantage. Also search out bookstores for a collectibles price guide listing the item you're interested in. This is especially important for a buyer if the bidding or sales price on the item is escalating rapidly. You need to do as much research as possible on the values of the specific item that you want to buy not only if you want to save money on the item, but also so that eventually you will make as much money as possible.

The time you spend making sure you're not getting ripped off, and not paying the price on an item you think is too high, is time well spent. It's hoped that you would have come across the auction in its infancy so you have adequate time to your research and make the proper decision.

Would I go to great lengths to research something in detail that is being sold or auctioned for a couple of dollars? Probably not. However, as the monetary stakes continue to rise in a high priced auction, the more you're informed the better…this way you might not pay too much for an item. From the selling side, the opposite is true. As a true Garage Sale Millionaire, you can always hope that your inexpensive items advance to increased amounts of value as an uninformed public continues to line your pockets with higher bids.

In the end, you are the ultimate judge as to what may be too high a monetary cost for you with regard to acquiring an item, or what you may find to be a financial steal. Once again, it's the "monetary cost" versus the "emotional currency value" argument I discussed earlier. Even when you weigh monetary cost against emotional value, in the end a dollar is still a dollar. If you've found the true value of an item that piques your interest and you've done the proper research to determine proper value, you're still the one who has to make the final decision.

Avoiding Fraud as a Seller

One of the more unfortunate facts about eBay is that the website will never be 100% free of individuals looking to make a quick buck by taking your money in an auction where the item is invalid, misrepresented, or never even existed. With so many individuals making up a global Internet community, that it's only human nature to have some evildoers lurking about within the system. eBay does an admirable job in policing their website to rid it of unsavory online predators seeking to defraud users via bogus auctions and fraudulent dealings. However, as diligent as eBay is, they cannot stop everyone from trying to take unfair advantage of honest, unsuspecting bidders.

As a seller, the only real type of fraud you need to be aware of is that which involves incoming sources of funds to pay for the items you've auctioned on the website. As long as you remember to use PayPal, which involves the use of credit card funds or a direct debit from a bidder's bank account, you're better protected. Other electronic options you can use to accept funds authorized by eBay are services from **ProPay** *(https://epay.propay.com)*, **Moneybookers** *(www.moneybookers.com)* and **Paymate** *(www.paymate.com)*. You can also directly accept a credit or debit card which will be processed through your Internet merchant account. Although I will not go into detail about these additional services, you can readily find more information about these optional payment services on the Internet.

Sellers may also offer to accept "payment upon pickup" when they list payment terms for their auctions. "Payment upon pickup" means that alternative payment methods could be offered if you pick up the item in person after you've won an auction. Other means of payment such as Cashier's Checks, Money Orders, or cash can only be accepted if the bidder picks up an auction win in this fashion. I highly recommend against this practice because of the potential fraud issues associated with accepting non-guaranteed funds.

Although stop payments are not supposed to be placed on Cashier's Checks or Money Orders, some banks will still place stop payments on these types of transactions. According to *John Burnett* of *BankersOnline.com*, "A bank may refuse payment of its cashier's check under certain circumstances, such as alteration, forged endorsement, or a claim against the payee/presenter. But it should be sure of its position before doing so, because the penalties for wrongfully refusing payment are stiff. Particularly when a holder in due course is involved, the bank that refuses payment of its own cashier's check is walking in a minefield. Another situation when a bank may refuse payment of a cashier's check is in the special circumstance of a lost, stolen or destroyed check."

Instead of having to deal with this type of potential fraud and financial headache, I believe it is really best to use electronic payment services for your business transactions. Just remember, when you list payment terms in your auction you must make sure to detail what is considered acceptable payment and what the specific terms are. That way you're protected from any misunderstandings which might occur when payment is due to you

Preparing Your Item for Sale

Before you even consider listing an item on eBay, you will have to do research first. Why must you go through this seemingly dull process? It is a given that you'll want to make the most money you can from the items you sell, but you also must give yourself every opportunity for your item to distinguish itself from the extensive multitudes of listings found throughout the eBay website.

Listing of Your Items on eBay

Considering all the detailed research you've conducted, now you know with certainty how to best describe your sale items and at what price you're going to start your auction for those items. It's time to fill in the proper listing information and get your item exposed so the eBay world can see your offering and of course, bid handsomely on it. Here are areas you have to decide on regarding listing your item:

Proper category and subcategory - What categories will you list your sale items under to best describe what you want to sell?

Listing your item in a second or third category - By listing your items in different categories, you will attract more bidders.

Starting bid price - What will the starting price be on your sale items? This is a very important because you don't want to undervalue your sale items.

Minimum bid you will accept for the item - When you set up your auction, this is the bid you place as the minimum starting bid. This option can only be used if you are signed up for a "current level" type of auction on eBay. Also called "The Reserve Price."

Specific item details - Color, size, speed and whatever makes the item you want to sell unique. Be very accurate when describing your sale items.

What pictures to upload -

eBay bidders absolutely love to see detailed pictures of how your sale item looks. If you want to move your sale merchandise quickly, upload some great pictures of what you're trying to sell!

What the duration of the auction will be - I recommend an auction length of seven days. By setting up an auction to last seven days, you have the best possible opportunity to receive the most traffic and highest number of webpage hits for your auction on eBay.

Terms of the sale - What types of payments will you accept for the sale of your auction items and what are the sale details of the auction? The acceptable methods of payment (i.e. PayPal), any additional shipping costs, listing a return policy and how long the winning bidder has to pay before he defaults on the auction must be listed in this section. The more clear you are when listing your auction details means less potential problems later down the road.

There are additional options you can choose from to include with the listing of your sale items. These options are not free, but these will in the long-run, help your auction stand out that much more. Some of these options include *extra pictures of your item, a border around your listing and having your item spotlighted in the "Featured Area" of the search and listings page.*

Also, eBay doesn't like it when you use the adjective "like" in your auction descriptions. For example, "Fontana Watch, just like a Rolex." Your item will be removed from the website if the term "like" is ever used. Instead try the terms "comparable to," "matching," or, perhaps "equivalent."

Managing Your eBay Listing and Completing the Sale

From your personal *My eBay* page, you can constantly track multiple auctions and see the status of all those auctions you're involved in. Your "My eBay" page is an essential element in order for you to become a successful seller, especially if you're buying and selling multiple items at the same time. This "eBay Control Center" helps you better organize and refine your efforts and also see what's selling, what's not selling and if you are the big winner on items you've been bidding on. The "My eBay" page is also the home to an abundance of other eBay options such as being the best place to save and list your favorite sellers, monitoring feedback on your eBay activities, viewing messages sent to you by other bidders and sellers or by messages generated by eBay and viewing specific eBay announcements as well.

The last major step in the selling process on eBay is to complete the sale.

When one of your auctions is completed and you have a high bidder for your item, eBay will auto-generate an email to you stating who the high bidder was, their shipping address and the winning bid amount. Because you clearly stipulated payment terms when you originally setup your auction, you may not hear from the high bidder until funds are received from the auction. You might also get an email from the buyer asking for some additional final questions about the payment process. This is a normal part of the eBay auction process even if you have one of the best, most detailed sales pages. Comply with the appropriate answers immediately.

Because you took great care and paid great attention to detail when posting your auction to the website, all you have to do is wait for payment from the customer and ship the high bidder's winning item. If for some reason the buyer delays sending in funds after several days, you can follow-up with a friendly reminder email about payment.

Always be a great communicator on eBay and your customers will love you! More importantly, they will love the way you do business. eBay is glutted with sellers who are terrible communicators, treat their customers terribly and make doing business on the website a nightmare. A competent, successful sales and business person stands out as being exceptional. After receiving repetitive positive feedback on your "Customer Feedback Page," people will more easily respect you and will want to continue to do business with you. By conducting business in a responsible manner you will obtain repeat customers in no time and your business will consistently grow.

Logging off eBay

As you explore eBay on your own, you will discover a treasure trove of valuable information at your fingertips just waiting to be discovered. eBay is a relatively simple website to get to know and one which is easy to navigate through and browse for hours at a time. With the information provided herein, as well as the knowledge you'll gain by cruising around the site and becoming an active day-to-day user on eBay, you will be a *Garage Sale Millionaire* in no time at all.

CHAPTER

7

How to Assign a Value

To Your New Treasures

A. This is a Boatgun, 1700's era (it does look like a blunderbuss). This is my
favorite weapon that I own. Value $4,500 to $7,000.
B. Replica western side arm. Found it at a gun auction for only $195.

Properly valuing your new found treasures is one of the most important aspects of becoming a successful *Garage Sale Millionaire*. If what you find during your treasure hunting endeavors is not valued correctly, when you decide to sell your items; you could be shortchanging yourself and losing out on a lot of money. Treasure hunters far and wide fight extremely hard every day to find those hidden gems which they believe can be resold for substantial profits.

If you price an item too low, you'll lose out on the money you could have potentially made on the sale. If you price an item too high you may never be able to make the sale at all. The actual practice of putting a price tag on any item is never an easy one. Even the most knowledgeable experts can sometimes find it difficult to determine what the best price is for certain items.

There are two different options available for properly and accurately valuing your treasures. You can complete a self-valuation or you can pay a professional to do the job for you. No matter which direction you choose, you'll have to value your items as accurately as possible in order to make as much money as possible.

Million $ Tip
Use more than one source to more accurately value your treasures.

Million $ Tip
Make sure when you compare your item to others that you do your due diligence because many collectibles look alike.

Self-Valuation

The main benefit to valuing items without any outside assistance is that you maintain lower overhead costs. The only cost associated with self-valuing items is your personal time spent valuing items and perhaps buying a book or two to assist you with the self-valuation process. Used books are available at truly extraordinary prices at **Alibris** *(www.alibris.com)*. Of course, if you do opt to hire a professional to value items for you, there are fees and expenses involved. There's nothing wrong with wanting to save some money valuing items yourself, but on certain occasions when you aren't confident that you're capable of making an accurate evaluation or appraisal on your own, using an expert could very well be the best course of action you could take. I will elaborate about using a professional to value your items a little later on in the chapter.

Self-Valuation - The Traditional Way

The simplest, most inexpensive way to research and assign a proper value to your collectibles is to visit your local bookstores and libraries. There's an amazing selection of books available to help you find exact dollar values for items you've collected and are trying to sell. If you go to bookstores like **Barnes & Noble** *(www.barnesandnoble.*

com) or **Borders** *(www.borders.com)* and visit the collectibles section, there are dozens of books covering price guides of collectible items ranging from Matchbox cars, Barbie Dolls, coins, stamps, antiques, G.I. Joes, as well as Star Wars and Star Trek memorabilia. The list is endless. When conducting a search for "Price Guides" in "Books" on **Amazon.com** *(www.amazon.com)*, over 15,200 books on this subject are listed. It goes without saying then that every *Garage Sale Millionaire* has an amazing amount of resource material on hand to properly self-value their items.

If you plan to specialize in a certain collectibles you should be willing to invest in a few books covering these items. Owning price guides that cover the items you want to specialize provides a timesaving resource. By personally owning these price guides, you can establish proper values for your items quickly and as the saying goes "time is money." Whether you're searching online for items or trying to find them at a garage sale, you may only have a few moments to spare for verifying information before your competition swoops in to buy that highly valuable item right out from under you. Having your resource materials on hand for use at a moment's notice is a strong weapon in your *Garage Sale Millionaire* arsenal.

Look at as many price guides as possible before buying a single book. You'll quickly get an idea of which books work the best for your needs by understanding what subject matter is contained in each book, how detailed each book is and how experienced the authors are about the subjects they cover.

The best place to look for current price guides is your local bookstore. Libraries should be considered a secondary source because you'll only be able to check out books for a set period of time before having to return them. Having price guides on hand that cover consecutive years is another great way to understand how your item has been valued over the course of time. You'll be able to make better educated guesses as to which direction the value of your items will go based on collective historical data.

A key part in determining an item's physical condition and potential resale value is called "grading." As we work our way through this chapter, I will discuss the subject of "grading" and how items are "graded" in more detail. I will also cover the top collectibles to buy and sell so you can make more substantial profits.

Self-Valuation Goes High Tech

Ah, the Internet! The glorious and wonderful Internet! How could society as we know it today possibly survive without email, using our finely-tuned web browsers to explore infinitely informative and richly interactive websites, as well as texting, instant messaging and "tweeting?" The better question is, "How would we as collectors, treasure hunters, and *Garage Sale Millionaires* be able to do business without the Internet?" Even up until a few years ago, you could get away with using the Internet only as a supplemental way of doing business. Not any more. As traditional ways of business evolve and make way for an electronic future, so must all your *Garage Sale Millionaire* activities.

Now it's time to use the Internet to help establish more accurate values on your collectibles so you can turn around and make the best profit possible by reselling those items!

eBay

Although **eBay** *(www.ebay.com)* was covered earlier, I feel it necessary to reinforce the importance of using this invaluable Internet community as an efficient and accurate resource for the purpose of determining the proper market value of items you're looking to buy and sell.

When buying and selling collectibles on eBay, the idea of Market Value plays a prominent role. "Market Value" refers to the dollar amount people are willing to pay for an item. Every item listed on eBay, as well as every bid made on those items, continuously helps to set the current market value. For example, if an original 1984 edition of an "Optimus Prime Transformers" collectible toy is put up for auction on eBay at a price of $1,995, then that becomes the current market value for that type of item. The market value of an item is affected if people continue placing higher bids on that item. Based on the actual selling price, the new current market value has now been established. Any subsequent listing of this collectible toy will similarly be priced at, or very close to, that final sales price.

In Chapter 6, I mentioned the fact that many individuals regard eBay as "The World's Largest Garage Sale." I would like to take that concept a step further. I also believe that eBay must also be considered to be the "World's Largest Pricing Guide." I'd venture to bet that not many people think of eBay along those lines. Although they're a fabulous resource to have, the obvious problem with price guides in book form is that once the word is printed on the page that price is finite. The market value of items is "locked in" when that book comes off the printing press for publication. eBay is the best kind of price guide available because it evolves minute-by-minute. Every time an item is listed, bid on and sold, eBay becomes a newly updated price guide.

To verify what items have sold for at past auctions on eBay requires a little digging accomplished by performing an advanced search. On eBay's homepage, click the *Advanced Search* link directly to the right of the main item search box. You'll next be redirected and taken to a secondary search page. About a quarter of the way down the page lays a *Completed Items* box. "Check" the box and then re-submit the search criteria you originally entered on the previous page. After you've submitted your search criteria, all the completed auctions which contain the item you are looking for will be displayed on the screen in front of you.

Terapeak

Depending on how popular an item is, there could be hundreds of pages and thousands of search results to look through before you're able to find an item that interests you. Unfortunately, the advanced search function on eBay only stores historical data for the past few weeks. If you're attempting to find results from eBay auctions that were completed further back, or you want to conduct more of a precise search on past auctions, try **Terapeak** *(www.terapeak.com)*. Terapeak tracks any item ever sold on eBay going back for at least a year. Basic searches on the website are free, but anything more will require a paid subscription.

Worthpoint

Another invaluable resource in valuing your treasures can be found at **WorthPoint** *(www.worthpoint.com)*. Experts contributing to the website are called "Worthologists" and bring decades of experience to the site. Worthpoint.com also houses one of the world's largest collecting databases. You can connect with other collectors interested in buying, selling, or swapping stories and share your insight and knowledge through their forums. As we go to press, the "Communities Forum" section was still in development and not functional.

After a free trial period, full access to the website is only available through a paid membership. Membership is offered on three levels: Basic, Professional and Power. Some membership benefits include access to extensive valuation data, a collecting community of over 350,000 members and access to a wealth of information and data on the subject of collecting.

Google

Another avenue to navigate when valuing your collectibles is **Google** *(www.google.com)*. With any search on Google, especially when it involves collectibles, there is an upside and a downside as well. The good news is that you will probably be able to find an extensive list of websites which deal in specific genres of collectibles. The bad news is that it may take a substantial time investment to search through all those hundreds, thousands and sometimes even millions of search results to find specific areas of importance you were interested in.

For example, try conducting a basic Google search for "Barbie Dolls." By entering this "basic" search string, approximately 8,800,000 search results were retrieved which includes pretty much everything under the sun and then some, regarding Barbie Dolls. Listed will be the official company's website that makes the dolls, some websites that cover the detailed history of Barbie Dolls, a multitude of Barbie Doll enthusiasts websites that discuss methods for collecting the dolls, numerous enthusiast websites that just show pictures of doll collections, various listings for similar dolls like Bratz which are similar to Barbie Dolls and retail toy websites that just sell the dolls. This is a lot of information to sift through. When you enter more detailed search criteria as in "Barbie Dolls + 1965 + Redhead," only

---

Million $ Tip

For collectibles which are not so common, you will need to take a little more effort to find the value. When you find a website which sells your item, make sure you compare size, color, and any markings which are on the collectible. Give the owner of the website a call and compare your item to what they have. There is a good chance they may have an interest in your treasure and you will have a fantastic sales opportunity! If an offer is made and, before you accept any offer, I recommend comparing the potential value of your item with a few other vendors as well as seeing if the same item is being sold for more on the Internet.

9,340 results are retrieved. You now retrieved more pertinent information which as a result, will help you find more accurate valuation data.

By making your search criteria more detailed with Google searches, you will have the best success in finding specific data which best suits your needs.

Blogs, News Sites, and Community Forums

After you've identified websites that have the information you need to value your items for eventual sale, delve a little bit deeper into each website. Many of them will also have blogs, news sites, or community forums available for you to read to gather more information about the items you have an interest in. There may also be hyperlinks to other websites with additional blogs, forums, or news sites available for you to investigate. Blogs, news sites, and forums contain quintessential reading material which could give you more insight on your items and the best opportunities to make valuable sales. Everything you learn from these resources will help shape your ideas and opinions on how to properly value your items.

> ### *Million $ Tip*
> Check with art gallery owners in your area as many times they will have expert knowledge and years of experience in the appraisal of items.

Using Professionals: Appraisers and Professional Grading Services

Appraisers

Hiring an experienced appraiser is one of the most accurate ways to find current and future market value for your collectibles. Depending upon an appraiser's level of experience, if that appraiser is involved in the collectibles industry, or perhaps if they own an art gallery, you could gain tremendous insight from their experience and knowledge of current and future selling trends. This information can certainly be used to your advantage when either selling an item or negotiating price with a customer.

Appraisers can be found in almost every city. How good they are in their ability to properly and accurately appraise items is another question altogether. Checking credentials for a quality appraisal service is as easy as making a few telephone calls to the appraiser or appraisal company. It's incumbent upon you to verify the experience a person or company has. You can do this via telephone, in person and over the Internet to see if the appraisal company you are interested in is certified with a National or International Appraisal Agency. **The American Society of Appraisers** *(www.appraisers.org)* is one of the better-known national certifying appraisal agencies and organizations. Also check to see if the appraiser is endorsed by the **Better Business Bureau** *(www.bbb.org)* and whether or not there are complaints filed against them. Another website that I have found useful is **Ripoff Report** *(www.ripoffreport.com)*. Founded in 1998 by Ed Magedson, Ripoff

Report is a website dedicated to informing consumers of potential marketplace ripoffs.

I have been appraising personal items, small, medium and large-sized personal collections and large family collections for years. Individuals worldwide have employed my services and they have trusted me time and time again as an expert appraiser. As a result of years of intensive study combined with expansive expertise and experience, I can look at collectibles and entire collections and know exactly what price the market will bear on such items. I represent the type of experienced appraiser you need to seek when hiring someone to make serious monetary judgments or decisions on what something is worth so you can sell it to make the best possible profit.

Million $ Tip

If you feel that item you want to resell has the potential to make you a substantial profit, then, definitely use a professional valuation or grading service. By using these types of services, even if there is a fee involved, in many instances you will get a professional certification or expert appraisal value which can be used to drive up sale prices.

Professional Grading Services

Professional grading services are available to every collector, treasure hunter and *Garage Sale Millionaire* who wants to determine actual physical quality and condition of a collectible. These grading services are usually dedicated to a certain type or category of collectible such as baseball cards, coins and comic books. Even though these grading services do not necessarily specify what the monetary value of an item is, by getting an item professionally graded, you give yourself the best opportunity to make more money upon resale.

Some of the benefits regarding hiring a professional to grade items include saving you a great deal of time from having to do the lengthy research needed to accurately grade items yourself and minimizing any evaluation mistakes you might make because you are not an expert in the respective field. Many times when a professional grading agency or company grades an item the resale amount increases. At some point during the grading process, grading companies will usually seal your collectible in a protective casing and place certifying marks and labels which you can show to prospective buyers to prove that the items in question have been professionally graded and certified by a respected organization or professional.

Of course, using someone else to grade your items will cost a fee depending on the items you want graded, the number of items to be graded and which certified professional or agency you take your items to. Costs can range from as little as just ten dollars to several hundred dollars.

Top Collectibles to Deal in for Substantial Profits and How to Accurately Value These Top Items through Their Respective Grading Services

I regard coins; comic books; action figures; baseball cards, sports trading cards and non-sports trading cards and antique firearms to be some of the top collectibles in which to deal for substantial profits. The different types of collectibles listed in this section are graded by companies and agencies which specialize in that particular type of collectible. Additionally, each one of these collectibles also has its own fervent, loyal and enthusiastic fan base. "Hungry" collectors will spend good money for the items and collectibles you are going to sell. If you're still in the mood to self-value your collectibles, you can use the following information in this chapter to better hone your self-valuing efforts.

Coins

There are many coin grading services available to the treasure hunter trying to determine the quality and condition of their coins. Grading fees typically range from $10 and up for each coin. Once a coin is graded, the professional coin grading service that graded your item will enclose your graded coin in a certified and sealed coin holder that not only protects your newly graded coin, but also displays pertinent data about your coin and its respective grade. This data includes the year the coin was minted, denomination of the coin, actual grade of the coin and a bar code. The bar code is imprinted on the outside of the protective casing by the grading company in case they need to reference the coin at some future date.

The *condition* and *grading* of a coin plays a major role in determining its eventual resale value. The "Condition" of a coin is defined as, "the state of preservation of a particular numismatic issue," and "Grade" is defined as, "the numerical or adjectival condition of a coin." Professional coin grading services use letter and numerical designations to show what they believe is a coin's most accurate grade. The numerical scale used by these grading companies is a 70-point scale which designates the incremental quality of each coin. The more pristine shape the coin is in, the higher the numerical grade will be. Letter designations are just as important as the numerical score. Each letter designation relates to the overall quality of the coin, as well.

One of the best coin grading services available to the collector is the **Professional Coin Grading Service (PCGS)** *(www.pcgs.com)*. Much of the industry grades coins according to the PCGS grading system. What follows below are the grading charts from the Professional Coin Grading Service (PCGS) website and the ones the company uses to grade coins. The first chart displays a particular coin grade and a description of what each grade means. The second chart explains what each letter grade means in the first chart:

Grade	Description
PO-1	Identifiable date and type.
FR-2	Mostly worn, though some detail is visible.
AG-3	Worn rims but most lettering is readable though worn.
G-4	Slightly worn rims, flat detail, peripheral lettering nearly full.
G-6	Rims complete with flat detail, peripheral lettering full.
VG-8	Design worn with slight detail.
VG-10	Design worn with slight detail, slightly clearer.
F-12	Some deeply recessed areas with detail, all lettering sharp.
F-15	Slightly more detail in the recessed areas, all lettering sharp.
VF-20	Some definition of detail, all lettering full and sharp.
VF-25	Slightly more definition in the detail and lettering.
VF-30	Almost complete detail with flat areas.
VF-35	Detail is complete but worn with high points flat.
EF-40	Detail is complete with most high points slightly flat.
EF-45	Detail is complete with some high points flat.
AU-50	Full detail with friction over most of the surface, slight flatness on high points.
AU-53	Full detail with friction over 1/2 or more of surface, very slight flatness on high points.
AU-55	Full detail with friction on less than 1/2 surface, mainly on high points.
AU-58	Full detail with only slight friction on the high points.
MS/PR-60	No wear. May have many heavy marks/hairlines, strike may not be full.
MS/PR-61	No wear. Multiple heavy marks/hairlines, strike may not be full.
MS/PR-62	No wear. Slightly less marks/hairlines, strike may not be full.
MS/PR-63	Moderate number/size marks/hairlines, strike may not be full.
MS/PR-64	Few marks/hairlines or a couple of severe ones, strike should be average or above.
MS/PR-65	Minor marks/hairlines though none in focal areas, above average strike.
MS/PR-66	Few minor marks/hairlines not in focal areas, good strike.
MS/PR-67	Virtually as struck with minor imperfections, very well struck.
MS/PR-68	Virtually as struck with slight imperfections, slightest weakness of strike allowed.
MS/PR-69	Virtually as struck with minuscule imperfections, near full strike necessary.
MS/PR-70	As struck, with full strike.

The letter designations from the chart above are as follows:

Grade	Condition
PO	Poor
FR	Fair
AG	About Good
G	Good
VG	Very Good
F	Fine
VF	Very Fine
EF	Extremely Fine
AU	About Uncirculated
MS	Mint State
PR	Proof

The condition and subsequent grade of a coin and how these qualities equate to market and potential resale value can be explained in the following example.

Let's say you owned two 1889-CC Morgan Dollars. Both coins look the same although one is a bit more worn than the other, have the same design, have the same mintmark and have the date of "1889." After getting the coin graded, you realize that one of your 1889 Morgan Dollars was graded as a "EF-40" and the other was graded as a "MS/PR-67." The difference in grade seems minor at first. Is the difference between an EF-40 (Extra Fine Condition) grade compared to an MS/PR-67 (Mint Strike/Proof Condition) grade that important? Yes! According to the **Professional Coin Grading Service (PCGS) Price Guide** *(www.pcgs.com/prices)*, as of January 2010, a "EF-40" graded 1889-CC Morgan Dollar was valued at $2,900 whereas an "MS/PR-67" 1889-CC Morgan Dollar was valued at $475,000.

The tremendous differences and nuances in the quality and condition of coins and their subsequent values based on particular sets of grading criteria, are found in every coin. By using a professional coin grading service, the potential of inaccurately grading valuable coins will be avoided.

Comic Books

The **Certified Guarantee Corporation Comics (CGC Comics)** *(www.cgccomics.com)* is the only professional grading company available for comics and comic books. Fees start in the $10 range for the grading of one comic and can escalate to hundreds of dollars if multiple comics or comic books are submitted. CGC Comics' success comes from their attention to detail and thoroughness throughout all facets of the comic book grading process. CGC Comic's four step process in the valuing of comics books involves *receiving* (getting the comic book shipped from the customer), *grading* (judging the physical condition of the comic book and assigning a grade), *encapsulation* (placing the comic in a protective sleeve or casing) and *shipping* (sending the comic book back to the customer). The industry standard for grading comic books is based on the "0.5-10.0

CGC Corporation Scale." A grade of "0.5" is the lowest score a comic can receive and it is an example of a comic in "poor" quality. A grade of "10.0" is the best grade score a comic can possibly achieve and denotes that this collectible is in the best possible condition or "gem mint" condition.

The CGC Scale is as follows:

Grade	Condition	Grade	Condition
0.5	Poor	6.5	Fine +
1.0	Fair	7.0	Fine/Very Fine
1.5	Fair/Good	7.5	Very Fine -
1.8	Good -	8.0	Very Fine
2.0	Good	8.5	Very Fine +
2.5	Good +	9.0	Very Fine/Near Mint
3.0	Good/Very Good	9.2	Near Mint -
3.5	Very Good -	9.4	Near Mint
4.0	Very Good	9.6	Near Mint +
4.5	Very Good +	9.8	Near Mint/Mint
5.0	Very Good/Fine	9.9	Mint
5.5	Fine -	10.0	Gem Mint
6.0	Fine		

Top comic books, when properly graded by a professional grading company, can be valued at more than $1 million. You can view a current listing of the **100 Most Valuable Comic Books** at *www.nostomania.com/servlets/com.nostomania. CatPage?name=Top100ComicsMain*. Comic Book values, like the values from any type of collectible, are always in a state of flux. The chart showing the values of the "Top 100 Comic Books" is just a "snapshot" of a particular comic book's value on a particular day.

Action Figures

Action Figure Authority (AFA) *(www.toygrader.com)* is the only professional grading service available for action figures. AFA uses three very detailed grading scales to accurately grade action figures: the **C-Scale** (Condition Scale), **AFA 3-Tier Grading Scale** (Action Figure Authority Grading Scale for items produced from 1960-present) and **AFAM 3-Tier Grading Scale** (Action Figure Authority Modern Grading Scale for items produced from 1995-present).

As with all grading scales in the collectibles market, the higher score given to any collectible equates to a higher assigned value. A higher value means that higher potential profits can be made. The three AFA grading scales (courtesy of Action Figure Authority) are:

C-Scale:

Grade	Condition
C1-C4	Very poor, badly damaged, basically only useful for spare parts
C5	Poor condition with heavy wear, broken parts will impair function
C6	Fair, significant wear, may have some broken parts
C7	Good, noticeable wear but no broken parts, items may be missing accessories
C8	Very good, some minor wear, no broken or missing parts
C9	Near mint condition, very minor imperfections apparent
C10	Mint condition, unused

AFA 3-Tier Grading Scale (For items produced from 1960-present):

Level   *Grade*
AFA Gold   Gem Mint (100), Mint (95) and Near Mint/Mint (90)

AFA Description/Condition

The AFA Gold level consists of the grades 100, 95 and 90. The select few figures that receive these grades are among the highest quality in existence. A very small percentage of figures submitted to AFA receive a Gold grade. The flaws are very minor, very subtle and are sometimes very hard to identify with the naked eye. The collector who is extremely condition sensitive will be satisfied with the condition of a Gold level figure.

Level   *Grade*
AFA Silver   Near Mint Plus (85), Near Mint (80) and Excellent Plus/Near Mint (75)

AFA Description/Condition

The AFA Silver level consists of the grades 85, 80 and 75. The figures that receive these grades are in excellent condition. A figure graded an 85 will often be referred to as 'case fresh' and should be very close to gold level condition. The term 'case fresh' is certainly justifiable as the average figure pulled from a sealed case will grade an 85 due to small flaws which occur when the figures are packaged or shipped in the case. The average figure pulled from a store shelf is usually an 80, which represents a nice specimen with minor flaws apparent upon close inspection. The final Silver level grade, a 75, represents an item with more minor flaws than the average Silver level piece. An item grading 75 does have significant wear but does not have major flaws which would draw the eye to them at first glance. For most high grade collectors, an 85 is satisfactory. For most discriminating collectors, an 80 is satisfactory. A 75 will be satisfactory to those who are not overly concerned with light stresses, small bubble imperfections and other flaws which do not jump out at first glance. Therefore, the Silver level grades do represent a much larger range than the Gold level grades.

Level	Grade
AFA Bronze	Excellent Plus (70), Excellent (60), Very Good (50), Good (40), Fair (30), poor (20) and Very Poor (10)

AFA Description / Condition

The AFA Bronze level consists of the grades 70, 60 and below. The figures that receive these grades typically have damage ranging from simply noticeable upon first glance to extremely significant. The card may have creases on the front and the blister may be crushed or cracked. The Bronze level covers a large range of figure conditions and the scope of the flaws range considerably. Condition for Bronze level figures is determined by how many 'major' flaws are present on the card and how severe each flaw is. Bronze level figures may have major flaws such as a torn off POP or other large paper tears. Bronze level figures may not be satisfactory to condition sensitive collectors.

AFAM 3-Tier Grading Scale (For items produced from 1995-present):

Level	Grade
AFA Gold	9.0, 9.25, 9.5, 9.75 and 10.0

AFA Description / Condition

The AFA Gold level consists of the grades 10.0, 9.75, 9.5, 9.25 and 9.0. The figures that receive these grades are among the highest quality in existence. The flaws are very minor, very subtle and are sometimes very hard to identify with the naked eye. A collector who is extremely condition sensitive should be satisfied with the condition of a Gold level figure.

Level	Grade
AFA Silver	7.5, 8.0 and 8.5

AFA Description / Condition

The AFA Silver level consists of the grades 8.5, 8.0 and 7.5. The figures that receive these grades are in decent condition. A collector would be able to spot a few small flaws on an 8.5 and would see several moderate flaws on a 7.5.

Level	Grade
AFA Bronze	1.0-7.0

AFA Description / Condition

The AFA Bronze level consists of the grades 7.0 and below. The figures that receive these grades typically have damage ranging from simply noticeable upon first glance to extremely significant. Since modern items are typically in good condition, very few items will be low enough to receive these grades.

As a *Garage Sale Millionaire*, leaving grading judgments to the professionals regarding action figures is one of the best decisions you can make. Because there are so many variables which can determine what condition your action figure is in, it's really best to leave those types of important decisions to the experts. When the discussion moves to potential future profits, having the proper grade on an action figure collectible is key in making the most money possible from every sale.

Baseball Cards, Sports Trading Cards and Non-Sports Trading Cards

Consider the following…there are 30 professional Major League Baseball teams playing every year, every team's roster is made up of 40 players, many players get called up from the Minor Leagues every year to the big leagues, the sport has been played professionally since 1871 and hundreds of baseball cards are made for each player in the big leagues every single year. You can only imagine how much profit potential there is to be made from buying and selling baseball cards.

And that's just baseball!

The baseball card, sports trading cards and non-sports trading card market is a treasure trove ready to be discovered and exploited by *Garage Sale Millionaires* everywhere. The baseball card and sports trading card market includes every sports trading card manufactured. Non-sports trading cards consist of television and movie trading cards, entertainment trading cards, pro-wrestling trading cards and various stiffeners from cigarette packs from the late-1800s through the early-1900s. Although football, basketball and hockey are all viable sports trading card markets and non-sports cards are still a novelty in comparison to sports trading cards, the baseball card market continues to be the most lucrative.

Some of the top grading companies in this field are **Professional Sports Authenticator (PSA)** *(www.psacard.com)*, **Beckett Grading Service (BGS)** *(www.beckett.com)*, **GMA Grading** *(www.gmagrading.com)*, **Sportscard Guarantee (SGC)** *(www.sgccard.com)* and **International Grading Service (IGS)** *(www.igsgrading.com)*. By choosing to get your cards professionally graded, you'll find increased value from your card. Also, your card will be protected in a sturdy and durable card holder and you will get your card expertly authenticated and graded.

Baseball cards are unique in the world of collectibles.
Only baseball cards are graded based on three unique criteria:

The physical condition of the card - Is the card in "good" condition or "mint" condition?

The "star quality" of the player - A rookie card of Babe Ruth is much more valuable than   a rookie card of John Kruk.

The era a player played the game - Older cards of "superstar" players will be more valuable overall, than the more recent "superstars" who have played the game of baseball within the last few years.

Beside grading a baseball card on the star quality of a player and what era that player played the game, baseball grading companies use four criteria to grade the physical quality of a card. According to **Baseball Cards Buyers.com** *(www.baseballcardsbuyers.com)*, the basic criterion for grading baseball cards is:

Centering - This refers to the evenness of the white space or border (if any) around the baseball card's main image. Centering is measured left-right and topbottom and is defined in "percentages." For example, if a card is slightly off-center (to the right) and way off-center (to the bottom), grading might be "55-45" and "65-35." That means that to the naked eye the baseball card's left border is just noticeably wider than the right border, but that the top border is almost twice as wide as the bottom border.

Corners - This refers to the sharpness of the corners and any creases in the corner. "Dinged" corners will drop the value of a baseball card almost more quickly than any other factor. To the naked eye, if the corners are a very sharp point, that's a good thing. Experts at professional card-grading companies check corners out under low magnification for complete accuracy. Some unscrupulous sellers will re-cut a card which gives it sharp, new corners. This trick is easily detected with a metal template that is cut to the exact size at which that particular card was originally manufactured.

Edges - While not as important a factor in grading baseball cards as the previous two items, chipped edges will reduce a card's value. The two causes of imperfect edges are poor card cutting at the time the card was originally manufactured and edge damage due to extensive or improper handling of the card. Of course, there's nothing you can do about how well the card was made, but you can reduce handling damage by keeping valuable baseball cards in protective sleeves.

Surface - This refers to coating on the image of the baseball card, as well as, but to a lesser degree, the printing on the back of the card. Other than unacceptable problems such as pin holes, tape, staples, writing, the biggest de-valuation factor is creases in the card which are typically visible to the naked eye. The very rarest of baseball cards are not subject to the same stringent "surface" criteria due to their age and uniqueness. Less obvious, but nearly as important are scratches in the surface of the baseball card. These scratches can be observed by the naked eye without magnification when held closely under a normal light bulb. You should also rotate the card so that the light hits it at different angles. A third flaw can be printing dots that are a different color than the area around it.

The Garage Sale Millionaire

If you're not familiar with how valuable the collectible and antique firearms market is, take one look at the auction listings on **GunBroker.com** *(www.gunbroker.com)* The amounts are staggering and are a real an eye-opener. Many firearms sales start in the hundreds of dollars and the price ranges increase until they hit six-figures. Antique firearms are a hot market because of their steady popularity over the decades and sales don't appear to be letting up anytime soon. Antique firearms and their associated values, are based on the physical qualities of the firearm and its provenance.

"Provenance" relates to the place of origin or earliest known history of an item. **Gun-Appraisals.com** *(www.gun-appraisals.com)* states that, "One thing we have noted throughout the years of doing appraisals is that if a gun can be tied to a historic person or event, the value of that firearm will escalate tremendously. This is no easy task however. Irrefutable proof must be provided and not just a letter from grandpa saying that he got this from a friend as payment for a debt; and the friend was related to Geronimo; and the friend swore it was a present from Geronimo to him. What you will need to provide is a myriad of supporting documentation. If you are able to prove that your weapon is tied to someone important, or an important event and this proof is accepted by the top dealers and collectors, then you have a great chance of getting a nice premium at one of the top auction houses. Of course the more historic and important the person or event is, the better your chances of a big score!"

Gun-Appraisals.com will value your collectible and antique firearm. Besides information concerning "provenance," Gun-Appraisals.com uses a certain set of criteria to determine if a firearm has value:

Desirability/Aesthetics - People collect weapons that personally appeal to them and ones that have a desirable aesthetic quality. This is not to say that an ugly yet unique firearm will not be sought after. It's more of a general statement regarding what the majority of collectors look for.

Condition - Condition definitely makes or breaks the value of any collectible. Now, thanks to the **National Rifle Association** *(www.nra.org)*, a gun collector has at their disposal a very sophisticated system of grading. Since grading remains a subjective art, there will always be differences in opinion as to the actual grade of an individual weapon. (Please see below for the NRA Standards of Conditions for Grading Firearms).

Price - Most firearms have been catalogued and priced in various guides. A search on the Internet can give you a good idea of the going rate for any particular weapon.

Maker/Manufacturer - Many collectors specialize according to manufacturer. The appeal and recognition of large name makers is usually much broader than the smaller and usually defunct companies. Firearms bearing the trademarks of a reputable firm will usually have a larger collector base than a lesser known maker.

Rarity - "Not every old gun is rare and not every rare gun is old." If your gun is indeed rare, it will be of interest to someone, somewhere. The trouble is that often locating that special someone is just as difficult as finding gun itself! Don't mistake rarity for desirability. Rarity is but one factor to take into account when determining the value of a gun. Some collectors will only collect weapons that are MIB (Mint in Box) condition and are not so interested in the rarity. Other collectors would do anything to have a rare gun in their collection no matter what the condition…believe it or not! The great original condition of an old gun is usually what is rare and not necessarily the gun itself.

Special Order Features - Firearms fall into a special category when it comes to special features. Almost every gun manufacturer has numerous options available to the buyer. From engraving, wood carving, checkering, special finishes, sights and everything in-between, there are literally hundreds of special features in the firearm world. To top it all off, not all of these special features were completed at the factory. Many were custom, after-market options. All of these features must be taken into consideration when determining the collectible value of your weapon. What is desirable to one collector may not necessarily intrigue another.

Market / Economic Factors - In North America, we usually talk about values of firearms in relation to the U.S. marketplace; however, even within the United States the values of a particular gun will be quite different, varying from region to region. This is particularly true when attending gun shows. Dealers notice higher demands for certain types of weapons in different states. The ability to post your gun for sale on the Internet has rapidly removed the distance barriers which are so typical to gun shows. For the person who has the disposable income available, this is the best time to buy. It is supply and demand in its purest form.

The National Rifle Association (NRA) Modern Gun Condition Standards (www.armchairgunshow.com/Condition-NRA-Guns.htm):

Grade	Condition
Fair	In safe working condition, but well worn, perhaps requiring replacement of minor parts or adjustments, that should be indicated in advertisement; no rust, but may have corrosion pits that do render the gun unsafe or inoperable.
Good	In safe working condition, minor wear on working surfaces, no broken parts, no corrosion or pitting that will interfere with proper functioning.
Very Good	In perfect working condition, no appreciable wear on working surfaces, no corrosion or pitting, only minor surface dents or scratches.
Excellent	New condition, used but little, no noticeable marring of wood or metal, bluing perfect (except at muzzle or sharp edges).
Perfect	In new condition in every respect.

The Garage Sale Millionaire

New	Not previously sold at retail, in same condition as current factory production

National Rifle Association (NRA) Antique Firearm Condition Standards (www.armchairgunshow.com/Condition-NRA-Guns.htm):

Grade	Condition
Poor	Major and minor parts replaced, major replacement parts required and extensive restoration needed, metal deeply pitted, principal lettering, numerals and design obliterated, wood badly scratched, bruised, cracked or broken, mechanically inoperative, generally undesirable as a collectors firearm.
Fair	Some major parts replaced; minor replacement parts may be required; metal rusted, may be lightly pitted all over, vigorously cleaned or re-blued; rounded edges of metal and wood; principal lettering, numerals and design on metal partly obliterated; wood scratched, bruised, cracked or repaired where broken; in fair working order or can be easily repaired and placed in working order.
Good	Some minor replacement parts; metal smoothly rusted or lightly pitted in places, cleaned or re-blued; principal letters, numerals and design on metal legible; wood refinished, scratched bruised or minor cracks repaired; in good working order.
Very Good	All original parts; none to 30% original finish; original metal surfaces smooth with all edges sharp; clear lettering, numerals and design on metal; wood slightly scratched or bruised; bore disregarded for collectors firearms.
Fine	All original parts, over 30% original finish, sharp lettering, numerals and design on metal and wood, minor marks in wood, good bore.
Excellent	All original parts; over 80% original finish; sharp lettering, numerals and design on metal and wood; unmarred wood; fine bore.
Factory New	All original parts, 100% original finish, in perfect condition in every respect, inside and out.

Now You Know the Rest of the Story

The best decision you can make to guarantee that you receive proper value for your collectible items at resale is to have your items graded. There are two directions you can take to have your collectible items graded: self-grading or hiring a professional. When you are ready to sell your valuable treasures, be it in person or online, all of your potential customers will want to know everything there is about what you are trying to sell. All this is accomplished through the process of grading. By providing your customers with as much detail as possible about your items, you will have a better chance to complete every sale and also make the most money from those sales.

Million $ Tip

If it is a baseball card, comic book, limited edition collectible or coin, you will have no problem finding a value.

Million $ Tip

The condition of your item will greatly change the value.

Million $ Tip

Retail value, and what you can get selling it to a retailer, is going to be different. Stores which are known for collectibles have a following and can receive top dollar. If a store is selling something for $100, they probably paid about $50 for that item.

Million $ Tip

If somebody offers you money for your item and the amount is enough, you can negotiate the price with them. I recommend you always ask for more during your negotiations. There is a good chance the dealer will give you more when they make an offer, they usually aim low in their offer.

CHAPTER

8

Putting on The World's

Greatest Garage Sale

My favorite place in my home, the President's Room.

My lifelong fascination with garage sales began at a very young age. I was only seven years old when I held my first sale with my Mom. I didn't really know why I even wanted to hold a garage sale. I saw other families in my neighborhood having garage sales; but I just didn't get it. What was the big deal, anyway? When you're seven years old, it seemed as though people were going though a lot of trouble and effort for nothing. Since garage sales were usually held on a Saturday and Sunday, *like all day Saturday and Sunday*, that meant the sale took away a chunk of some very serious play time. Why would I ever want to sacrifice having lots of "fun?" What a totally boring way to waste the weekend!

It couldn't have been about the money. The concept of free market economics in buying and selling physical goods for money and hopefully turning a profit, was just barely starting to sink in at such a young age.

I did notice one characteristic all the families who did hold garage sales had in common. Every single one of our neighbors seemed to be having serious amounts of fun when they did this sort of thing. Of course, being seven years old, I wanted to have fun too! After a lengthy discussion with my Mom, I convinced her that we needed to have some "fun like the neighbors," so we should have a garage sale of our own. My Mom agreed and my first garage sale was a "go."

After my first sale ever was over, I finally understood why everyone seemed to have such a great time holding garage sales. I also learned my first worldly lesson. In the end, it is really all about the money! People actually came up and gave you handfuls of cash for a bunch of old stuff that you didn't want anyway. I can't remember how much my Mother and I made at our first sale together, but I do remember seeing more cash than I had ever seen before in my life. Safe to say, I was immediately hooked on the idea of holding garage sales. I had been bitten by the garage sale bug and bitten badly. A new world seemed to open up for me. After all these years, I still can't wait for the arrival of summer so I can have yet another sale!

The Need-To-Know List: Essential Information for Holding "The World's Greatest Garage Sale"

There are certain things you need to know in order to hold a successful, moneymaking garage sale. In this section, I will discuss some of the key elements necessary for making your garage sale the best it can be.

When to hold the sale

One of the crucial elements in conducting a successful garage sale is to know when the right time is to have one. Picking the right days of the week to conduct your sale is absolutely crucial.

You really need to hold your garage sale when as many people as possible can attend. The more foot traffic you can generate at your sale the better chance you have for success and of course turning substantial profits. Well, that and having some seriously cool things to sell, but I will talk about these points later in the chapter.

The best day to hold a garage sale is on Saturday. Sundays through Thursday are generally not good days at all to have a sale. You will waste plenty of time and effort on any of these days. While some people may show up if your sale is between Sunday and Thursday, most people have other obligations which will take priority, especially, on a Sunday. On Sunday the priority will be attending church and family events. During the week, the obvious priority will be work. This doesn't mean you won't have some success on other days of the week, but usually the most sales will be made on Saturdays.

If you insist on having a sale on a weekday, pick Friday. Friday is an excellent secondary day to hold a garage sale. Some people might take Friday off as part of a three day weekend and some good sales may be made, providing you publicize your sale with

---

Million $ Tip

If you want to have a garage sale and have just one day for such an event, make sure you hold your sale on a Saturday. People just do not attend garage sales between Sunday and Thursday like they do on a Saturday. On these days you will just be "spinning your wheels" and you will only be wasting your own time, hard work and effort.

---

street signs and in the local paper. Even if individuals don't take the whole day off, by Friday afternoon they may leave work early and be ready to get a jump on finding some great sales in their area. If you want to do a two day garage sale, definitely plan for a Friday and Saturday.

If you live where you have four distinctive seasons, it's best to schedule your sales for the warmer weather months. That means anytime during the late spring, throughout summer, or into early fall. Scheduling your garage sale for a potentially non-rainy day is also a key to success.

You can usually rely on the accuracy of advanced local weather predictions up to a week in advance. Many people just don't attend garage sales when the weather is bad. If you live in a part of the country that has great weather all year long, then every weekend offers you the potential to bring garage sale success and profitability.

Getting People to Your Garage Sale - and Managing Them Once They've Arrived

Getting as many people possible to attend your garage sale is a key component for achieving great financial garage sale success. Additionally, how you address your customers is another key to making your garage sale more profitable.

Many individuals plan their entire weekend solely based on going to garage sales. When they see a sign or advertisement for your garage sale, they may arrive at least ninety minutes early. If you think I'm kidding, just wait until you have your first sale. For as long as I've been involved in the business and for too many times to count, I've seen people actually "camp out" on the seller's front yard before the sun even rises so they can be the first one there. Even if your sign states that the sale doesn't start until 9:00 a.m., people will still get there while you're setting up everything. Even when you're pulling items out of your garage to place on the sale tables, they will be walking with you trying to carry on a conversation and may ask if they can help you set up. Experienced garage sale shoppers do this sort of thing to try to not only get a look at what you have to sell, but this places them in the best possible position so they can have a first go at all of your great sale items.

It is important how you handle garage sale "early birds" because these early arrivals could make or break your garage sale. Don't shoo them away like my mother always wanted to and did, on many occasions. I suppose she just didn't understand the business as well as I did even at my young age. As a child, I wanted to let all my early bird customers into our house and have them start picking up our furniture and taking it home with them. *For a price, of course.*

Million $ Tip

When someone is trying to buy one of your treasures, they are going to ask questions. Sometimes, many questions! Try to give as many answers as you can and do not ever rush them. This kind of interaction is considered great entertainment for the garage sale enthusiast! This is what garage sale customers look forward to every weekend. If you are short with them, do not treat them kindly and show disinterest, I can guarantee they will not buy anything and they will never come back to another one of your garage sales.

Million $ Tip

You will want to try to inform the customers at your garage sale about the history behind the items you are trying to sell. The amount of information you do or do not provide could make or break any sale! Customers at garage sales absolutely love hearing value-added information and background stories about the items they are getting ready to buy.

Enjoy your customers, even if they prove to be difficult to handle. People like to shop in a jovial environment. Definitely, make sure you hold a garage sale which has an element of fun attached to it. In many cases at a garage sale, a relaxed shopping and sales environment equals bigger profits! I will discuss some of the ways to spice up a garage sale later in the chapter.

Preparation and Setup

How do you prepare for and set everything up for the "World's Greatest Garage Sale?" You need to arrange the details for your sale a few weeks in advance, not just days in advance. If you want to make the most profit possible from your garage sale, you need to make sure everything regarding the upcoming sale is in order and ready to go when the sale begins. This, of course, takes a little bit of planning.

Having a garage sale is a great opportunity for you to go room to room, closet to closet and drawer to drawer throughout your home to identify all the items for which you have no need or use for anymore. This includes unwanted gifts...things you may never have liked or needed at all. Have you used, worn, or even looked at something you have tucked away collecting dust in the past year? If not, then you more than likely need to get rid of it. You can choose to sell it, give it to charity, or just throw it out if it isn't in good condition. Why have something lying around if you do not use that item?

I truly believe that if you can find all the "stuff" in your house that you don't use you can make very good money from it. If for some reason you sell something and decide you need it again, go to the store and buy it new again. Or go to another garage sale and buy it!

I usually begin preparing for my garage sales about a month before the actual date of the sale so I can be thorough in my preparations. I want to make sure I've gone through my house from top to bottom so I don't overlook something of value I can sell. The worst thing that can happen is that you discover things that might have been sold after your garage sale is history. After I've exhausted the search throughout my own home for salable items, I move on to my office and look for even more items to sell.

Parents, family members, neighbors and friends are a fantastic source for finding more valuable items to sell at any garage sale. Over time, miscellaneous items always seem to get stuck in people's basements and as a result, all those long-forgotten items just end up gathering dust and cobwebs. Always ask people you know if there's anything of theirs you can put in your garage sale. You can always arrange to split the money you make on their items with them. It really is a "win-win" situation for all involved. They give you their old stuff. You do all the work. They make a percentage on the sales! Many times family and friends want to help you out and will even "work" at your garage sale because these types of events are so much fun.

Throughout the years, I've developed a proven timeline that has helped me stay organized and get ready for any garage sale. By always adhering to my timeline, I can 99.99% guarantee myself that I make sure that everything I want to sell will be at my garage sale.

Let's look at the timeline and then I will discuss some key points in more detail:

Time to Go Before Sale	Things to Do
1 Month	✓ Start looking for and gathering up, items around your house and office which you do not use.
	✓ Ask your family members if they have any items for you to sell.
	✓ Try to get as many items as possible for your sale. Size matters!
	✓ Over do it if you have to. More items are better.
	✓ The more items people see at your garage sale, the more motivation they will have for stopping and shopping.
	✓ Clean and fix your sale items (if necessary).
	✓ Look for original packaging on the items you have, especially if you have collectibles to sell.

The Garage Sale Millionaire

Time to Go Before Sale	Things to Do
2 Weeks to 2 Days	✓ Create your signs and flyers for your sale (extra credit pointsare awarded for very colorful and eye-catching signs and flyers). ✓ Get a change purse together so you are prepared to make correct change when your garage sale starts.
2 Weeks to 2 Days	✓ Place your advertisements in your local newspapers, or in any free newspapers in your area, to announce your sale. ✓ Start using social networking Internet websites such as Twitter, Craigslist and Facebook to get the word out on the location and date of your garage sale. ✓ Start methodically pricing your sale items. ✓ Make sure you have enough tables for all of your sale items.
The Night Before	✓ Put your signs and flyers out in the busiest of traffic areas and around your neighborhood, where you believe the most people will see the announcement of your garage sale. ✓ Look over and meticulously double check everything you want to sell at least one more time to guarantee accuracy in the pricing of your sale items.
The Morning of Your Garage Sale	✓ Two hours before your sale, start physically setting up your garage sale.
Your Garage Sale Begins	✓ **Smile and watch the money pour in!**

Key Elements from My Tried-And-True Garage Sale Timeline

Size Matters

Implement this *key element* one month before the date of your garage sale

I cannot tell you how many garage sales I've seen where people will slow down, stick their heads out the car window, take a look around and keep on driving. This is definitely not what you want to have happen at your sale.

To make sure your garage sale is an even bigger eye-catcher, you'll want to have as many items as possible in view to sell and have them spread out on as many tables as possible. By having enough tables to display all your merchandise, your garage sale will take on the image of being bigger. When you have people driving by to see if your sale is worth the time and energy to get out of their cars to shop, bigger is most definitely better. Also, when you have a larger sale, people will take more time to browse and eventually to shop. In my decades of garage sale experience, the more time people spend at a garage sale the more money they seem to spend.

By including as many "other people's stuff" that you can get your hands on, the better opportunity you'll have to make a bigger profit.

Million $ Tip

The more treasures, trinkets, items and goodies you have in your garage sale, the bigger it will look. By having a fully stocked sale, your chances for garage sale success and making as much money from your sale as possible, will increase exponentially. When people drive by and see all the great items at a garage sale, they will almost always stop, get out of their cars and walk quickly into your sale.

Clean and Fix Everything

Implement this *key elemen*t one month before the date of your garage sale

After you've gone to family and friend's homes to look for salable items for your enterprise, next look through your house inside-out and upside-down identifying the items people might be interested in buying, Then, take time to scour your office for finds you didn't even know you had lying around. Now it's time to make sure everything is clean and in working order. If something minor needs to be fixed, you need to fix it before the sale, so

Million $ Tip

By inviting more people to help you at your garage sale, you increase your chances for garage sale success and you will more than likely have a great turn out.

you avoid having customers bargain you way down on the price. There's nothing worse than going to a garage sale and finding something you really want to buy which is in absolutely awful shape. I have seen it all in my experience with garage sales: If you're selling stuffed animals, furniture with cushions, or, even, pillows, give them a good spritz of Febreze® ! Dirty, malfunctioning and broken items don't bring in very much revenue! These are deal breakers for me...

I've found so many items that look dusty, unclean and noticeably in a state of ill-repair that I've passed on buying these items even if there was an inkling that I could have sold them for a profit later on.

Items which physically fell apart in my hands when I picked them up get a pass from me every time.

Discovering that when I went to plug an electrical item into the outlet, the item for sale started smoking…no thanks.

I've found items which smelled so horribly awful that they were a complete turn off…a definite NO!

I've found rusted out items which lost all their value many years ago. Sometimes it seems, decades ago. It doesn't take a very keen eye to pick up on this.

My list could have been longer, but you get the idea. Always make sure the items you have are in decent working order. People will ask you to plug in an item to see if it really works and they will pick up items to see if they completely fall apart. The opportunity to test your items is in the days leading up to your garage sale. The opportunity to get the most money for every item lies in whether or not it's in proper working order and how good it looks when it's sitting on the sales table. If you have something to sell and it's missing a part, believe me, your garage sale visitors are going to ask if you have that missing part. It's an inevitable garage sale truth…they will always ask! If you happen to have the part, it will usually guarantee the sale. If not, then good luck.

> ### Million $ Tip
> Have an extension cord available for your customers to use if you are selling any electrical items. Your customers may want to test out these items before they buy.

Customers will ask you questions you never thought they would come up with in a million years. Be ready for anything and always be honest with your reply. If you are dishonest at any time during your sale, buyers will be very upset. If you ever have another garage sale, they will never stop by again. More importantly, they may warn many others to stay away from any garage sale you may hold in the future.

Original Packaging Greatly Adds Value to Your Items

Implement this *key element* one month from the date of your garage sale

It's very important, especially if you're selling collectibles, to include the original box or packaging which came with the item. Why? Items with the original packaging, along with the instructions (if there were any), will sell for much more money than items being sold without their original sales packaging. A lot more money! In my experience, an item with its original packaging will sell for at least 20% to 40% more than an item sold by itself. If it's a collectible and you have the box and certificate, this will raise the value about 50%. If your collectible came with a wind up key, it's essential to find that key to keep the item fully intact. Anything you can find to help add value is crucial to include with the item at your garage sale.

It's worth your while and will result in bigger profits, to take the extra time needed to make certain that everything is in perfect order for your big day. Do everything in your power to present the "World's Greatest Garage Sale." Run your event like a well-oiled machine and your pocketbook as well as your bank account will be happy that you did.

Pricing Your Items

Implement this *key element* one week from the date of your garage sale

Pricing is another crucial element to any garage sale. *To place prices on items, or put them out without pricing…that is the question.* You would think that prices should be placed on everything at a garage sale. This is not always the case. I've gone to a multitude of garage sales where pricing falls into two categories…items with pricing and items without any price attached.

Why would someone not put a price on something at a garage sale? By not placing a price on an item, the person holding the garage sale forces the potential buyer to personally inquire about the price, or to make an offer. This gives the seller a potential amount of leeway in determining the price of the item. This non-pricing of items occurs most often on items of very little value. With less expensive items selling for as little as a dollar or less, it will take you hours to price out everything. On these types of items, try omitting the price altogether and bargaining with your customers. You're not going to make much from these items anyway. You know people are going to probably spend the minimum so why waste your valuable time marking a price on insignificant smaller items?

> ### *Million $ Tip*
> Always leave room to barter when pricing an item. Make sure you price your sale items 15% to 20% higher so you can barter the price when someone makes you an offer.

When pricing items, don't be greedy. If you're too greedy on your pricing, people will walk away from your sale with nothing in hand. Place a fair price on your items, but always leave yourself some room to bargain. If you have an item that cost $100 when it was new, your sale price should not exceed $45. Also, be ready to accept $30. If you're not prepared to take a lower offer of $30 for the item, then slightly raise your sales price to $47, $48, or even $50. Remember, the goal at any garage sale is to have nothing left over at the end of the day. Try to sell everything on hand so you can begin building a fresh new inventory for your next sale.

If you're unsure of something when it comes to pricing your sale items, search out **eBay** *(www.ebay.com)*. eBay will give you an upto-the-minute idea of what an item is worth. If an item is even worth only a few dollars, price it to sell. It's better to put it on your table and have someone make you an offer than to hold onto it for another ten years! If you really don't know how to value an item, price it at what you believe to be fair and be very observant of your customers during your sale. If someone wants to buy an item that you marked at a certain price and it looks like they are ready to walk away from the sale, go over and ask, "Would you like to make me an offer?" If they come up with a number that's below the price that you had listed for the item, counteroffer. You can always suggest "meeting in the middle" between your final price and your customer's offer. If they offered $2 and you made a final counteroffer of $3, then $2.50 will be the final sales price. That's the normal flow of the garage sale.

There are so many great deals for people to buy "new" merchandise. "New" means there are items in perfect or near-perfect condition. "New" may also mean this year's model of whatever is made. I can guarantee you that almost every item sold at a garage sale is not going to be this year's latest model. If an item is in perfect condition, you can't expect to make all your money back or even consider charging retail value. Don't forget! You are conducting a garage sale where full price is almost never paid. That's just the way it works. You're doing extremely well if you get between 25% and 35%, or even sometimes 45% of what you originally paid for an item.

When you're thinking about what's valuable and what could be worth good money at any garage sale, don't look at used books. If you charge more than a few dollars per book, people will quickly walk away. No sale, my friends! Used books don't hold much value either.

Computers, old appliances and "tube" televisions (not flat screens) don't sell for much, as well. Of course, you can always try to sell these items, but don't expect much in return for them. This doesn't mean you shouldn't sell everything and anything you want, but just be cognizant of what you might or more than likely might not get for older items way past their prime.

One of the reasons you would want to try to sell everything you can has to do with trash removal. Whatever you have left after your sale that needs to be disposed of will cost you money to haul away. Trash companies won't even take the majority of larger items which you were unable to sell and you'll be forced to hire a private junk hauler to get rid of your items for you. Trash companies also don't like taking obsolete computer monitors and printers, or anything which could be considered hazardous to a dump site. Second hand stores are also not taking everything as readily as they once did. In the end, you'll be stuck spending your hard-earned garage sale profits on hiring a hauler to move anything which was unsold. It's sometimes better to take a little less money for your sale items so you don't have to dispose of them yourself if they are left over after the sale.

Advertising

Implement this *key element* beginning two weeks and up until to two days before the date of your garage sale

Your sale items have all been exhaustively acquired, painstakingly organized for your garage sale and are all ready to go. They are priced, cleaned up and looking good…as though like they are ready to literally leap from the table into your customers' hands. Now, all you have to do is figure out a way to get people to your sale.

From my experience, people believe overwhelmingly that the advertising aspect of any garage sale is an extremely complicated process. Nothing could be further from the truth.

Advertising for any garage sale is the easiest component within the sales process. Publicizing your garage sale does take some attention to complete, but it's a very straightforward exercise.

Two weeks to go before your sale is when you need to start taking advantage of many of the free advertising resources at your disposal. You must have all your advertising in place a couple of days before your target day. Not only are almost all of these resources free of charge, but they are also very effective and proven methods for making your forthcoming event known. These free resources include:

Advertising on the Internet. There are many garage sale websites that will let you post your garage sale information for free.

Various Internet social networking websites such as Facebook *(www.facebook.com)*, Twitter *(www.twitter.com),* and Craigslist *(www.craigslist.org)*.

Post your advertisements in flyer form at local libraries, coffee shops and your neighborhood recreation centers. Always be sure to get permission to place your garage sale advertisements so your hard work will not be torn down and thrown in the trash before your sale.

The week before your sale is when you need to start posting information about your sale on *Twitter*. You must have your sale posted to *Craigslist* three days before your sale. On *Facebook*, you need to have everything in place within a few days of your sale. Although the use of free advertising options are excellent cost-effective ways to get the word out, don't overestimate the power of spending a little money by placing an ad in your local newspaper's classifieds section. One of the main benefits of advertising in your local paper is for whatever the small expense might be, you will be reaching many more potential customers than with free advertising alone. Serious garage sale aficionados, who are big shoppers at every sale they attend, scour the classifieds sections of the paper every week to map out a plan and decide which sales they will attend. Of course, every newspaper's fee structure is different, so contact your local classifieds section advertising sales rep to get an idea of what the actual fees are. Because of today's very tough economic climate, you may get a great deal to advertise your garage sale in your local newspaper. Why? For some time now, free online advertising websites such as Craigslist have taken a big bite out of the newspaper industry's advertising profits. Because of this trend in advertising, you may get a great deal on the ad rates. I can't guarantee anything, but you can always try.

You will need to begin creating all the signs for your sale a week prior. These signs will be placed around your immediate area and neighborhoods. They need to be placed in their designated, high traffic locations within twelve hours of your garage sale. The higher and faster the traffic area, the bigger your signs should be. I recommend you get some white poster board from an art or office supply store. You can even try going to some frame stores that have tons of left over scrap board you might be able to get for free. Once they use part of the mat boards or cardboard, they throw away the other part. Trust me. I own an art gallery and since I go through so much of it myself, it really is a huge waste. My art gallery is just starting to recycle the mat board we don't use. So, going to a frame shop is one great way to get colorful mat board for your low budget sale. You also need to make your sign extremely visible. Choose signs or boards which are either red or white. For lettering, use thick-tipped magic markers. On white signs or white boards, always use a RED magic marker. If you're using red signs or red boards, always use a BLACK magic marker. Green or brown colors get lost in the background of trees and yards.

If you're placing signs in speedy traffic areas, you'll want to use big mat boards. When I mean big, I mean BIG! I am talking boards at least 3' high x 3' wide. If you're in an area where people are using pedestrian walkways and are leisurely walking with their children or dogs, or going out for their daily jog, then you can use smaller signs to advertise your sale.

I recommend making about 20 signs and placing them on several busy streets within three to five miles of your home. Be sure to take a staple gun with you as well as some duct tape. Never put your signs on traffic markers. That is against the law. Take the signs to as many busy streets as close to your home as possible. By placing the majority of your signs near stop signs or stop lights, people will have ample time to read them. If libraries, grocery stores, or shopping malls are within three to five miles of your home, then these are also great places to put up signs. Be sure to place these signs near the exit of parking lots as well.

Don't place signs in locations where traffic is moving very fast and streaking past. When you place a sign along a busy street and the cars are going about 45+ MPH, what are the chances anyone is going to see that garage sale sign? The answer is "little to none."

What should be written on your signs to achieve the best financial success at your sale? The address is the very first piece of information that needs to be listed. The day and time of your sale goes directly under the address. Also, with bullet points, include some key items you will have at the sale. Be focused. Only list the five most sought after main selling items. Anything more and your sign gets too crowded. People often make the big mistake of trying to squeeze too much information on a sign. Here are the top items people sell and what people look for most at garage sales. When these items are listed on a garage sale sign, people take notice and will make it a point to stop by and spend their money:

- *Antiques*   - *Bikes*
- *Tools*   - *Collectibles*
- *Electronics*   - *Furniture*
- *Baby "anything" (i.e. clothes, cribs, toys)*

Extras to have at your sale which will help it achieve "The World's Greatest Garage Sale" status

A Refreshment Stand

When people come to a garage sale, especially in the hot summer months, they're going to get thirsty. The larger your sale, the longer people will pause and spend time looking at as many items as they can. As a result, they will want something to drink. *A refreshment stand at your sale will help make the shopping experience for your guests a much better one. It may also add some extra money in your pocket because people will stay longer if they are not hungry or thirsty.* If you have children of your own or know of some neighbor kids between the ages of five to sixteen years old, see if they want to have a lemonade or refreshment stand right next to your garage sale. Having kids selling soft drinks (that's "pop" or "soda"), iced tea, lemonade and/or bottled water will save you from having to run into your house for a cup of water when someone inevitably asks for a drink. Also, consider selling food items at your refreshment stand. These items could include cookies,

---

Million $ Tip

Half the fun of going to any garage sale is doing the buying. People also want to be entertained! No, you do not have to do cartwheels, juggle, or put on a magic show. All you have to do is be kind, chatty and make the process for the buyer an enjoyable experience. I guarantee if you are a great garage sale host people will buy more of your wares and will always come back when they know you are having another sale.

---

candy, chips, popcorn, or a variety of homemade baked goods. Shoppers will invariably be more relaxed and will have a more enjoyable time at your sale if they can quench their thirst and enjoy a snack! Always remember that if your customers are enjoying themselves, there will be a greater than average chance that they will spend more time and spend more money at your sale.

If you want to do the refreshment stand on a larger scale, contact your church or a local charity to see if they would like to host one at your garage sale. Good refreshment stands at garage sales easily net between $50 and $200. I've seen some refreshment stands take in almost as much as the actual garage sale itself.

More Tables Equal Better Profits

Earlier I mentioned the necessity of having an adequate number of tables. When you hold your garage sale, you're going to need as many tables as possible to sufficiently display your items. *The more tables you have, the better a garage sale becomes…it never fails.* If you put all of your items in boxes, potential customers will have to make an exerted effort to rummage through everything. Sometimes people like that, but more often they don't. One of the most universal garage sale rules is *all items need to be laid out in plain sight.* If you're asking good money for something, you don't want to display your valued objects in a crowded pile or hidden in a box. If items are hidden in a box, there's a very real chance someone might not even see what you're trying to sell. Having all your treasures nicely laid out is going to be a monumental plus. This means you're going to need those tables we mentioned to show off your wares.

When you put the tables out, people might ask if you're going to sell the tables as well as what's on each table. When I say everything must go at a garage sale, I was not joking!

You will need to determine ahead of time if you want to sell the tables and at what price you will want to sell them. Of course, only sell them if they're yours and aren't borrowed. If you have really ugly looking tables, always cover them with attractive looking tablecloths. If you have items lying on top of an ugly, old and weathered table without a proper covering, the items for sale will appear to be ugly, too.

Volunteers

When your garage sale is quite large, one or two people working the sale just won't do. There's no chance to be able to cover everything and help every customer with just a few people. This is especially true if you have multiple families selling their treasures at your garage sale. This is where having multiple volunteers comes in handy. If there are several families selling items at your garage sale, then each family really needs to have several helpers present. There are a few positive reasons for this:

People usually come to garage sales in groups. There won't be anyone at your sale for a while and then all of a sudden, you'll find yourself inundated with five to 15 people all at once. One or two people staffing your sale won't be able to handle that many buyers as well as provide the level of customer service your potential customers require. As a result of being understaffed, you'll end up losing money.

Shoppers need ample time to look at everything. Not only that, but they are going to want to chitchat with you and negotiate the price on almost everything. If you rush them, they'll become dissatisfied with your sale and walk away without buying anything. At a large garage sale, it is good to have *at least* three to five volunteers standing by, ready to help, answer questions and assist with getting items into shopper's cars.

There is a really good chance if you sell something large it's going to take a little time to settle on a price and help load it into a customer's car or truck. Having a volunteer who can just "hang out" and talk with the other customers, process any sales, or just supervise the sale with help as needed (while you're busy helping others) will be a huge asset.

What Not To Do At Any Garage Sale

Do Not Let Strangers in Your Home...EVER

The major point I want you all to know and never forget, is to **NEVER LET ANYONE INTO YOUR HOME UNDER ANY CIRCUMSTANCE**. There are a few essential reasons why this is a good strategy:

People have been known to get into your house and "case" it. These strangers look over the contents within your home, see what they can find of value and check how your home is laid out for easy access and a quick exit. This is commonly referred to as "casing the joint." Experienced thieves take everything they see into considerationso they can return later and rob you. Not good!

People have also been known to come into your house and take items while you're distracted or when you're not paying attention. Again, not good!

The shoppers and customers who come into your home to use the bathroom facilities might not be up to your level of cleanliness. The last thing you want to do is to clean up after a stranger who improperly uses your bathroom. This goes way beyond not good!

As you can see by the above examples, nothing good can result by letting strangers into your house. In advance of your garage sale, make up some plausible excuses you're comfortable with using to avoid these types of situations. For example, you have a baby asleep inside, you have a sick parent, or you own a dog which doesn't really get along with strangers. Whatever the reason is, always be prepared to convey it at a moment's notice.

Never Take Checks

It gets very difficult to turn down any sale especially in this economy; and most especially when you are talking hundreds of dollars. People will try to convince you that the only form of payment they have at the moment is a personal check. Some customers will go to great lengths to reassure you that their check is legitimate. If you accept a check from someone you don't know and it turns out to be no good as is often the case, then you have only yourself to blame for your predicament. Not only will you have to pay your bank any NSF (Non-Sufficient Funds) fees for accepting a bad check, but you also get to keep the worthless check as a "truly wonderful" souvenir from your sale. Avoid these problems by never accepting a personal check.

These days due to our poor economic climate, you can't afford to accept checks from people frequenting garage sales. Unfortunately, it's very likely that they don't have the money in their account to cover the amount written. A possible sales saving solution for those experiencing financially rougher times is to ask them for a smaller cash deposit instead of a check. Tell them you'll hold the item they want for 48 hours so they can get the money when their bank opens or when they get paid. If they don't return at a certain time, advise them that their deposit is non-refundable. To prevent them disputing the deposit situation after the 48 hours time period has passed, or if you feel they might demand their money

---

Million $ Tip

Even if you post a sign stating "NO CHECKS WILL BE ACCEPTED" at your sale, people will still offer them as a "viable" payment option. Be firm. Sticking to "your guns" will save you a substantial amount of money.

The Garage Sale Millionaire

back, write a very informal agreement and have them date and sign it. That way you're completely covered from a legal standpoint. Under no circumstances would I ever accept a check from someone I don't know personally.

Allow me to present one prime example of a standard garage sale check ripoff scheme, called "*The Cash Back Artist*."

The Cash Back Artist

One of the biggest ripoffs at garage sales is one I would like to call "The Cash Back Artist."

Many garage sales get very busy and the owner of the garage sale is somewhat overwhelmed and usually distracted. Customers are constantly asking you for details about this item and that, negotiating prices on what they want to buy and confusion reigns supreme. Occasionally, you'll have a customer who may ask you to take a check, but then ask to write the check for more than the sales price of the item. The prospective customer will then request the amount over the cost of the item to be handed back to them in cash.

Enter "The Cash Back Artist."

For example, a seemingly very decent looking, well-groomed shopper at your sale wants to buy a couch. You've priced the couch at $200. Then, the shopper says very convincingly, "Oh, man, I don't have enough cash on me. I'm so sorry. When I left the house this morning, I thought I put enough cash in my wallet. I must have gotten busy and I only have about $60 or $80 on me. The customer let's you see the actual cash in their wallet to suggest subliminally that you're dealing with what appears to be an "honest" person. "Can I write this check for $250; and could you give me the difference in cash?" The unknowing garage sale owner takes the check for the couch and feels good about the sale, but seven days later the check bounces.

Congratulations. Thanks to the "Cash Back Artist" you don't have your sofa, you are out an extra $50 in cash (which you handed out to the customer when you accepted his/her check) and you now owe your bank money to cover the NSF fees which you accrued when the check bounced.

Additionally, "Cash Back Artists" may also use fake certified checks. This kind of activity happens often when you're dealing with transactions through Craigslist.

Do Not Give Out Your Telephone Number!

I never put my telephone number on any of my garage sale signs or in any of the advertisements I place. If you list your telephone number, you'll have people calling you at all hours of the day and night. Incoming calls about your sale will sometimes last for weeks after the sale is over. You really need to think seriously about whether or not you want to divulge your number to the general public and exactly what the repercussions may be if you choose to do so. The only exception to this rule is if you give someone your telephone number because they were interested in buying an item from you after your garage sale for a lower price than you originally asked.

        Another reason not to display your number is that people don't value your time the same as you do. With your best intentions, you give the customer your telephone number so they are able to call back regarding an item if they have any questions or to arrange payment. The customer then decides to call you at 6:30 p.m. when you're in the middle of dinner, after you've gone to bed for the night, or at any other extremely inconvenient time of day.

        So, remember, when you do give out your telephone number, you must consider what could happen in a worst case scenario. If you must advertise your telephone number, only share a cellular telephone number that you can control.

Do Not Sell Anything Illegal

        You may read this and think it's the most ridiculous thing I could say. You might also say, "Of course, who would be dumb enough to sell illegal items?" It's not as stupid a statement as you might think. I've been to many garage sales where honest people have unknowingly sold illegal items. Besides the obvious illegality of selling drugs, drug paraphernalia and fireworks, I need to clue you in on some very popular "legal" items that might be misconstrued as "illegal" if the circumstances were right.

        Firearms and ammunitions are one of the biggest categories sold at garage sales; however, if not sold properly, the sale can constitute an illegal act. People don't usually set out to sell entire arsenals of illegal firearms, but if they sell their firearms and ammunitions improperly, they could end up serving jail time. If you want to sell firearms or ammunitions, you need to let a licensed gun store "clear" them for you first. Licensed gun stores will make all the proper background checks to ensure that people who are not allowed to purchase these items at will not wind up getting them. Better yet, by going through licensed gun stores, you can almost assure yourself that you won't get into any legal trouble by selling firearms. The worst case scenario you could encounter is if you were to sell a firearm improperly at your event and then, that firearm was used in the act of committing crime. In the event that this was to happen, the "authorities" will come directly back to you and you will be entangled in a web of legal problems.

        Fireworks are another tricky item to sell at garage sales, especially if you want to stay out of legal trouble. Time and time again, I have seen people selling fireworks that are not legally allowed in their city or county. The worst case scenario associated with selling fireworks is if someone becomes injured or has an accident with the fireworks you have sold. Profits from fireworks, whether illegal or not, would never be worth the risk of selling if they might potentially cause someone bodily harm. If a person gets hurt after they buy something from you, the most likely outcome will be that they will come back and aggressively sue you. We live in a very litigious society (if you haven't noticed already) and people are always for looking for an easy way to make quick money from lawsuits. Be very mindful to ensure that anything you sell cannot harm anyone in any way.

        Recalled items must never be sold at any garage sale. If you have something that has been recalled and you know it has been recalled, please don't ever try and sell it. The best thing you can do with any recalled item is throw it away or send it back to the manufacturer if there is a recall notice. Obviously, you don't want to sell an item such as baby furniture or children's toys that pose a potential health risk to anyone's family. So please, if you know something could be harmful, especially if it's been officially recalled, don't sell that item.

What do you do if you can't sell all of your items?

Here are some other possible options for disposing of things you couldn't sell at your garage sale. I mentioned using a private trash hauling company to come to your home and remove any remaining items and I even talked about giving your items to second hand stores to see if they could resell any of your unsold items, giving you a portion of the proceeds. What I didn't mention was using charities to take those leftover items. The benefit of donating anything remaining from your garage sale to a charitable organization comes in the form of potential tax write-offs. Of course, please consult with your personal tax professional to get an exact idea of what you can or cannot deduct from any charitable donation. By donating items to charity, not only will you be helping others in need, you will be helping yourself as well.

Now You Can Have "The World's Greatest Garage Sale"

I have to say that buying and selling items at estate auctions, garage sales and everything in-between, is a highly enjoyable activity to engage in -- not to mention a highly

My Last Million $ Tip of The Garage Sale Millionaire

The information that I've presented in this book has helped me buy and sell tens of millions of dollars worth of collectibles over the course of 30+ years - not only as a fine art and collectibles gallery owner, but, also, as a *Garage Sale Millionaire*. If you adhere to the principles detailed in this book, you, too, can become a *Garage Sale Millionaire*.

Fortunately, all the profitable fun doesn't stop where this book ends. Please visit my website at *www.thegaragesalemillionaire.com* for more insider tips and need-to-know money-making information so I can continue to guide you in your quest in becoming the best *Garage Sale Millionaire* you can be! Also, if you have any questions for me about the book, the collectibles buying and selling process, or if you want to share your successes with me which I could possibly highlight in my next *The Garage Sale Millionaire* book, I'd love to hear from you *thegaragesalemillionaire@gmail.com.*

I hear remarkable success stories all the time from other Garage Sale Millionaires. You now have the essential tools to successfully navigate your own course to become a Garage Sale Millionaire. Those "hidden gems" and "buried treasures" are always out there just waiting for you to discover them. **Get out there and claim your fortune!**

profitable endeavor! Personally, I've had so much fun holding garage sales that I have hosted nearly 50 of them in my life and I don't plan on stopping any time soon. I absolutely know you're going to have a tremendous time holding your own garage sale, as well.

By actively participating in estate auctions, buying and selling items online and using other means to buy and sell collectibles as outlined in this book -- in addition to holding garage sales -- you'll be making yourself some serious money.

Glossary of Terms

# #

3-D Card

A sports trading card which appears to be three-dimensional (3-D) as it is moved or tilted.

3-D Comic

Comic art drawn (and printed) in two color layers. This type of illustration produces a three-dimensional (3-D) effect only when viewed through special 3-D glasses.

3-D Effect Comic

Comic art drawn so it appears to be three-dimensional (3-D), but actually is not.

9-Up Sheets

Uncut sheets imprinted with nine cards, usually used as promos. A term commonly used with sports and trading cards.

A

About Good

Refers to a coin with a grade of " AG-3."

About Uncirculated

(1) Coins with grades of "AU-50," "AU-53," "AU-55," and "AU-58" on the "Professional Coin Grading Service (PCGS) Grades and Grading Terms" scale. (2) A coin that, at first glance, appears Uncirculated but, upon closer inspection, has slight friction or rub. See "Professional Coin Grading Service (PCGS) Grades and Grading Terms."

Abraded Corner

The grinding of a corner area on a comic book which is caused by improper handling or storage.

Absentee Bid

When this type of bid is allowed at an auction, a person can bid on any item without actually attending the event. The buyer submits in advance, a written or oral bid which is the top price he/she will pay for a given auction item. Only the auctioneer knows this amount and the bid amount is kept private. The auctioneer bids on behalf of the absentee bidder until the buyer either wins the auction item or when that person's maximum bid is exceeded.

Absolute Auction

An auction where property is sold to the highest qualified bidder with no limiting conditions.

Accessories

Any additional item included in the action figure or toy package, or something which is associated with the action figure and sold separately.

Accessory Pack

A set of accessories, typically intended for a specific line of action figures and/or toys, which come packaged by themselves instead of with an individual action figure and/or toy.

Acid Cutting

A process used for decorating glass where objects were coated with an acid-resistant substance.

Acrylonitrile Butadiene Styrene (ABS)

One of the two most common plastics used in the manufacture of action figures, the other is Polyvinyl Chloride (PVC). ABS plastic is generally harder and more brittle than PVC.

Action Figure

A doll-like plastic figure, which can be made to pose in different configurations. Action figures have come a long way over the years and many are now collected for the quality of manufacturing and for their resale potential. Action figures are usually licensed by comic book or entertainment companies.

Action Figure Authority (AFA)

Professional grading agency which verifies, authenticates, and certifies items such as action figures, toys, die cast items, and dolls. www.toygrader.com.

Action Figure Authority (AFA) C-Scale Grading Scale:

C1-C4- Very poor, badly damaged, basically only useful for spare parts.

C5- Poor condition with heavy wear, broken parts will impair function.

C6- Fair, significant wear, may have some broken parts.

C7- Good, noticeable wear but no broken parts, items may be missing accessories.

C8- Very good, some minor wear, no broken or missing parts.

C9- Near mint condition, very minor imperfections apparent.

C10- Mint condition, unused.

Action Figure Authority (AFA) 3-Tier C-Scale Grading Scale (for items produced from 1960-present):

AFA Gold

Graded as Gem Mint (100), Mint (95), and Near Mint/Mint (90). The AFA Gold level consists of the grades 100, 95, and 90. The select few figures which receive these grades are among the highest quality in existence. A very small percentage of figures submitted to the AFA receive a Gold grade. The flaws are very minor, very subtle, and are sometimes very hard to identify with the naked eye. The collector who is extremely condition sensitive will only be satisfied with the condition of a Gold level figure.

AFA Silver

Graded as Near Mint Plus (85), Near Mint (80), and Excellent Plus/Near Mint (75). The AFA Silver level consists of the grades 85, 80, and 75. The figures that receive these grades are in excellent condition. A figure graded as an 85 will often be referred to as 'case fresh' and should be very close to gold level condition. The term 'case fresh' is certainly justifiable, as the average figure pulled from a sealed case will grade an 85 due to small flaws which occur when the figures are packaged or shipped in the case. The average figure pulled from a store shelf is usually an 80, which represents a nice specimen with minor flaws apparent upon close inspection. The final Silver level grade, a 75, represents an item with more minor flaws than the average Silver level piece. An item grading 75 does have significant wear but does not have major flaws which would draw the eye to them at first glance. For most high grade collectors, an 85 is satisfactory. For most discriminating collectors, an 80 is satisfactory. A 75 will be satisfactory to those who are not overly concerned with light stresses, small bubble imperfections, and other flaws which do not jump out at first glance. Therefore, the Silver level grades do represent a much larger range than the Gold level grades.

AFA Bronze

Graded as Excellent Plus (70), Excellent (60), Very Good (50), Good (40), Fair (30), poor (20), and Very Poor (10). The AFA Bronze level consists of the grades 70, 60, and below. The figures that receive these grades typically have damage ranging from simply noticeable upon first glance to extremely significant. The card may have creases on the front and the blister may be crushed or cracked. The Bronze level covers a large range of figure conditions and the scope of the flaws range considerably. Condition for Bronze level figures is determined by how many "major" flaws are present on the card and how severe each flaw is. Bronze level figures may have major flaws such as a torn off POP or other large paper tears. Bronze level figures may not be satisfactory to condition sensitive collectors.

Action Figure Authority (AFA) Modern Grading Scale (AFAM) 3-Tier Grading Scale (for items produced from 1995-present):

AFA Gold

Graded as 9.0, 9.25, 9.5, 9.75, and 10.0. The AFA Gold level consists of the grades 10.0, 9.75, 9.5, 9.25, and 9.0. The figures that receive these grades are among the highest quality in existence. The flaws are very minor, very subtle, and are sometimes very hard to identify with the naked eye. A collector who is extremely condition sensitive should be satisfied with the condition of a Gold level figure.

AFA Silver

Graded as 7.5, 8.0, and 8.5. The AFA Silver level consists of the grades 8.5, 8.0, and 7.5. The figures which receive these grades are in decent condition. A collector would be able to spot a few small flaws on an 8.5 and would see several moderate flaws on a 7.5.

AFA Bronze

Graded as 1.0-7.0. The AFA Bronze level consists of the grades 7.0 and below. The figures which receive these grades typically have damage ranging from simply noticeable upon first glance to extremely significant. Since modern items are typically in good condition, very few items will be low enough to receive these grades.

Actual Gold Weight (AGW)

The amount of pure gold in a coin, medal or bar. Any alloys are part of the gross weight of a gold coin, but not part of the AGW.

Adjustment Marks

Pre-striking file marks seen mainly on gold and silver coins prior to 1840.

Advance One Sheet

A 27 x 41-inch poster usually issued several months prior to the release of the movie.

Adzine

A magazine primarily devoted to the advertising of comic books and collectibles as its first publishing priority, as opposed to one containing written articles.

Aerophilatelist

Someone who collects airmail stamps.

AFA Bronze

See "Action Figure Authority (AFA) 3-Tier C-Scale Grading Scale (for items produced from 1960-present)" or "Action Figure Authority (AFA) Modern Grading Scale (AFAM) 3-Tier

Grading Scale (for items produced from 1995-present)."

AFA Gold

See "Action Figure Authority (AFA) 3-Tier C-Scale Grading Scale (for items produced from 1960-present)" or "Action Figure Authority (AFA) Modern Grading Scale (AFAM) 3-Tier Grading Scale (for items produced from 1995-present)."

AFA Silver

See "Action Figure Authority (AFA) 3-Tier C-Scale Grading Scale (for items produced from 1960-present)" or "Action Figure Authority (AFA) Modern Grading Scale (AFAM) 3-Tier Grading Scale (for items produced from 1995-present)."

After-Market

The market in which an item is sold after its initial retail availability.

AG-3

Refers to the "grade" or quality of a particular coin based on the "Professional Coin Grading Service (PCGS) Grades and Grading Terms" scale. This designation is for "About Good" (the grade) and "3" (the corresponding numerical designation). Most of the lettering on the coin is readable, but there is moderately heavy wear into the rims. This grade is frequently found on Barber coins where the obverse is fully Good (or better) but the reverse is heavily worn. See "Professional Coin Grading Service (PCGS) Grades and Grading Terms."

Airbrushing

The art of touching up a photo prior to a sports trading card being printed to remove imperfections, or to update the player's jersey or cap logo.

All Bisque

A doll, usually under eight inches in length, made entirely of bisque parts.

All Published

A book, or set of books, is complete "As-Is." Any additional parts or volumes were never published.

Allegorical Print

A print which represents a universal truth by using imagery.

All-Star Card

A sports trading card picturing a player who has participated in the previous season's All-Star game.

Alteration

A coin that has a date, Mintmark, or other feature which has been changed, added, or removed, usually to simulate a rarer issue of a coin.

Ambrotype

A photographic process which consisted of one-of-a-kind glass negatives made positive by coating the backs of the negatives with black lacquer. This process was very popular between 1850 and the mid-1860s. Also see "Tintype."

American Numismatic Association (ANA)

A non-profit numismatic organization founded in 1888. www.money.org.

American Numismatic Association Certification Service (ANACS)

A third-party coin grading service. www.anacs.com.

American Numismatic Society (ANS)

An organization dedicated to the study of coins, currency, medals, tokens, and related objects from all cultures. www.numismatics.org.

ANACS Certificate

The certificate issued regarding the authenticity and/or grade from the American Numismatic Association (ANA) Certification Service on a coin.

Ancients

World coins struck between 600 B.C. and 450 A.D.

Aniline

A poisonous oily liquid, colorless when pure, obtained from coal tar and especially from nitro benzene, used in making inks, dyes and perfumes, in certain medicines, plastics, resins, etc.

Animated Toys

Any toy which simulates lifelike movements. Animated toys can be powered by, but, not limited to springs, strings, flywheels, gyroscopes, electricity, or batteries.

Animation Production Cel

A transparent sheet on which objects are drawn to create an animated cartoon. Animation production cels are currently hand-painted from behind onto celluloid acetate. In the early years of animation, these cels were made out of a thin plastic or nitrate, with paint on the back or front of a cel. Each cel also represents one frame of a character's movement on film. Also known as a "Cel."

Annual

(1) A comic or comic book which is published yearly. (2) Some square-bound comics.

Annual Edition

A new collectible piece created annually.

Antiquarian Book

An old and "rare" book, preferably at least 100 years old, similar to an antique, but with common usage the term has come to mean any book that is out-of-print, old, rare, scarce, common, used, or remaindered. Virtually any book that is not a new or in-print book.

Antique

Any work of art, piece of furniture, decorative object, created or produced in a former period, or according to United States Customs laws, 100 years before date of purchase.

Antiquities International

A retailer of one-of-a-kind collectibles, nostalgia, and memorabilia from the worlds of history, entertainment, and sports. Antiquities coined the term "Autographistry" to describe its technique of turning a piece of history into a work of art. The company was founded in 1984 and is headquartered in Las Vegas, Nevada. www.antiquitieslv.com.

Anvil Die

The lower die of a coin, usually the reverse.

A/O

An abbreviation for "All Original." An "A/O" action figure or toy comes complete with everything it came with as new and in its original packaging.

Applied Ears

Ears which are applied to a doll after the mold for the head has been poured.

Appliqué

The process of applying small patches of fabric to a base fabric to make a design.

Appraisal

The process of evaluating the quality, condition, rarity, provenance and source of a particular item in order to establish its value.

Apron

A length of wood found beneath the bottom framing of a piece of antique furniture such as a drawer, table top, or chair seat.

Arcading

A series of arches, usually supported on columns.

Archival Mount

The way to have your art properly framed using acid-free materials that affix your art inside the frame.

Archival Quality

The conservation materials and techniques accepted by libraries for the preservation and permanent housing of their old and rare materials.

Armoire

A French term for a large freestanding closet for hanging clothes.

Arrival Date

The date written or stamped on the cover of a comic by either the local wholesaler or the retailer.

Arrows

A design element usually found in the left claw of the eagle which is seen on many United States coins.

Arrows and Rays

Refers to the quarters and half dollars of 1853.

Arrows at Date

The arrows to the left and right of the date on a coin.

Articulation

(1) The pose-ability and movement of an action figure. (2) The amount and quantity of movable joints and parts of an action figure to make it more easy to pose.

Artificial Toning

The coloring added to the surface of a coin by chemicals and/or heat.

Ashcan

A pre-publication issue of a comic book usually used to show to potential advertisers.

Ask

The selling quotation of a coin either on a trading network, pricing newsletter, or other medium.

Assay

To analyze and determine the purity of a metallic alloy.

Association Issue

A paper or magazine that can be verified and authenticated to have been owned by a person of historical importance.

Assortment

Defines the series of an action figure line.

Assortment Number

The numerical listing used by toy companies to identify the series of an action figure line.

Atom Age

The period recognized by the comic book industry between 1946 and 1956.

Attic Mint

A term used to refer to a collectible found in an attic or area of building that has been left untouched for many years. This item may be dirty but in perfect condition.

Attributes

The elements which make up a coin's grade.

AU-50

Refers to the "grade" or quality of a particular coin based on the "Professional Coin Grading Service (PCGS) Grades and Grading Terms" scale. This designation is for "About Uncirculated" (the grade) and "50" (the numerical designation of which grade). Also called "Almost Uncirculated 50." This is the lowest of the four "AU" grades, with the others being AU-53, AU-55, and AU-58. Between 50% and 100% of the surfaces will exhibit luster disturbances, and perhaps the only luster still in evidence will be in the protected areas. The high points of the coin will have wear which is easily visible to the naked eye. See "Professional Coin Grading Service (PCGS) Grades and Grading Terms."

AU-53

Refers to the "grade" or quality of a particular coin based on the "Professional Coin Grading Service (PCGS) Grades and Grading Terms" scale. This designation is for "About Uncirculated" (the grade) and "53" (the numerical designation of which grade). Also called "Almost Uncirculated 53." There is obvious wear on the high points with light friction covering 50-75% of the fields. There are noticeable luster breaks, with most of the luster still intact in the protected areas. See "Professional Coin Grading Service (PCGS) Grades and Grading Terms."

AU-55

Refers to the "grade" or quality of a particular coin based on the "Professional Coin Grading Service (PCGS) Grades and Grading Terms" scale. This designation is for "About Uncirculated" (the grade) and "55" (the numerical designation of which grade). Also called "Almost Uncirculated 55." There is slight wear on the high points with minor friction in the fields. Luster can range from almost nonexistent to virtually full, but it will be missing from the high points. The grade of "Choice AU" equates to AU-55. See "Professional Coin Grading Service (PCGS) Grades and Grading Terms."

AU-58

Refers to the "grade" or quality of a particular coin based on the "Professional Coin Grading Service (PCGS) Grades and Grading Terms" scale. This designation is for "About Uncirculated" (the grade) and "58" (the numerical designation of which grade). Also called "Almost Uncirculated 58." There is the slightest wear on the high points, even though it may be necessary to tilt the coin towards the light source to see the friction. In many cases the reverse of an AU-58 coin will be fully Mint State. Less than 10% of the surface area will show luster breaks. The grade of "Borderline Unc" equates to AU-58. See "Professional Coin Grading Service (PCGS) Grades and Grading Terms."

Auction
The process of selling items through open, competitive bidding.

Auction Block
The specific area, usually on a podium or platform, where the auctioneer stands while conducting an auction.

Audiophile
An audio enthusiast. (2) A person who collects audio equipment.

Authentication
The process of determining the authentic qualities of a collectible item.

Authorized Issue
An issue or set of sports trading cards that are produced and distributed with the permission or written consent of the given league or player's association.

Autograph Guest
A current or former player, athlete, or other celebrity who attends a sports convention to sign autographs for fans.

Autographed Card
A sports card which has been autographed, almost always by the player depicted on the card.

B

B&W
The abbreviation for "Black and White."

Backup Feature
A story or character not usually featured on the cover of a comic. Additionally, a "Backup Feature" is never the first story in the comic.

Backstamp
A legal mark or logo put on the bottom of a figurine or the back of a plate as proof of authenticity.

Bag
The cloth sack in which a coin is stored and transported.

Bag Mark
The mark on a coin, made from another coin, while placed in a coin bag.

Bag Toning
The coloring on a coin acquired from the bag in which a coin was stored.

Ball Jointed
A common method of jointing composition bodies. Small wood "balls" are used in the doll's joints for more accurate movement.

Ball-And-Claw Foot
A carved decoration commonly found on cabriole legs from antique furniture items manufactured since early in the 18th century.

Bank Wrapped Rolls
The rolls of coins wrapped at a Federal Reserve Bank of the United States from original Mint bags.

Barber Coinage

An alternate name used to describe the Charles Barber-designed Liberty Head dimes, quarters, and half dollars struck between 1892 and 1916.

Bare Toy

A toy which comes with no accessories.

Barn Find

A car found in long-term storage, in highly original, although not necessarily orderly or complete condition. This term applies to cars and motorcycles.

Baroque

An architectural and decorative style invented in Europe in the 17th century.

Base Brand

The basic set of sports trading cards manufactured by a trading card maker which are usually the lowest priced.

Base Card

This term is sometimes used interchangeably with the term common, but as some base cards are produced in lower quantities than others, this is not technically correct. All commons are base cards, but not all base cards are commons.

Base Sets

A complete set of base cards for a particular trading card series.

Baseball Cap Coin

A slang term used to describe a "Pan Pac Commemorative" Gold dollar coin.

Baseball Card

A sports trading card which features a professional baseball player or team.

Baseball Hall of Fame (HOF)

Located in Cooperstown, New York, the Baseball Hall of Fame features thousands of artifacts from the game of baseball including many game-used pieces of memorabilia. Any memorabilia associated with a player who is enshrined as a member of the Baseball Hall of Fame will carry more resale and collectible value. www.baseballhalloffame.org.

Basining

The process of polishing a die to impart a mirrored surface or to remove clash marks or other injuries from the die.

Baxter Paper

A high quality, white, heavy paper used in the printing of some comics.

Bazooka

A bubble gum-making subsidiary of "Topps" which made baseball cards between 1959 and 1971, and once again, between 1988 and 1991. www.topps.com/candy/brands/Bazooka.

BBC

(1) The abbreviation for "Bottom Back Cover." (2) The abbreviation for the British Broadcasting Corporation, headquartered in the United Kingdom.

BC

The abbreviation for "Back Cover."

Beaded Border

The small, round devices around the edge of a coin, often seen on early United States coins.

Bébé
French dolls which represent small children.

Beckett
A well-known publisher of sports and specialty market collectible publications. Founded in 1984. www.beckett.com.

Bendie(s)
A type of toy manufacturing process whereby rubber is molded around a wire armature making the piece extremely flexible.

Bibliophile
Someone who collects books.

Bid
(1) A prospective buyer's indication or offer of a price he or she will pay to purchase property at auction. (2) The buying quotation of a coin either on a trading network, pricing newsletter, or other medium.

Bid Increments
The amount that a bid must be raised in an auction to be considered as acceptable. The proper bid amount depends on what the current bid is and the individual auction house's rules.

Bidder
A participant in an auction.

Bidder Number
The unique number assigned by auction houses to the various participants in their auction.

Binder
The individual who oversees the comic book bindery process.

Binder Holes
Either two or three holes punched into the spine of comics and comic books so as to fit them into a two or three ring binder.

Bindery
The location where comics are assembled, trimmed, and stapled and/or glued.

Bindery Corner
The small, triangular spine corner tears which occur during binding of a comic book.

Bindery Defect
The defects associated with the binding process.

Bisque
Unglazed porcelain which is molded into a particular shape, then baked in high temperatures in a kiln, to form doll heads and doll body parts.

Bisque Pottery
Unglazed porcelain or china which has had only one firing in the kiln.

Bi-Monthly
A comic, or periodical, which is published every two months.

Bi-Weekly
A comic, or periodical, which is published every two weeks.

Black Cover
Comic book covers with a predominate use of black ink.

Blacklist

A list which actively blocks certain bidders from participating in an auction. On eBay, a "Blacklist" is the "Blocked Bidder" list.

Blank

The flat disk of metal before it is struck by the dies and made into a coin. Also known as "Coin Blank."

Blank Back

A trading card which has nothing imprinted on the reverse side of the card.

Blind Box

A style of packaging that does not allow the purchaser to see the enclosed action figure inside its packaging.

Blister

The clear plastic shell, attached to a card, which encases an action figure or toy.

Blister Packs

A means of packaging action figures or toys within a clear plastic bubble glued to a cardboard backing. Many times "Blister Packs" are fitted with "J-cards" for better product placement in retail stores. Also known as a "Blister Card."

Bluebook

A wholesale pricing book for United States coins. The "Bluebook" is issued annually.

Bluesheet

Also known as the "Certified Coin Dealer Newsletter (CDN)."

Bobble Heads

A series of dolls which have heads that bobble and wobble. Bobble heads are manufactured in both limited and mass quantities.

Body Bag

A slang term used to describe a coin returned from a grading service in a plastic sleeve within a "Flip."

Body-Off Restoration

A comprehensive restoration process where the body of a car is removed from the chassis and every component is either replaced or renewed.

Bondage Cover

Denotes a person on comic book covers shown as being held in bondage or some type of restraint.

Border

The part of a trading card which surrounds the photo in the middle of the card. The "Border" of a card is found around the outer edges of the card.

Bound Copy

A comic book copy which has been bound into a book.

Bound Short

See "Siamese Page."

Bowman

A well-known sports trading card manufacturer, established in 1948. "Topps" purchased the company in 1956.

Box Topper

An item inserted into a box of sports trading cards as an incentive for the purchase of an entire box of cards.

Boxes

Original manufacturer's container of multiple packs of trading cards. "Boxes" often include 24 packs of cards.

Braided Hair

A style of hair on half cents and large cents beginning in 1840 which consists of hair pulled back into a tight bun with a braided hair cord.

Branch Mint (BM)

Any United States Mint other than the Mint located in Philadelphia, Pennsylvania.

Brass

A metal alloy comprised of approximately 50% copper and 50% zinc.

Brasses

The handles and other metalwork hardware on a piece of furniture.

Breast Feathers

The central feathers seen on numerous eagle coin designs.

Breweriana

A category of beer-related antiques and collectibles such as advertisements, coasters, openers, labels, signs, steins, mugs, odd-sized cans, bottles, and trays. www.americanbreweriana.org.

Brilliant

A coin with full luster, unimpeded by toning, or impeded only by extremely light toning.

Brilliant Uncirculated

Any coin which has never been in circulation.

British Issue

Comic books which are printed for distribution in Great Britain.

Brittleness

A severe condition of paper deterioration where paper loses its flexibility and easily chips, flakes and tears.

Brockage

A Mint error which includes an early capped die impression where a sharp image has been left on the next coin fed into the coining chamber.

Bronze

A metal alloy comprised of approximately 83% copper, 13% tin, 3% zinc, and 1% lead.

Bronze Age (B.A.)

(1) The "Age" of comic books after the Silver Age (S. A.). (2) A non-specific term which denotes comics published between 1970-1980.

Brown

A copper coin which no longer has the red color of copper.

Browning

(1) The aging of paper characterized by the ever-increasing level of oxidation characterized by darkening. (2) The level of paper deterioration one step more severe than tanning and one step before brittleness.

Brummagem

Fake political items which are made with low-grade materials. Brummagem items are gaudy, pretentious, and are worthless in potential value.

Buckled Die

A coin die which has warped in some way, possibly from excess clashing. A "Bucked Die" produces coins which are slightly "bent."

Buffet

A French term for a small dining room sideboard used for dish storage, with drawers and cupboards and a flat surface for serving. The term is often used interchangeably with sideboard.

Buffalo Nickel

An Indian Head nickel struck between 1913 and 1938.

Bulged Die

A small indentation that forms on a coin die when a die has clashed too many times.

Bullion

A slang term used to describe coins, ingots, or private issue numismatist items which trade below, at, or slightly above their intrinsic metal value.

Burl

An abnormal growth on a tree such as found in the roots and crotches that produces a beautiful strongly grained wood prized in veneers.

Burnished

Refers to specially prepared planchets which were used for specimen coins or other special coins.

Burnishing

A process by which the surfaces of a planchet or a coin are made to shine. Acheived through rubbing or polishing.

Burnishing Lines

Lines resulting from burnishing, seen mainly on open collar "Proofs" and almost never found on close collar "Proofs." This term is commonly used with coins.

Burnt

A slang term used to describe a coin which has been over-dipped to the point where the surfaces are dull and lackluster.

Burr

A type of "Veneer."

Bust

A slang term used to describe the process of opening a pack, box, or case of sports trading cards.

Bust Dollar

A particular type of silver dollar which was struck and minted between 1795 and 1803.

Butt Joint

A glue joint between two surfaces which are joined with no overlap, tenons, or shoulders.

Buyer's Premium

The additional fee paid to the auction house by the buyer or winning bidder at an auction.

C

"C" Mint

The term applied to gold coins struck and minted at the Charlotte, North Carolina branch Mint. This Mint uses the "C" mintmark.

"C" Scale

A common grading system used to convey the condition of a toy being sold or traded among collectors. See "Action Figure Authority (AFA) C-Scale Grading Scale."

Cabinet Card

An oversized trading card featuring detailed paintings. "Cabinet Cards" were issued between 1910 and 1915.

Cabinet Friction

The slight disturbance seen on coins, usually on the obverse, which were stored in wooden cabinets used by early collectors to house their specimens.

Cabriole

A style of leg on a chair or table that has a "S" shape.

Cameist

A person who collects cameos.

Cameo

The brief appearance of one character in the comic strip of another.

Cameo Glass

A technique used on glass or stone to create a decorative effect of contrasting colors.

Canadian

Coins and other numismatic items from Canada.

Canadian Issue

Comics which are printed for distribution in Canada.

Canadian Silver

Describes silver coins struck and minted from Canada.

Capped Bust

Any of the various incarnations of the head of Miss Liberty represented on early United States coins by a bust with a floppy cap. Also known as "Cap Bust."

Capped Die

An error in which a coin gets jammed in the coining press and remains there, receiving successive strikes, eventually forming a "cap" either on the upper or lower die.

Caravan Auction

A series of "On-Site" auctions advertised through a common promotional campaign.

Carbon Spot

A spot seen mainly on copper and gold coins, though also occasionally found on United States nickel coins and silver coins.

Card

Refers to the cardboard backing of an action figure's packaging in which the "Blister" is attached.

Card Show

An event, gathering, or exchange composed of sports or non-sports trading card dealers displaying their items for sale and trade.

Card Stock

The paper or cardboard material on which a sports or non-sports trading card is printed.

Carded

Denotes an unopened action figure. A "Carded" action figure is understood to be in mint condition.

Cartwheel

The visual effect seen on some coins when they are rotated in good light. The "Luster" of the coin then rotates around the coin like spokes of a wagon wheel.

Case Fresh

A toy or action figure which has come directly out of the factory case or box.

Cases

A factory-sealed crate filled with card "Boxes." A case usually includes six to twelve card boxes per case with 24 packs of cards per box.

Cast Counterfeit

A replication of a genuine coin usually created by making molds of the obverse and reverse, then casting base metal in the molds.

Casting Machine

A device which adds the edge lettering and devices to early United States coins before they were struck.

Category Listing

A list of auctions by a specific category.

Catalog

A publication which describes in varying detail the items available for sale at an auction as well as the "Terms and Conditions" of the sale.

Caveat Emptor

A Latin term meaning "let the buyer beware." A buyer takes the risk regarding quality or condition of the property purchased, unless that item is protected by a warranty.

"CC" Mint

The term applied to coins struck and minted at the Carson City, Nevada branch Mint. This Mint uses the "CC" mintmark.

CCA Seal

Emblem which was placed on the cover of all Comics Code Authority-Approved (CAA-Approved) comics beginning in April and May of 1955.

Cel

See "Animation Production Cel."

Cello

A type of trading card pack whose wrapper is plastic and see-through. Those packs which haven't been open, with a major star's card showing, have a premium value.

Celluloid

(1) The first plastic used to make dolls. (2) The full name used for an "Animation Production Cel."

Census

A compilation of the known specimens of a particular coin or numismatic item.

Census Report

The list of comic books graded by CGC which shows scarcity between books and also relative scarcity of grade.

Cent

A coin with a denomination valued at one-hundredth (1/100) of a dollar.

Centerfold

(1) The two folded pages in the center of a comic book at the terminal end of the staples. Also known as "Center Spread." (2) Usually a portrait such as a "pin-up" or "nude" inserted in the middle of the publication. Commonly found in adult magazines.

Centering

Refers to the evenness of the white space or border (if any) around a baseball card's main image. Centering is measured left-to-right and top-to-bottom, and is defined in "percentages."

Ceramic

A product of baked clay, porcelain, pottery, tile, or earthenware.

Certificate of Authenticity (COA)

(1) A document issued by a seller which guarantees that the item you want to purchase is authentic. (2) A document which accompanies a piece denoting the name of the manufacturer, artist, date, size of the edition, etc.

Certification

The professional evaluation of grade and condition of a collectible (i.e. comic book, movie memorabilia, signatures and autographs, etc.), including examination for restoration and other characteristics of an item's integrity.

Certified Coin Dealer Newsletter (CDN)

The Certified Coin Dealer Newsletter lists "ask," "bid," and "market prices" for third party certified coins. www.greysheet.com.

Certified Coin Exchange (CCE)

The largest online dealer-to-dealer numismatic network in the world dealing in rare coins. You must be a professional numismatist with extensive experience and excellent trading references from current dealers to be a member of CCE. www.certifiedcoinexchange.com.

Certified Guaranty Company (CGC)

The first independent third-party grading service specializing in comic books and photographs. www.cgccomics.com.

Certified Guaranty Company (CGC) Grading Scale:

0.5 - Poor	4.0 - Very Good	8.0 - Very Fine
1.0 - Fair	4.5 - Very Good +	8.5 - Very Fine +
1.5 - Fair/Good	5.0 - Very Good/Fine	9.0 - Very Fine/Near Mint
1.8 - Good-	5.5 - Fine -	9.2 - Near Mint -
2.0 - Good	6.0 - Fine	9.4 - Near Mint
2.5 - Good+	6.5 - Fine +	9.6 - Near Mint +
3.0- Good/Very Good	7.0 - Fine/Very Fine	9.8 - Near Mint/Mint
3.5 - Very Good -	7.5 - Very Fine -	9.9 - Mint
		10.0 - Gem Mint

Chain Cent
The name for the Flowing Hair Chain Cent of 1793.

Character Doll
A doll which is made to look like a living child or adult.

Chase Cards
Trading card(s) included as a bonus in a factory sealed case. Also known as "Insert Cards."

Chasing
(1) A method used by forgers to create a false mintmark on a coin. (2) Process of engraving or embossing to decorate a toy or bank. (3) In antique furniture, a method of decorating silver and other metals by creating a raised pattern using a hammer or punch.

Chip Cut
A missing piece of a comic or comic book which is smaller than one square millimeter.

Chippendale
A neoclassical style of furniture developed in the mid-18th century by London, England designer and furniture maker, Thomas Chippendale.

Chromium Cover
A special foil used on covers of comics.

Chromolithographs
Lithographs printed in at least three colors.

Chromoxylograph
An image printed in color from a wood block.

Circa
Applied before each approximate date, while dates without a "Circa" immediately preceding them are generally assumed to be known with certainty.

Circulated Proof
See "Impaired Proof."

Circulation
A term applied to describe coins which have been used in everyday commerce.

Clamshell
Action figure and toy packaging which is more resistant to dents and bending. "Clamshell" packaging is also extremely difficult to open.

Clash Marks
The images of the dies seen on coins struck from clashed dies.

Clashed Dies
Coin dies which have been damaged by striking each other without a planchet between them.

Classic Car
(1) Any car which is 25 years old or older. (2) A range of vehicles built mostly from 1925 to 1948. (3) Made to describe a newer vehicle, one that is immediately sought after like that of a Ferrari, Lamborghini, or Aston Martin, from the moment that vehicle leaves the manufacturing plant and is ready for sale.

Classic Cover
A comic book cover considered by collectors to be highly desirable because of its historical importance, subject matter, and artwork.

Classic Era

The period between 1792 and 1964 when silver and gold coins of the United States were issued.

Classic Head

A depiction of "Miss Liberty" on a coin which recalls the "classic" look of a Roman or Greek athlete wearing a ribbon around the hair.

Cleaned

A coin whose original surface has been removed.

Cleaning

A process in which dirt, grime, and dust are removed from comics not only to clean the comic book, but to raise potential value.

Clip

A coin struck from a clipped planchet.

Clipped

A coinage term for an irregularly cut planchet.

Clogged Die

A die of a coin which has grease or some other contaminant lodged in the recessed areas.

Close Collar

The edge device, sometimes called a collar die, which surrounds the lower die of a coin.

Closing

The time that the last bid at an auction will be accepted.

Club Piece

A piece, usually considered a collector's item, which is included in the annual membership dues of a "Collector's Club."

CNP

An abbreviation for "Complete No Package."

Coach's Card

A sports trading card that features a coach or group of coaches.

Coat-Tail

A political item or pin where local political candidates take advantage of popularity and/or awareness of the national candidate to enhance their own chance for being elected. A "Coat-Tail" pin would have a local candidate's picture displayed alongside a national candidate's name or picture.

Coin Blank

The flat disk of metal before it is struck by the dies and made into a coin. Also known as a "Blank."

Coin Silver

The proportion of silver used in American coins.

Coin Universe Daily Price Guide

A price guide which lists approximate selling prices for the "Professional Coin Grading Service (PCGS)" graded coins. www.pcgs.com/prices.

Coin World Magazine

A weekly numismatic periodical first published in 1960. www.coinworld.com.

Coinage

The issuance of metallic money from a particular country.

COINage Magazine

A monthly numismatic magazine first published in 1964. www.coinagemag.com.

Coins Magazine

A monthly numismatic periodical, first published in 1955. www.coinsmagazine.net.

Cold-cast

A type of resin which is set by a chemical process as opposed to the application of heat.

Cold Paint

The finish of a pottery and/or ceramic item.

Collar

A metal piece which either positions a planchet beneath the die and/or restrains the expanding metal of a coin during striking.

Collectible

An item, or items, people like to acquire and collect. Some individuals obtain items to add to their specific collections while other individuals acquire items to resell for profit.

Collectible Doll Authority (CDA)

Professional grading agency which verifies, authenticates, and certifies all packaged dolls and related items. www.dollgrader.com.

Collector

Someone who buys an item, whether in used or mint condition, because they enjoy that item.

Collector's Club

A group or organization that usually charges annual dues which include special pieces, announcements, newsletters, and exclusives.

Color Flake/Color Fleck

This happens when the color layer has been lost on a comic, making the white paper substrata (the underlying layer) visible.

Colorist

The artist who applies color to black and white (B&W) pen and ink art.

Color Touch

A comic book restoration process by which colored ink is used to hide color flecks, color flakes, and larger areas of missing color.

Comic Book Restoration

Any attempt, whether professional or amateur, to enhance the appearance of a comic book.

Comics Code Authority (CCA)

Also known as the Comics Magazine Association of America, which was founded in 1954.

Comics Magazine Association of America

See "Comics Code Authority (CCA)."

Commemorative

Specific coins issued to honor a person, place, or event. "Commemoratives" are also issued to raise funds for activities related to a particular theme.

Commercial Strike

A synonym for a coin's regular strike or business strike.

Common Cards

Also known as base cards. Cards which aren't rare and form the main set (for example, Cards #1–200 of a set).

Complete

An action figure or toy which comes with all its accessories included.

Complete Run

All comic book issues from a specific title grouping.

Complete Set

A term for all possible coins within a series, all types, or all coins from a particular Mint.

Composition

A mixture of wood pulp, sawdust, glue, and similar items which are used to make the bodies for antique dolls.

Con

A convention or public gathering of fans. The annual San Diego Comic-Con International, held in San Diego, California, draws over 100,000 attendees during its four-day event. www.comic-con.org/cci/.

Condition

The state of preservation of a particular collectible item.

Condition Census

A listing of the finest known examples of a particular issue.

Conditions of Sale

The legal terms which govern the conduct of an auction. "Conditions of Sale" include acceptable methods of payment, buyer's premiums, seller's premiums, terms, and any other important rules of an auction.

Consensus Grading

The process of determining the condition of a coin by using multiple graders.

Contact Marks

Marks on a coin which are incurred through contact with another coin or a foreign object.

Contemporary Counterfeit

A coin, usually base metal, struck from crudely engraved dies and made to pass for face value at the time of its creation.

Continental Dollars

Dollar coins struck in 1776.

Copper Spot

A spot or stain commonly seen on gold coinage.

Copper Nickel

This alloy, composed of approximately 12% nickel and 88% copper, was used for small cents between 1856 and 1864.

Copper Nickel Cent

A copper nickel alloy used in cents struck between 1859 and 1864.

Coppers

A slang term used to describe half cents, large cents, and pre-Federal copper issues.

Copy

See "Fake."

Corner Blunting

The actual compression of a comic book, at the ends and sides of a comic book, occurring at a 45-degree angle.

Corners

Refers to the sharpness of the corners and any creases in the corner of a trading card.

Coronet Head

An alternate name for a Braided Hair design coin which was designed by Christian Gobrecht.

Corrosion

The damage which results when reactive chemicals act upon a metal.

Counterfeit

A coin which is not genuine or authentic. Many times the term "counterfeit" is used when discussing paper currency. This term has the same meaning for both coinage and currency.

Counterstamp

An impression or stamp placed on a coin after it has left the originating Mint.

Counting Machine Mark

Refers to a dense patch of lines caused by the rubber wheel of a counting machine. This defect occurs when the rubber wheel of a counting machine was set with insufficient spacing for the selected coin at the time in which the coin was struck and minted.

Coupon Cut/Clipped

A comic book with a missing coupon. Also known as "Coupon Missing."

Cover Gloss

The reflective quality of the cover ink.

Cover Loose

(1) Cover has become completely detached from the staples. (2) Cover moves around on the staples but is not completely detached from the staples.

Cover Off

Refers to when a comic book cover is completely detached from the staples.

Cover Reattached

Refers to when a comic book cover has been repaired/restored to hold staples and reattached to comic interior.

Cover Trimmed

Refers to a comic book cover when it has been reduced in size by neatly cutting away rough or damaged edges.

Crazing

(1) A close network of very fine cracks on the top surface as in the glaze of ceramics. (2) Aging lines which run through the paint on vintage toys and banks.

Crease

(1) A fold in a comic which causes ink removal usually resulting in a white line. See "Corner Crease" and "Reading Crease." (2) A paper wrinkle defect caused by bending a trading card.

Crossover

(1) A coin which was graded the same at two different grading services. (2) A comic book story where one character appears prominently in the story of another character. Also called "X-Over."

Crystal

A type of fine quality glass created in 17th century England that is highly transparent and contains a larger proportion of lead oxide. The percentage of lead oxide required to be defined as crystal varies according to the country. In the United States an item is considered being "authentic" crystal with only 1% lead oxide content, while in Europe a 10% lead oxide content is required.

Cud

An area of a coin struck by a die which has a complete break across part of its surface.

Cull

A coin which is basically non-collectible due to its extremely bad condition.

Custom

An action figure not released in stores, but made by a collector usually by using parts from existing action figures.

Cut Signature

A signature that was cut away from a document, book, or photo and, as a result, the signature stands alone.

CVR

An abbreviation for a comic book "cover."

D

"D" Mint

(1) Coins struck and minted at the Dahlonega, Georgia Mint between 1838 and 1861. (2) Coins struck and minted at the Denver, Colorado branch Mint starting in 1906. These Mints use the "D" mintmark.

Date Stamp

The arrival date or other date printed in ink somewhere in or on the comic by use of a stamp and stamp pad.

De-Acidification

The process of neutralizing harmful acids from the paper in a comic book, by applying a special solution of a calcium carbonate.

Deadbeat Bidder

A bidder who does not pay for their auction winnings. Also known as a "Non-Paying Buyer."

Dealer

(1) Someone whose occupation involves the buying, selling, and trading of numismatic materials. (2) An individual who sells toys, action figures, and collectibles on the after-market.

Debut

The first time that a character ever appears in a comic. "Debut" may also refer to the first issue of a comic book.

Deep Cameo

A "Proof" and "Proof-like" coin, which has deeply frosted devices and lettering that contrast with the fields. Also known as "black and white cameos."

Deep Mirror Proof-like
Any coin which has deeply reflective mirror-like fields.

Defect
Any fault, flaw, or negative characteristic in the quality of a comic which detracts from its perfection.

Deformed Staple
A staple which has not properly penetrated all the pages of a comic book. This term also refers to a staple that is bent and/or misshapen. Also known as a "Maverick Staple" or "Shallow Staple."

Denomination
The value assigned to a specific coin by a government. For example, the denomination of a U.S. "nickel" is five cents.

Dent
An indentation usually on the cover of a comic, which does not penetrate the paper nor remove any material or gloss.

Denticles
Small, toothlike design elements all the way around the perimeter of some coins, especially of the 18th and 19th centuries.

Depression Glass
Glassware manufactured around the time of the Great Depression between the late 1920s and the early 1940s.

Designer
An individual whom is responsible for a particular design used in a numismatic series.

Device Punch
A steel rod with a raised device on the end used to punch the element into a working coin die.

Die
A steel rod which is engraved, punched, and/or hubbed with devices, lettering, and the date for use in the minting of a coin.

Die Alignment
Indicates the relative positioning of the "Obverse" and "Reverse" dies used on a coin.

Die Break
A defective area of a coin which is the result of a broken die.

Die-Cast
An action figure or toy which is manufactured out of metal.

Die-Cast Authority (DCA)
Professional grading agency which verifies, authenticates, and certifies die-cast and various other related items. www.diecastgrader.com.

Die Crack
A raised and irregular line on a coin.

Die-Cut Cover
When areas of a comic book cover are precut by a printer to a special shape or to create a desired effect.

Die Line

Raised lines on a coin which results from the polish lines on the die.

Die Rust

Rust which has accumulated on a coin die which was not properly stored.

Die Stage

Refers to the specific status of a certain coin's die state.

Die State

A readily identified point in the life of a coin die.

Die Striations

Raised lines on coins which were struck with polished dies.

Die Trial

A test striking of a particular die of a coin in a different metal.

Die Variety

A coin which can be linked to a given set of dies due to the characteristics possessed by those dies and imparted to the coin at the time it was struck.

Die Wear

Deterioration in a die caused by excessive use.

Dime

See "Roosevelt Dime."

Dipped

A coin which has been placed in a commercial "dip" solution. This solution consists of a mild acid wash which results in the removal of the toning from most coins.

Direct Metal Mastering (DMM)

During the vinyl record production process the master disc is cut on a copper-coated disc which produces a high-quality audio record. The use of the DMM process also seemed to improve the lifetime of the vinyl discs

Discophile

Traditionally, this term refers to a person whom collects phonograph records. This term can also include those individuals who collect compact discs.

Disme

The original spelling of the American dime.

Distressed

An object which has been artificially aged.

Distributor Stripes

Color brushed or sprayed on the edges of comic book stacks by the distributor/wholesaler to code them for expedient exchange at the sales racks. Also referred to as "DISTRO Ink."

DISTRO Ink

See "Distributor Stripes."

Doctored

A numismatic item which has been enhanced by chemical or other means.

Dollar

An American numismatic item with a value of 100 cents.

Double

A duplicate copy of the same comic book.

Double Cover

A bindery "defect" where two covers are stapled to the comic book interior instead of the "usual" one.

Double Eagle

Refers to a Twenty dollar United States gold coin which was issued between 1850 and 1932.

Doubled Die (DD)

A die which has been struck more than once by a hub in misaligned positions, resulting in doubling of design elements. The most famous "Double Die" coin in United States numismatics is the 1955 Doubled Die Lincoln cent.

Double Struck (DS)

A condition which results when a coin is not ejected from the dies and is struck a second time.

Dovetail

An antique furniture making term used to describe a joint that fits two pieces of wood tightly together. The wedge-shape resembles a dove's tail and is used to join corners of case pieces and drawers.

Draped Bust

A coin design which features Miss Liberty with a drape across her bust.

Drew Struzan

One of the most prolific and well-known movie poster artists. Drew Struzan has created the images for some of the biggest and most successful movies in cinematic history including all six Star Wars films, Indiana Jones, Harry Potter, Hellboy, Blade Runner, The Muppets, Back to the Future, E.T., and Hook.

Dribbler

The nickname for solid brass, steam-powered toy locomotives manufactured in Britain from the 1840s to early-1900s.

Drift Mark

The area on a coin which has a discolored or streaky look.

Drug Propaganda Story

When a comic makes an editorial stand about drug use.

Dry Press

The machine used to flatten out comics with rolled spine and folds.

Due Diligence

The process of gathering information about the condition and legal status of assets to be sold.

Duotone

Comics printed with black ink and one other color of ink.

Dust Jacket

A paper cover used to protect the binding of a book from dust and wear.

Dust Shadow

A darker, usually linear area at the edge of some comics stored in stacks.

Dutch Auction

This occurs when a seller has several, sometimes many identical items for sale at an auction. Every winning bidder pays the exact same price for each auction item no matter what their bid was. The final sales price of each item will be the lowest bid that is successful on all of the same items up for that particular multiple item auction.

E

E-Unit

The mechanism which provides the reverse sequence on its toy trains. There are two-position (forward-reverse) models and three-position (forward-neutral-reverse) models.

Eagle

A gold coin which has a face value of ten dollars U.S..

Ear

The area of a coin which is most important to the strike.

Early Strike

One of the first coins struck from a pair of dies.

eBay

The biggest worldwide online sales and marketing site. www.ebay.com.

Ebonized

A term used to describe antique furniture stained with a black color imitating the color of ebony.

Edge

The third side of a coin. Not the "Obverse" or "Reverse" of a coin, but the side or rim of a coin.

Edge Defects

Defects which occur to the edges of a comic or comic book.

Edge Device

A group of letters or emblems on the edge of a coin.

EF-40

Refers to the "grade" or quality of a particular coin based on the "Professional Coin Grading Service (PCGS) Grades and Grading Terms" scale. This designation is for "Extremely Fine' (the grade) and "40" (the numerical designation of the grade). Also called "XF-40." About 90% of the original detail is still evident and the devices are sharp and clear. See "Professional Coin Grading Service (PCGS) Grades and Grading Terms."

EF-45

Refers to the "grade" or quality of a particular coin based on the "Professional Coin Grading Service (PCGS) Grades and Grading Terms" scale. This designation is for "Extremely Fine" (the grade) and "45" (the numerical designation of the grade). Also called "XF-45." About 95% of the original detail is still evident and the devices are sharp and clear. See "Professional Coin Grading Service (PCGS) Grades and Grading Terms."

Eisenhower Dollar

One of the United States of America's official dollar coins minted from 1971-1978 which featured the image of President Dwight D. Eisenhower. This dollar coin carries a value of one hundred cents, or one dollar.

Electrotype

Refers to a duplicate coin created utilizing the electrolytic method.

Elements

The various components used for grading a coin.

Embossed

The raised, relief, or dimensional design on paper or cardboard.

Embossed Cover

When a pattern is embossed onto the comic book cover which creates a raised area.

Emission Sequence

The order, or sequence in which coin die states are struck.

Engraver

The individual who is responsible for the design and/or punches used for a particular numismatic item.

Envelope Toning

The toning or discoloration of a coin, which results from storage, mainly in a small 2x2-inch manila envelope.

Environmental Damage (ED)

The corrosion effects seen on a coin which has been exposed to the elements.

Eraser Mark

Damage that remains when pencil marks are removed from the cover or inside of a comic.

Eroded Die

Also known as a "worn die."

Errinophilist

A person who collects revenue or tax stamps.

Error Coin

A coin which accidentally varies from the norm.

Error Card

A sports trading card that contains some sort of mistake or error, such as a misspelling, or a photo of someone other than the athlete named on the card.

Escrow

A transaction that involves a buyer, seller, and an escrow company. The buyer pays the cost of the item directly to the escrow company and the escrow company holds the money from the sale until the buyer receives the item and is completely satisfied with his/her purchase. Once the buyer is completely satisfied that the item is "as advertised," the escrow company, then, releases the held funds and pays the seller.

Essai

The term for trial, pattern, or experimental strikings on a coin.

Estate Sale

The sale of property left by a person after his/her death.

Event Piece

An item, or piece which is made specifically for a particular event. This item is available only to those who attend the particular event.

Ex-Libris

A book which was once owned by someone whose ownership adds value, often from someone who is famous or notable. An "Ex-Libris" item is typically indicated by some ownership marking such as a stamp or seal, a signature or handwritten note.

Excellent Condition

An item not in mint or perfect condition, but one that is found to have no major flaws.

Exclusive

A specific type of action figure or toy, sold through only one store or a limited number of specific stores, often considered rare.

Exhibit Card

A larger size of sports or non-sports trading card, which is basically the size of a postcard.

Extra Fine

Also known as "Extremely Fine."

Extremely Fine

Refers to the coin grades of "EF-40" and "EF-45" on the "Professional Coin Grading Service (PCGS) Grades and Grading Terms" scale. This grade has nearly full detail with only the high points worn, the fields rubbed often with luster still clinging in protected areas. See "Professional Coin Grading Service (PCGS) Grades and Grading Terms."

Extremely High Relief

A feature on a coin where the Mint engraver lowers the design on a coin.

Eye Appeal

(1) The element of a coin's grade which makes a coin more appealing to a collector. (2) A term which refers to the overall look of a comic book when held at approximately at arms length.

F

F-12

Refers to the "grade" or quality of a particular coin based on the "Professional Coin Grading Service (PCGS) Grades and Grading Terms" scale. This designation is for "Fine" (the grade) and "12" (the numerical designation of the grade). The design detail is partially in evidence. The coin is still heavily worn. If there is any eye appeal in this grade it comes from the smooth surfaces associated with this grade, as any distracting marks have usually been worn off through circulation. See "Professional Coin Grading Service (PCGS) Grades and Grading Terms."

F-15

Refers to the "grade" or quality of a particular coin based on the "Professional Coin Grading Service (PCGS) Grades and Grading Terms" scale. This designation is for "Fine" (the grade) and "15" (the numerical designation of the grade). Most of the letters in LIBERTY are visible, about 35-50% of the wing feathers are visible, or whatever applies to the coin in question. In other words, the coin is still in highly collectible shape. See "Professional Coin Grading Service (PCGS) Grades and Grading Terms."

Face Value

The stated value on a coin which can be spent or exchanged.

Facsimile Autograph

A simulated, usually machine printed autograph designed to duplicate a player's signature on a sports trading card. Not an authentic autograph.

Factory Sets

Trading card sets, typically complete base sets, sorted and sold directly from the factory.

Faded Cover

see "Fading."

Fading

Color fading that occurs on a comic which is caused by exposure to sunlight or certain fluorescent lights that give off a moderate to high concentration of ultra violet light. Also known as a "Faded Cover."

Fake

(1) A copy of a legitimate item which is created to deceive the buyer. (2) A slang term used to describe a counterfeit or altered coin. Also known as a "Copy," "Replica," or "Faux."

Fanboy

A fan, aficionado, or supporter is someone who has an intense, occasionally overwhelming liking and enthusiasm for a sporting club, person (usually a celebrity), group of persons, company, product, activity, work of art, idea, or trend. Fans of a particular thing or person constitute its fanbase or fandom. They often show their enthusiasm by starting a fan club, holding fan conventions, creating fanzines, writing fan mail, or promoting the object of their interest and attention.

Fandom

The subculture composed of fans characterized by a feeling of sympathy and camaraderie with others who share a common interest.

Fantasy Piece

(1) An item made to look like an authentic item which was never manufactured, produced, or licensed by the company that holds intellectual rights property of that particular item. Many modelers and hobbyists on the Internet make items which replicate a specific collectible out of their love and "fandom" for a particular item. (2) A term applied to coins struck at the desire or whim of Mint officials.

Fanzine

An amateur publication produced by a fan, usually about a specific topic.

Fashion Doll

A French or German "lady doll" made, generally, with a bisque head and dressed in fashions of the day.

Faux

Another term for a fake item. See "Fake."

FAQ

The abbreviation for "Frequently Asked Questions." FAQs are listed questions and answers, all supposed to be frequently asked in some context, and pertaining to a particular topic. This is a commonly used term on the Internet.

Fasces

The term used to designate the Roman symbol of authority used as a design on the reverse of Mercury dimes.

FC

An abbreviation for "Front Cover," the first page of a comic.

Feedback

The positive or negative comments left by both buyer and seller for each other. "Feedback" helps establish the reputation of the buyer or seller. Receiving positive "Feedback" is extremely important for any seller on eBay if that seller wants to run a successful business on the website.

Fiat Currency

Coins and paper money (for example one dollar bill) which do not have metal value.

Field

The area on a coin where there is no design.

File Copy

A high-grade comic book that was originally from the publisher's own files.

Fine

The term referring to the coin grades of "F-12" and "F-15" on the "Professional Coin Grading Service (PCGS) Grades and Grading Terms" scale. Most of a coin's detail is worn away although some detail is present in a coin's recessed areas. See "Professional Coin Grading Service (PCGS) Grades and Grading Terms."

Finest Known

The best known example of the condition of a particular coin.

Finger Oils

"Finger Oils" cause a damaging effect when comics and comic books are handled with bare hands. The oil from an individual's hands and fingers degrade the comic or comic book over time.

First Appearance

Also known as "Debut."

First Shot

A slang term used to describe the opportunity to get the first opportunity to buy items from a particular numismatic deal or from a particular dealer.

Five Indian

Also known as Indian Head Half Eagle coins, which were struck between 1908 and 1929.

Five Lib

Also known as the Liberty Head Half Eagle coin, which was struck between 1839 and 1908.

Flange Neck

A flange neck, or the "cup and saucer" joint as it is occasionally called, is when the bottom of the dolls head piece and the top of the doll's shoulder piece fit together on a flat surface. This is most commonly found on cloth bodied dolls with a rim around the neck.

Flashback

When a previous story in a comic is being recalled.

Flasher

See "Lenticular."

Flat Luster

A subdued type of luster which can be seen on coins struck from worn dies.

Flatware

Any flat or shallow tableware.

Flats

Two-dimensional lead soldiers with engraved decorations.

Fleck

Also known as "Color Fleck."

Flicker Cover

See "Lenticular Cover."

Flip

(1) The plastic sleeve in which coins are stored. (2) To quickly sell a recently purchased coin, or any collectible for that matter, usually for a quick profit.

FlipRub

The discoloration of the highest points of a coin resulting from contact with a "Flip."

Flirty Eyes

The eyes of a doll which can move from side-to-side.

Flop

To sell a new coin purchase for a quick profit.

Flow Lines

The lines on a coin which result from the metal flowing outward from the center of a planchet as it is being struck.

Flying Eagle

Another term used to describe a "Flying Eagle Cent."

Flying Eagle Cent

A small cent which replaced the large cent. Also known as a "Flying Eagle."

Focal Area

The area of a coin which a viewer's eye is drawn.

Foil Cover

A thin metal foil which is hot stamped onto the cover of a comic book during manufacturing.

Folding Error

A bindery defect in which the comic is folded off-center, resulting in part of the front cover appearing on the back cover, or more seriously, part of the back cover appearing on the front cover.

Folds

Linear dents in comic book paper which do not result in the loss of ink. Not considered a "crease."

Foreign

Any coin not from the United States of America.

Four Color Process

The name given to the process of comic book printing which include three primary colors (red, yellow, and blue) plus black.

Four Dollar Gold Piece

An experimental coin issue between 1879 and 1880.

Foxed

A defect caused by mold growth which results in a spotting effect usually at the edges of a comic.

FR-2

Refers to the "grade" or quality of a particular coin based on the "Professional Coin Grading Service (PCGS) Grades and Grading Terms" scale. This designation is for "Fair" (the grade) and "2" (the numerical designation which means Fair). A coin which is worn out. There will be some detail intact, the date will be discernible (if not fully readable) and there is almost always heavy wear into the rims and fields. See "Professional Coin Grading Service (PCGS) Grades and Grading Terms."

Franklin

Another term for a "Franklin Half Dollar."

Franklin Half Dollar

One of the United States of America's official fifty-cent coins minted from 1948-1963 which featured the image of Benjamin Franklin. This fifty-cent coin was replaced by the "Kennedy Half Dollar" in 1964. Like the "Kennedy Half Dollar," this coin carries a value of fifty cents, or fifty one-hundredths (50/100) of a dollar.

Freakbeat

The name for rare, collectable, and obscure British Invasion vinyl records.

Frost

A crystallized metal effect seen in the recessed areas of a coin die.

Frosted Devices

Raised elements on coins struck with treated dies which have frost in their recessed areas.

Frosty Luster

The crystalline appearance of coins struck with dies which have frost in their recessed areas.

FS

An abbreviation for "Factory Sealed." A commonly used term with action figures and toys.

Fugio Cents

Refers to one of the first coins authorized by the Continental Congress for minting in 1787.

Full Bands (FB)

The term applied to Mercury dimes when the central band is fully separated.

Full Bell Lines (FBL)

When the lower sets of bell lines are complete on Franklin half dollars.

Full Head (FH)

The term applied to Standing Liberty quarters when the helmet of the head has full detail.

Full Steps

When at least five steps of Monticello are present on a Jefferson nickel.

Full Strike

A coin which displays the full detail intended by the designer.

Fumetti

An illustration system in which individual frames of a film are colored and used for individual panels to make a comic book story.

Fusilatelist

A person who collects telephone calling cards.

G

G-4

Refers to the "grade" or quality of a particular coin based on the "Professional Coin Grading Service (PCGS) Grades and Grading Terms" scale. This designation is for "Good" (the grade) and "4" (the numerical designation of the grade). The major details of the coin will be worn flat. Minor wear into the rims is allowable, but the peripheral lettering will be nearly full. See "Professional Coin Grading Service (PCGS) Grades and Grading Terms."

G-6

Refers to the "grade" or quality of a particular coin based on the "Professional Coin Grading Service (PCGS) Grades and Grading Terms" scale. This designation is for "Good" (the grade) and "6" (the numerical designation of the grade). A higher grade (i.e., less worn) than a G-4 coin. The rims will be complete and the peripheral lettering will be full. See "Professional Coin Grading Service (PCGS) Grades and Grading Terms."

G-4

Refers to the "grade" or quality of a particular coin based on the "Professional Coin Grading Service (PCGS) Grades and Grading Terms" scale. This designation is for "Good" (the grade) and "4" (the numerical designation of the grade). The major details of the coin will be worn flat. Minor wear into the rims is allowable, but the peripheral lettering will be nearly full. See "Professional Coin Grading Service (PCGS) Grades and Grading Terms."

G-6

Refers to the "grade" or quality of a particular coin based on the "Professional Coin Grading Service (PCGS) Grades and Grading Terms" scale. This designation is for "Good" (the grade) and "6" (the numerical designation of the grade). A higher grade (i.e., less worn) than a G-4 coin. The rims will be complete and the peripheral lettering will be full. See "Professional Coin Grading Service (PCGS) Grades and Grading Terms."

Galvano

The large metal relief used in the portrait lathe from which a positive reduction in steel, called a "hub", is made.

Gatefold Cover

A double cover which folds over into itself.

Gem

The description applied to a Mint State and "Proof 65" (MS/PR-65) coin.

Genre

A category defining a comic book's subject matter- Science Fiction, Super Hero, Romance, Funny Animal, Teenage Humor, Crime, War, Western, Mystery, Horror, etc., are all of these examples are of a specific "Genre."

Gift Pack

A model and toy train set sold without a track or transformer.

Gilt

Also known as gilding, it is a process by which an object is decorated with a thin layer of gold, gold leaf or gold foil. This technique is used on glass, ceramics, furniture and picture frames.

Glasses Attached

In 3-D comics, the special blue and red cellophane glasses that come attached to an individual comic to allow for true 3-D readability.

Glasses Detached

In 3-D comics, the special blue and red cellophane glasses are not attached to an individual comic.

Glue (or) Glued

A restoration method in which some form of glue was used to repair or reinforce a comic book defect.

Gobrecht Dollar

A particular type of silver dollar minted in 1836, 1838, and 1839.

Gold

(1) A precious metal. (2) A slang term used to describe any United States gold issue coins.

Gold Dollar

The small coins of one dollar denomination struck between 1849 and 1889.

Golden Age of Comics (G.A.)

The Golden Age of comics occurred between June, 1938 (with the publication of Action Comics #1) until the end of World War II (approximately 1945).

Good

The term which corresponds to the coin grades of "G-4" and "G-6" on the "Professional Coin Grading Service (PCGS) Grades and Grading Terms" scale. Coins in these grades usually have little detail but outlined major devices. See "Professional Coin Grading Service (PCGS) Grades and Grading Terms."

Googly Eyes

A doll which has big, round, and side-glancing eyes.

Goudey

A very popular sports trading card manufacturer that produced cards between 1933 and 1941.

Grade

The numerical condition of a coin.

Grader

An individual who evaluates the condition of coins.

Grading

The process of numerically quantifying the condition of a coin.

Grease Pencil

A wax based marker commonly used to write on cardboard.

Grease Pencil on Cover

Indicates that someone marked the cover of a comic with a grease pencil, usually with a resale price or an arrival date.

Grey Tone Cover

A comic book cover art style in that uses an underlying pencil or charcoal under the normal line drawing to enhance the effects of light and shadow.

Greysheet

Also known as the "Certified Coin Dealer Newsletter (CDN)."

Gum Stain

A trading card that is marred by bubble gum which was once inserted in the pack. This term usually refers to sports trading cards.

Gusseted Joint

A type of joint found on dolls, which is sewn into leather and cloth bodies. This allows the joint to bend.

H

Hairline(s)

(1) The term associated with pottery items when a small crack, with the approximate thickness of a strand of hair, occurs. (2) A type of crack in bisque dolls which can often only be seen upon close examination with the help of direct lighting. (3) Fine cleaning lines found mainly in the fields of "Proof" coins.

Half Cent

The lowest value coin denomination ever issued by the United States.

Half Dollar

See "Kennedy Half Dollar."

Half Eagle

A coin with a face value of half the value of an Eagle. The Eagle has a face value of ten silver dollars, U.S.

Halftone

The process by which photographs are converted into printable images.

Hallmark

(1) The distinguishing mark used by silversmiths and goldsmiths to identify who made a particular piece. (2) Used to guarantee an item was made from metal of a high-quality. (3) The mark(s) stamped on silver or gold objects when passed at "Assay." See Assay.

Halogen Light

A powerful light which enables a viewer or coin grader to examine a coin very closely. As a result of using a halogen light, all of a coin's faults or imperfections can be more easily recognized.

Hammer Price

The price established by the last bidder. This final bid is acknowledged by the auctioneer before he officially drops the hammer or gavel.

Hard Plastic

A type of durable plastic used to make dolls from the 1940s and 1950s.

Heavy Creasing

A crease in a comic book which is longer than two inches.

Heavypack

An action figure included in a pack in excess quantities. There are more per case of this one item than the rest of its companions. The opposite of a "Shortpack."

Hickory

A hardwood tree that grows in the eastern half of the United States. It is a very tough, heavy wood used on furniture requiring both thinness and strength, such as veneers and woven seats.

High End
A term applied to any coin at the upper end of a particular grade.

High Number
The last, or near the last series in a sports trading card set.

High Quality 180 (HQ 180)
Refers to high quality vinyl records weighing 180 grams. The "High Quality 180" gram premium format offers a significant improvement in the playback and sound of vinyl record recordings.

High Series
Also known as "High Number."

Highboy
(1) A tall chest of drawers on a four-legged base. (2) A two-part case piece.

Highest Reorder Number (HRN)
Most often used to distinguish first editions from later printings in Gilberton's Classic Comics series.

Hit
A general term used to describe the number of autographed cards, memorabilia cards and, depending on the product, rookie cards, in a box of sports cards.

Hoard
A group of coins, large or small, held by a coin collector for either numismatic or monetary reasons.

Hoarder
(1) Someone who buys action figures and/or toys solely with the intent to resell. This person will buy as many of a single item as they can and stockpile them away, in the hope that the item's collectible and resale value will increase. (2) A coin collector who amasses a very large collection of coins.

Hobby Cards
Items sold mainly to collectors through stores that deal exclusively in collectible cards.

Hobo Nickel
An "Indian Head" or "Buffalo" nickel which has been engraved with a portrait of a hobo or character other than a buffalo or Indian head.

Hockey Card
A sports trading card which features a professional hockey player or team.

Holder Toning
Any toning on a coin's surface that appears as the result of its storage in a coin holder.

Holo
A shortened term for "Hologram."

Hologram
A three dimensional image; unlike regular images which are usually two dimensional, a three dimensional image or hologram, appears to "pop out" of the media which it is printed on or illuminated from. When collectible merchandise and memorabilia is professionally graded, the agency verifying an item's authenticity will affix a sticker that displays a one-of-a-kind image in the form of a hologram. This proves that he item is deemed to be authentic.

Hologram Cover

True 3-D holograms are prepared and affixed to comic book covers and trading cards for special effects.

Hot Stamping

The process of pressing foiled prism paper and inks on comic book cover stock.

HTF

An abbreviation for "Hard to Find."

Hub

A coin minting term for the steel device from which a die is produced.

Hutschenreuther

The family name of the German company known for their fine porcelain plates, dinnerware, and figurines, established in 1814.

I

IBC

The abbreviation for "Inside Back Cover."

Iconophile

Someone who collects prints, engravings, and is a connoisseur of icons or images.

IFC

An abbreviation for "Inside Front Cover."

Illo

The abbreviation for "Illustration."

Imbrication

A decorative design carved into a piece of furniture which resembles overlapping fish scales.

Impaired Proof

A "Proof" coin which grades less than a "MS/PR-60." Also known as a "Circulated Proof."

Incomplete

An action figure or toy that comes with some accessories.

Incomplete Strike

A coin which is missing design detail because of a problem during the striking process.

Incremental Bidding

Occurs when you bid enough to be high bidder, but not your maximum, bidding again when someone tops your bid. In this instance it's important to stay close to the computer in the last hours of bidding to continue bidding if you're outbid. This is also the time when sniping can come into play. If you're not willing to put your maximum bid up early, someone could come in and bid their maximum in the last few seconds and not giving enough time to respond.

Note: Online auction houses will use an automatic incremental bidding system that allows you to "secretly" bid your maximum, but only comes into play when there are other bids.

Incuse Design

The "Intaglio" design used on an Indian Head quarter, Eagle, or Half Eagle.

Indian Cent

The common name used for an "Indian Head Cent."

Indian Head Cent

Cents minted between 1859 and 1909 which have an Indian head on the front side of the coin.

Indian Head Eagle

The Saint Gaudens-designed ten dollar gold coin minted between 1907 and 1933.

Indian Penny

Also known as an "Indian Head Cent."

Indicia

Publishing and title information usually located at the bottom of the first page or the bottom of the inside front cover. In some pre-1938 comics, the "Indicia" was sometimes located on an internal page.

Initials on Cover

Someone's initials in pencil, pen, or grease pencil on the cover of a comic. Also known as "Init. on CVR."

Ink Skip

A printing defect in which the printing roller momentarily receives no ink causing a streak or blank spot.

Ink Smudge

A printing defect in which ink is smeared, usually by handling or binding before the ink is completely dry.

Inker

The artist who lays the inks over the penciler's artwork.

Insert Cards

Non-rare to rare cards which are randomly inserted into packs in various ratios such "as one per 24 packs." An "Insert Card" is often different from the main set and contains a different number on the back such as SS01 to SS10. Also known as "Chase Cards."

Inset Eyes

A doll's eyes which are set into the doll's head and do not move.

Intaglio

An incised gemstone or any incised decoration on furniture.

Intaglio Eyes

A doll's eyes which are molded into the head. "Intaglio Eyes" are meant to be painted.

Intaglio Print

An image which is printed from a recessed design incised or etched into the surface of a plate.

International Posters

Posters which are printed in English, but intended for use in countries outside of North America. International posters may be printed in the United States or overseas.

Intrinsic Value

The value of the metal(s) contained within a coin.

Intro

Also known as a "Debut."

Investment Grade Copy

(1) A comic of sufficiently high grade and demand to be viewed by collectors as instantly liquid should the need to sell it arise. (2) A comic purchased primarily to achieve a profit.

Investor

An individual who buys strictly for profit.

Irvington Cars

Lionel's pre-war (#2623 and #2624) and post-war (#2625, #2627, and #2628), and 12-wheel semi-scale passenger cars. Made of compression-molded Bakelite. "Irvington Cars" were styled after 1920s-era Pullmans.

ISH

The abbreviation for "Issue."

Issue Number

The actual "Edition Number" of a given comic or comic book title.

Issue Price

The Manufacturers Suggested Retail Price (MSRP) of an action figure or toy when it is first introduced in the marketplace.

J

J-Card

A "Blister Pack" with a "J-shaped" notch in the top of the item's packaging. "J-Cards" were designed to hang on a store peg for product display.

James Spence Authentication (JSA)

Internationally recognized memorabilia authentication experts, based in Parsippany, New Jersey. www.spenceloa.com.

Jefferson Nickel

The United States of America's official five-cent coin picturing President Thomas Jefferson. The Jefferson nickel was first minted in 1938 and carries a value of five cents, or five one-hundredths (5 / 100) of a dollar. Also known as a "Nickel."

Jersey Cards

A sports trading card containing a piece of material taken from a jersey worn by a player or athlete.

Joined Pages

(1) A bindery defect in which pages of a comic book are "trimmed long" and are not separated at right hand corners or along right edge. (2) A rare printing defect where a new roll of paper is glued to the spent roll while still on the press.

Jugate

A political item, such as a button or pin, which includes two images. A jugate pin may have the presidential and vice-presidential candidates pictured. Jugate images are also found on various forms of political campaign items such as postcards, pennants, and posters. Similar to a "Trigate" item.

K

Kakiemon

Japanese porcelain made in the 17th century by the Kakiemon family. The wares were produced at the factories of Arita, Saga Prefecture, Japan with much in common with the Chinese "Famille Verte" style. The superb quality of its enamel decoration was highly prized in the West and widely imitated by the major European porcelain manufacturers. In 1971 it was declared an important "intangible cultural treasure" by the Japanese government.

Kazak

Rugs manufactured from central Caucasus. "Kazak" rugs are usually decorated with distinctive geometric designs. A flat woven rug with no pile. The Caucasus or Caucas is a geopolitical region at the border of Europe and Asia. It is home to the Caucasus Mountains, including Europe's highest mountain (Mount Elbrus).

Kelim

Flat tapestry-woven carpets or rugs produced from the Balkans to Pakistan. Kelims can be purely decorative or can function as prayer rugs.

Kennedy Half Dollar

One of the United States of America's official fifty-cent coins picturing President John F. Kennedy. The Kennedy half dollar was first minted in 1964 and carries a value of fifty cents, or fifty one-hundredths (50/100) of a dollar. The Kennedy half dollar replaced the "Franklin Half Dollar" which was minted from 1948-1963. Also known as a "Half Dollar."

Key Coin

The number one, most important, coin of a particular series. Also known as "King."

Key Issue

A comic or comic book issue which contains a first appearance, origin, or other historically or artistically important feature considered especially desirable by collectors. Also known as a "Key Book."

L

Label

Displays the title, issue number, publisher, and grade of a comic book.

Lamination

(1) A thin piece of metal which has nearly become detached from the surface of a coin.

(2) A clear plastic cover with adhesive used by early collectors to protect comics.

Large Cent

A large copper United States coin, which carries a value of one cent, or one-one hundredth (1/100) of a dollar.

Large Date (LD)

The size of the digits on the date of a coin. The "Large Date" designation refers to the large digits of the date of a coin.

Large Letters (LL)
The size of the lettering of the date on a coin. The "Large Letters" designation refers to the large letters displayed in a coin's date.

Large Motto (LM)
A common name for the particular variety of two cent coins minted in 1864. The "Large Motto" designation refers to the large letters displayed in the coin's motto.

Large Scale
Model and toy trains made since 1970 which use No. 1 gauge track. The model and toy trains are scaled to different ratios including 22.5:1.

Large Size
A term which refers to the particular diameter of a coin in a series.

Laserdisc
A laser-read large optical disc playback device used for the reproduction of audio and video signals. The laserdisc was a precursor of the smaller DVD format, which was a precursor for the High-Definition DVD Format.

LBC
An abbreviation for the "Lower or Left Side or Edge of Back Cover" on a comic book.

Legend
A specific phrase which appears on a coin. For example, "E PLURIBUS UNUM."

Lenticular
A piece of plastic that changes the image seen when the plastic piece is moved back and forth. Theatrical release movie posters are sometimes made from lenticular materials and are quite valuable. Also known as a "Flasher."

Lenticular Cover
Images on a comic or comic book cover which move when viewed at different angles, specially prepared and affixed to the cover. Also known as a "Flicker Cover."

Letter of Authenticity (LOA)
May be provided by a seller to prove an item is verified as authentic. Similar to a "Certificate of Authenticity (COA)."

Letter Column
A feature in a comic book that prints letters written by its readers.

Lettered Edge
The edge of a coin which displays an inscription or some other design.

LFC
An abbreviation for the "Lower, Left Side or Edge of the Front Cover" on a comic.

LFT
An abbreviation for "Left."

Liberty
The symbolic figure used in many United States coin designs.

Liberty Cap
The head of Miss Liberty, with a cap on a pole by her head, used on certain United States half cents and large cents.

Liberty Head
The design used on most United States gold coins from between 1838 and 1908.

Liberty Nickel

Refers to the "Liberty Head Nickel" or "V" nickel minted between 1883 and 1912.

Light Creasing

A crease 2-inches long or less on a comic book.

Light Line

The band of light seen on photographs of coins. A "Light Line" is especially visible on "Proof" coins.

Limited Edition

(1) This term is usually associated with art and fine art prints although limited edition items may be associated with various collectible items such as action figures, toys, coins, trading cards, and Barbie dolls. (2) A manufacturing run which is restricted to a limited number of pieces or figures which are not produced in large quantities.

Limited Production

A manufacturing run which is restricted to a limited time span.

Lincoln Head Cent

The United States of America's official one-cent coin picturing President Abraham Lincoln. The Lincoln Head cent was first minted in 1909 and carries a value of one cent, or one one-hundredths (1 / 100) of a dollar. Also known as a "Penny."

Line Drawn Cover

A comic book cover published in the "traditional" way, whereby pencil sketches are overdrawn with India ink and then colored in. Also known as a "Grey Tone Cover," "Photo Cover," or "Painted Cover."

Liner

A coin which is classified in-between two different grades.

Lint Mark

A repeated depression on a coin caused by a thread which attached itself to the die during the manufacturing process.

Lionel Trains

A toy train manufacturer, established in 1900. www.lionel.com.

Lithograph

A method for printing utilizing a lithographic limestone or a metal plate with a completely smooth surface.

Live

A sports trading card product is referred to as "live" when it has been released by its manufacturer and is available for sale. The date when a product goes "live" is called its "release date."

Live Auction

An auction that takes place in "Real Time." Live auctions also include those conducted online.

LLBC

An abbreviation for the "Lower Left Corner of Back Cover" on a comic.

Logo

The title of a strip or comic book as it appears on the cover or title page.

Long Arm

A firearm with a long barrel.

"Long Beach"
The common name used for the Long Beach Coin and Stamp Exhibition held in Long Beach, California.

Loose
An action figure or toy which is sold or purchased without its original packaging and having no accessories.

Loose Staples
Refers to staples which can be easily moved and no longer hold comic pages tightly. Also known as a "Popped Staple."

Lot
(1) The unique number assigned by an auction house to an item which is to be sold in a particular sale. (2) A grouping of trading cards.

Loupe
A loupe (pronounced loop), is a type of magnification device (usually set in an eyepiece) used by numismatists, jewelers and horologists to see things more closely.

LRBC
An abbreviation for a comic book's "Lower Right Corner of Back Cover."

LRFC
An abbreviation for "Lower Right Corner of Front Cover" on a comic.

LSH
The acronym for the "Legion of Super Heroes" in comics.

Luster
The result of light reflecting on the flow lines of a coin, whether it is visible or not. Alternate spelling is "Lustre."

Lustrous
A term used to describe coins which still have their original "Mint bloom."

M

Mail Bid Sale
An auction or sale where bidding is limited to bids by mail.

Major Variety
A coin that is easily recognized as having a major difference from other coins of the same Mint, date, design, and type.

Manufacturing Fold
A defect in which some pages of the comic are folded during the printing and/or the paper manufacturing process.

Mark(s) or Markings
(1) The imperfections found on a coin that are acquired after its striking. (2) The letters, numbers, and symbols placed by the manufacturer of a doll on the doll's head or body. These markings are used as a means of identification. (3) The imperfections found on a coin acquired after its striking.

Market Grading

(1) A "numerical grade" that matches the grade at which a particular coin generally is traded in the marketplace. (2) The grading standard used by the "Professional Coin Grading Service (PCGS)."

Market Price

The economic price for which a good or service is offered in the marketplace.

Market Value

(1) The price at which an asset would trade in a competitive auction setting. (2) The price at which an asset is valued in the marketplace.

Married Item

A term in the antique trade used to describe furniture when it is composed of parts that were not originally made together.

Marvel Chipping

A bindery defect which causes a series of chips and tears at the top, bottom, and right edge of the cover of a comic.

Master Die

The main coin die produced from the master hub.

Master Hub

The original hub created by the portrait lathe. This term is commonly used regarding coins.

Maverick Pages

Interior pages of a comic which are not the same size or shape as the majority of the rest of the pages. Most commonly known as a "Bindery Defect." Also known as a "Maverick Signature."

Maverick Staple

See "Deformed Staple."

Maximum Bid

The upper bid limit set by the buyer when using proxy or "automatic" bidding.

McFarlane Toys

An action figure manufacturing company which produces many extremely sought after and highly collectible lines of action figures and toys from sports, comic books, the Military, video games, horror, fantasy, Sci-Fi, music, television, and movies. McFarlane Toys was established in 1994, and currently is the fifth largest action figure manufacturer in the United States of America. www.spawn.com.

Medium Date (MD)

Refers to the size of the digits of the date on a coin.

Medium Letters (ML)

Refers to the size of the lettering of the date on a coin.

Melt

A slang term used to describe the intrinsic value of a particular numismatic item.

Mercury Dime

The common name for the "Winged Liberty Head" dime which was issued between 1916 and 1945.

Metal Stress Lines

Radial lines, sometimes visible, which result when the metal flows outward from the center of the planchet during the minting process.

MIB

An abbreviation for "Mint in Box." A box, containing a collectible, toy, or action figure, which has never been opened.

Mid-Spine

The section of the comic book's spine which is in between the staples.

Milling Mark

A mark which results when the reeded edge of one coin hits the surface of another coin.

MIMB

An abbreviation for "Mint in Mint Box." Similar to "MIB."

MIMP

An abbreviation for "Mint in Mint Package." Similar to "MIB."

Minimum Bid

The smallest amount that a buyer can bid.

MINMB

An abbreviation for "Mint In Near Mint Box."

MINMP

An abbreviation for "Mint in Near Mint Package."

Minor League Card

A sports trading card that features players and teams from the minor leagues.

Minor Variety

A coin that has a minor difference from other coins of the same design, type, date, and Mint.

Mint

An official coining facility of the United States Government.

Mint Bloom

The original luster still visible on a coin.

Mint Mark

A variation of the coinage term "Mintmark."

Mint Set

A set of Uncirculated Coins from a particular year comprising coins from each Mint.

Mint Set Toning

The colors and patterns Mint Coins have acquired from years of storage in the cardboard holders.

Mint State

Coins with numerical grades of "MS/PR-60" through "MS/PR-70." "Mint State" coins also represent business strike coins which have never been in circulation.

Mintage

The number of coins of a particular date struck at a given Mint during a particular year.

Mintmark

The tiny letter stamped into the die of a coin to denote the Mint at which a particular coin was struck.

MIP

An abbreviation for "Mint in Package." If applied to a box, or alternatively "Mint in Plastic," if applied to a carded figure.

MISB

An abbreviation for "Mint in Sealed Box." The box has never been opened, and the coin is considered the same as if it was just purchased from a store.

Miscut

A "Bindery Defect" where cover and/or pages are not cut square or are cut to the wrong size. Also known as "Mistrimmed."

Mis-Struck

Error coins which have striking irregularities.

Mishandled Proof

A "Proof" coin, which has been circulated and/or cleaned. If a proof is mishandled, the grade of a coin is reduced to below "MS/PR-60."

MISP

An abbreviation for "Mint in Sealed Package."

Missing Edge Lettering

A coin which does not display any of the intended design on the edge of the coin.

Miswrapped

A "Bindery Defect" where staple and fold do not intersect the center of the cover causing some of the back cover to appear on the front of the comic or front cover to "ride around" to the back.

MOC

An abbreviation for "Mint On Card." Used in the description of an action figure or toy's condition. If an action figure or toy is listed as "MOC," then, the item has never been unopened.

Model Products Corporation (MPC)

A subsidiary of General Mills which manufactured "Lionel Trains" between 1970 and 1973.

Modern Era of Toy Trains

All model and toy trains manufactured since 1970.

Mohair

The hair of the Angora goat used in the wigs of antique dolls.

Moisture Damage

The wrinkling and/or stains on a comic caused by absorption of a liquid.

Moisture Ring

The circular wrinkling and/or stain caused on the paper of a comic by absorption of moisture from the bottom of a cup or glass.

Molded Ears

Doll ears which are molded right onto a doll's head. The opposite of "Molded Ears" would be "Applied Ears."

MONMC

An abbreviation for "Mint on Near Mint Card."

MNB

An abbreviation for "Mint, No Box."

Morgan Dollar

The common name used for the Liberty Head silver dollar minted between 1878 and 1904. The "Morgan Dollar" was also minted in 1921.

Mother-of-Pearl

Refers to the iridescent lining of certain shells such as oyster or mussels used as a decorative inlay in furniture and other smaller decorative items.

Motto

An inscription or phrase on a numismatic item.

MS/PR-60

Refers to the "grade" or quality of a particular coin based on the "Professional Coin Grading Service (PCGS) Grades and Grading Terms" scale. This designation is for "Mint State" (the grade) and "60" (the numerical designation of which grade). "PR" also denotes "Proof." This is the lowest of the eleven Mint State grades which range from MS-60 through MS-70. An MS-60 coin will usually exhibit the maximum number of marks and/or hairlines. The luster may range from poor to full, but is usually on the "poor" side. Eye appeal is most likely minimal. See "Professional Coin Grading Service (PCGS) Grades and Grading Terms."

MS/PR-61

Refers to the "grade" or quality of a particular coin based on the "Professional Coin Grading Service (PCGS) Grades and Grading Terms" scale. This designation is for "Mint State" (the grade) and "61" (the numerical designation of which grade). "PR" also denotes "Proof." This grade meets the minimum requirements of Mint State plus includes some attributes not found on MS-60 coins. For instance, there may be slightly fewer marks than on an MS-60 coin, better luster, or less negative eye appeal. See "Professional Coin Grading Service (PCGS) Grades and Grading Terms."

MS/PR-62

Refers to the "grade" or quality of a particular coin based on the "Professional Coin Grading Service (PCGS) Grades and Grading Terms" scale. This designation is for "Mint State" (the grade) and "62" (the numerical designation of which grade). "PR" also denotes "Proof." This grade is nearly in the "choice" or MS-63 category, but there is usually one thing which keeps it from getting a higher grader. Expect to find excessive marks, an extremely poor strike or dark and unattractive toning. Some MS-62 coins will have clean surfaces and reasonably good eye appeal but exhibit many hairlines on the fields and devices. See "Professional Coin Grading Service (PCGS) Grades and Grading Terms."

MS/PR-63

Refers to the "grade" or quality of a particular coin based on the "Professional Coin Grading Service (PCGS) Grades and Grading Terms" scale. This designation is for "Mint State" (the grade) and "63" (the numerical designation of which grade). "PR" also denotes "Proof." The equivalent of "Choice" or "Choice BU" from the days before numerical grading was prevalent. This grade is usually found with clean fields and distracting marks or hairlines on the devices, or clean devices with distracting marks or hairlines in the fields. The strike and luster can range from mediocre to excellent. See "Professional Coin Grading Service (PCGS) Grades and Grading Terms."

MS/PR-64

Refers to the "grade" or quality of a particular coin based on the "Professional Coin Grading Service (PCGS) Grades and Grading Terms" scale. This designation is for "Mint State" (the grade) and "64" (the numerical designation of which grade). "PR" also denotes "Proof." This grade is also called "Borderline Gem" at times, as well as "Very Choice BU." There will be no more than a couple of significant marks or, possibly, a number of light abrasions. The overall visual impact of the coin will be positive. The strike will range from average to full and the luster breaks will be minimal. See "Professional Coin Grading Service (PCGS) Grades and Grading Terms."

MS/PR-65

Refers to the "grade" or quality of a particular coin based on the "Professional Coin Grading Service (PCGS) Grades and Grading Terms" scale. This designation is for "Mint State" (the grade) and "65" (the numerical designation of which grade). "PR" also denotes "Proof." This grade is also called "Gem" or "Gem Mint State" or "Gem BU." There may be scattered marks, hairlines or other defects, but they will be minor. Any spots on copper coins will also be minor. The coin must be well struck with positive (average or better) eye appeal. This is a NICE coin! See "Professional Coin Grading Service (PCGS) Grades and Grading Terms."

MS/PR-66

Refers to the "grade" or quality of a particular coin based on the "Professional Coin Grading Service (PCGS) Grades and Grading Terms" scale. This designation is for "Mint State" (the grade) and "66" (the numerical designation of which grade). "PR" also denotes "Proof." This is not only a Gem quality coin, but the eye appeal ranges from "above average" to "superb." The luster is usually far above average, and any toning cannot impede the luster in any significant way. This is an extra nice coin. See "Professional Coin Grading Service (PCGS) Grades and Grading Terms."

MS/PR-67

Refers to the "grade" or quality of a particular coin based on the "Professional Coin Grading Service (PCGS) Grades and Grading Terms" scale. This designation is for "Mint State" (the grade) and "67" (the numerical designation of which grade). "PR" also denotes "Proof." A superb quality coin! Any abrasions are extremely light and do not detract from the coin's beauty in any way. The strike is extremely sharp (or full) and the luster is outstanding. This is a spectacular coin! See "Professional Coin Grading Service (PCGS) Grades and Grading Terms."

MS/PR-68

Refers to the "grade" or quality of a particular coin based on the "Professional Coin Grading Service (PCGS) Grades and Grading Terms" scale. This designation is for "Mint State" (the grade) and "68" (the numerical designation of which grade). "PR" also denotes "Proof." A nearly perfect coin, with only minuscule imperfections visible to the naked eye. The strike will be exceptionally sharp and the luster will glow. This is an incredible coin. See "Professional Coin Grading Service (PCGS) Grades and Grading Terms."

MS/PR-69

Refers to the "grade" or quality of a particular coin based on the "Professional Coin Grading Service (PCGS) Grades and Grading Terms" scale. This designation is for "Mint State" (the grade) and "69" (the numerical designation of which grade). "PR" also denotes "Proof." Virtually perfect in all departments, including wondrous surfaces, a 99% full strike (or better), full unbroken radiant luster and show stopping eye appeal. You may have to study this coin with a 5X glass to find the reason why it didn't grade MS-70. See "Professional Coin Grading Service (PCGS) Grades and Grading Terms."

MS/PR-70

Refers to the "grade" or quality of a particular coin based on the "Professional Coin Grading

Service (PCGS) Grades and Grading Terms" scale. This designation is for "Mint State" (the grade) and "70" (the numerical designation of which grade). "PR" also denotes "Proof." A perfect coin! Even with 5X magnification there are no marks, hairlines or luster breaks in evidence. The luster is vibrant, the strike is razor sharp, and the eye appeal is the ultimate. Note Minor die polish and light die breaks are not considered to be defects on circulation strike coins. See "Professional Coin Grading Service (PCGS) Grades and Grading Terms."

Mule Error

This is a rare Mint error where the obverse die is of one coin and the reverse die is of another coin.

Muscle Car

American mid-size cars manufactured from 1964 to 1972 which were supplied with large, powerful V8 engines, super chargers, and special exhaust systems. The first true "muscle car" was the 1964 Pontiac GTO.

Mutilated

A term used to describe a coin which has been damaged to the point where it no longer can be graded.

Multiple Bindery Staples

A "Bindery Defect" in which the comic book is stapled additional times unnecessarily.

Multiple Reading Creases

Also known as "Reading Creases" on comic books.

Multi-Seller Auction

Properties owned by many sellers, offered through a common promotional campaign, are auctioned in a single event.

Mylar™

An inert, very hard, space-age plastic used to make high-quality protective bags and sleeves used for comic book storage.

N

Name Stamp

Indicates an ink stamp with someone's name, and sometimes someone's address, that has been stamped in or on the comic or comic book.

National Rifle Association (NRA) Standards of Condition for Grading Antique Firearms:

Excellent - All original parts; over 80% original finish; sharp lettering, numerals and design on metal and wood; unmarred wood; fine bore.

Factory New - All original parts, 100% original finish. Perfect condition in every aspect, inside and out.

Fair - Some major parts replaced; minor replacement parts may be required; metal rusted, may be lightly pitted all over, vigorously cleaned or re-blued; rounded edges of metal and wood; principal lettering, numerals and design on metal partly obliterated; wood scratched, bruised, cracked or repaired where broken; in fair working order or can be easily repaired and placed in working order.

Poor - Major and minor parts replaced, major replacement parts required and extensive restoration needed, metal deeply pitted, principal lettering, numerals and design obliterated, wood badly scratched, bruised, cracked or broken, mechanically inoperative, generally undesirable as a collectors firearm.

Fine - All original parts, over 30% original finish, sharp lettering, numerals and design on metal and wood, minor marks in wood, good bore.

Good - Some minor replacement parts; metal smoothly rusted or lightly pitted in places, cleaned or re-blued; principal letters, numerals and design on metal legible; wood refinished, scratched bruised or minor cracks repaired; in good working order.

Very Good - All original parts; none to 30% original finish; original metal surfaces smooth with all edges sharp; clear lettering, numerals and design on metal; wood slightly scratched or bruised; bore disregarded for collectors firearms.

National Rifle Association (NRA) Standards of Condition for Grading Modern Firearms:

Excellent - New condition, used but little, no noticeable marring of wood or metal, bluing perfect (except at muzzle or sharp edges).

Fair - In safe working condition, but well worn, perhaps requiring replacement of minor parts or adjustments, which should be indicated in advertisement; no rust, but may have corrosion pits which do render the gun unsafe or inoperable.

Good - In safe working condition, minor wear on working surfaces, no broken parts, no corrosion or pitting which will interfere with proper functioning.

New - Not previously sold at retail, in same condition as current factory production.

Perfect - In new condition in every respect.

Very Good - In perfect working condition, no appreciable wear on working surfaces, no corrosion or pitting, only minor surface dents or scratches.

New
A term for a numismatic item which never has been in circulation.

Nickel
See "Jefferson Nickel."

Nickel-Plating
The technique used for coating cast-iron or steel toys with molten nickel to prevent rusting and enhance appearance.

Nippon
A country of origin mark of Japan. The "Nippon" mark was used on exported porcelain items from Japan between 1891 and 1921.

NM
An abbreviation for "Near Mint."

No Arrows
Coins without arrows by their dates during years when other coins had arrows by the date.
No "CENTS" Nickel
"Liberty Head" or "V" nickels struck in 1883 without any sort of denomination engraved on the coin.
No Cover (NC)
A comic book with the cover missing. Also known as "Cover Missing."
No Date (ND)
This occurs when there is no date given on the cover or "Indicia" page.
No Grade
The term applies to a coin returned from a grading service which was not encapsulated due to a variety of reasons.
No Motto
Coins struck without the motto, "IN GOD WE TRUST."
No Number (NN)
Occurs when there is no number given on the cover or "Indicia" page.
Non-Paying Bidder
A bidder who does not pay for items they have won. Also known as a "Deadbeat Bidder."
Non-Sport Card
A trading card that pictures a topic other than sports such as movies, television, entertainers, and celebrities.
Notching
Indentations along the edge of a sports or non-sports trading card sometimes caused by a rubber band. "Notching" decreases a trading card's value.
NRFB
An abbreviation for "Never Removed From Box."
Numbered
(1) Collectibles which are "numbered," with lower serial numbers, within a specific edition, are considered more desirable to a collector. (2) A sports trading card whose print run is limited to a specific quantity, which is stamped or printed on the card itself. A trading card or collectible, which is stamped "25/1000," is read as "25 out of 1,000."
Numbered Print
A print which is part of a limited edition and has been numbered by hand. Also see "Numbered."
Numismatic Guaranty Corporation (NGC)
A third-party coin grading service based in Parsippany, New Jersey. www.ngccoin.com
Numismatic News
A weekly numismatic periodical which provides weekly reports on market trends and news concerning collectible United States coins and paper money,
established in 1952. www.numismaticnews.net
Numismatics
The science of money. Coins, paper money, tokens, and all related monetary items are included.

Numismatist
A person who collects coins, paper money (currency), tokens, and medals.

N.Y. Legis. Comm.
A shortened name for the New York Legislative Committee (NYLC) to study the publication of comics and comic books. The NYLC was founded in 1951 but no longer exists.

O

"O" Mint
Refers to coins struck and minted at the New Orleans, Louisiana. branch Mint. This Mint uses the "O" mintmark.

Oak
The more common name of several hundred trees and shrubs of the genus Quercus. Its durability lends itself well to furniture making. The wood color varies from light tan to deep leathery brown with black grain. Variations are due to differences in the soil and climate.

Obverse
(1) The front, or "heads side," of a coin. (2) The front of a trading card which displays the picture.

Off Center
A coin struck on a blank which was not properly centered over the anvil, or lower die.

Oil Stain
A defect in which oil has penetrated the cover and/or interior pages of a comic or comic book, causing them to become translucent in the area of the stain.

Oleographs
Chromolithographs printed on a textured surface. See "Chromolithographs."

On-Site Auction
An auction conducted on the premises of the property being sold.

One Sheet
A 27 x 41-inch poster usually printed on paper stock and usually folded. The "standard" movie advertising poster size in the United States.

One Shot
When only one issue is published of a comic book title, or when a series of comics are published where each issue carries a different title.

Open Head
A doll's head with the crown cut out so its eyes can be inserted.

Opening Bid
The first acceptable bid at an auction.

Orange Peel Surfaces
The dimple-textured fields seen on many "Proof" gold coins. The surfaces on these coins resemble the surface of an orange.

Origin
When the story of a comic book character's creation is introduced.

Original

A term used to describe a coin which never has been dipped, cleaned, or struck from original dies in the same year as the date it bears.

Original Art

A one-of-a-kind piece of art created by an artist. This term is commonly used to reflect items of art.

Original Property

A line of toys and characters developed in-house with no pre-existing outside support.

Original Roll

Coins in fixed quantities which are wrapped in paper and stored at the time of their issuance.

Original Rolls

Rolls of coins that have been together since the day they were removed from their storage bags.

Original Toning

The term used for the color acquired naturally by a coin which has never been cleaned or dipped.

Over Cover

A condition common in 1950s era comic books, where the cover extends approximately one-sixteenth (1/16) of an inch beyond its interior pages.

Over Mintmark

A coin struck with a die on which one mintmark is engraved over a different mintmark.

Over-Dipped

A coin which has become dull from too many baths in a dipping solution.

Overdate

A coin struck from a die with a date which has one year punched over a different year.

Oversized Cards

Any base, common, insert, or other trading cards not of standard or wide-vision size.

P

"P" Mint

Refers to coins struck and minted at the main United States Mint, located in Philadelphia, Pennsylvania. This Mint uses the "P" mintmark.

Packs

The original wrapper with base and insert cards within, often called 'wax packs', typically containing two to eight trading cards per pack.

Pages Missing

When one or more pages of a comic have been removed from a comic book.

Pages Out of Order (POOO)

A rare "Bindery Defect" in which the pages are bound together in the wrong order, causing the pages of a comic or comic book to become out of sequence.

Pages Trimmed

The top, bottom, and right hand edge of the comic book, or possibly some interior pages, have been trimmed with a paper cutter, hand blade, or pneumatic cutter to hide "Edge Defects."

Pages Upside Down
A rare "Bindery Defect" in which the cover orientation of a comic or comic book is reversed relative to the orientation of the interior pages.

Painted Cover
(1) The cover taken from an actual painting instead of a line drawing. (2) An inaccurate name for a grey-toned cover. Also known as a "Line Drawn Cover."

Painted Rug
Rugs which have been doctored with a permanent dye or other color to hide wear and tear.

Paneloligist
An individual whom researches comic books and/or comic strips.

Pannapictagraphist
Someone who collects comic books.

Paper Abrasion
A rough patch or area where the paper has been abraded on a rough surface, leaving a rough texture which is often faded.

Paper Cover
A comic book cover made from the same newsprint as the interior pages.

"Parade of Pleasure - A Study of Popular Iconography in the U.S.A."
A book about the censorship of comics. Published in 1954 by Geoffrey Wagner.

Parallel Cards
Usually a modification of the main set of base trading cards which contains extra foil stamping, or hologram stamping. Often seen one per pack up to one per 36 packs.

Parian
A doll made of unglazed bisque and finished without a wash of color.

Partial Edge Lettering
A coin which has at least one complete letter or star missing.

Patina
(1) A greenish coating on the surface of bronze or copper that develops with age. (2) The mellowing of age on any object or material due to exposure, handling, repeated waxing, or polishing. Also known as "Toning."

Pattern
A test striking of a coin produced to demonstrate a proposed design, size, or composition.

Pave
Stones or jewels set closely together so no metal is seen between the settings.

PCGS
An acronym for the "Professional Coin Grading Service."

Peace Dollar
The common name for silver dollars struck and minted between 1921 and 1935.

Pedigree (Coin)
A detailed and exhaustive listing of a coin's current owner plus all known previous owners of the same coin.

Pedigree or Pedigreed Collection
The status given to certain highly-publicized and usually high-grade comic book collections

and finds.

Penciller

The artist who creates the original line drawings used in a comic book.

Penny

Also known as a "Lincoln Head Cent."

Perfect Binding

A process whereby pages are glued into the cover of a comic or comic book as opposed to being stapled to the cover. Also called "square bound" or "square back."

Perforations

A small hole in the page margins of a comic which sometime occurs as part of the manufacturing process.

Period

An item or piece made at the time when its style first originated.

Peripheral Toning

Light, medium, or dark coloring around the edge of a coin.

Pewter

An alloy of tin and lead that produces a metal with a dull gray appearance. Used for tableware and other small objects copying silver forms. It was later replaced by chinaware.

PG

The abbreviation for "page."

Philadelphia Gum Co.

A major manufacturer of professional football trading cards in the 1960s.

Philatelist

A person who collects postage stamps.

Photo Cover

A comic book cover made from a photograph instead of a painting or line drawing. Also known as a "Line Drawn Cover."

Photomechanical Prints

Prints made from photographically prepared printing surfaces.

Photo Reactive Colors

Also known as "Photo Reactive Inks" on comic books.

Photo Reactive Inks

Certain inks used in the printing of comics which contain a higher proportion of metals, thus decreasing their stability and resistance to fading.

Pickle Smell

A description of the odor of ascetic acid, which is often associated with browning and/or brittle paper on a comic.

Pictorial Cover

See "Photo Cover."

Piedfort

Refers to French coins which were once made with the double thickness of regularly minted coins to signify double value.

Pioneer Gold

Privately issued gold coins struck and minted prior to 1861.

Plain Edge

A flat, smooth edge seen mainly on a small denomination coinage.

Planchet

The blank disk of metal before it is struck by a coining press transforming it into a coin.

Planchet Defects

Any abnormality found on a "Coin Blank."

Planchet Flaw

An irregular hole in a "Coin Blank."

Planchet Striations

Fine lines found on some "Proof" coins.

Plated

A coin to which a thin layer of metal has been applied.

Platinum

A precious metal sometimes used in the striking, manufacture, and minting of coins.

Platinum Age

The first age of comics, beginning in 1897.

Play Value

The features, accessories and/or interactivity a toy possesses for the best possible personal enjoyment while in use.

Playmates Toys

A popular maker of toys and action figures, established in 1966. Major properties include Teenage Mutant Ninja Turtles (TMNT), Terminator Salvation, Star Trek, Rainbow Brite, The Simpsons, Strawberry Shortcake, and Nickelodeon's iCarly. www.playmatestoys.com.

Plugged

A coin which has had a hole expertly filled which can only be analyzed and detected under magnification.

Pneumatic Cutter

An industrial tool used to cut large amounts of paper.

PNG Certificate

A certificate from the Professional Numismatists Guild (PNG) which guarantees the authenticity of a coin.

PO-1

Refers to the "grade" or quality of a particular coin based on the "Professional Coin Grading Service (PCGS) Grades and Grading Terms" scale. This designation is for "Poor" (the grade) and "1" (the numerical designation which means Poor). A coin of this grade is basically uncollectible due to its terrible condition, but coins of great rarity (such as an 1802 half dime) are still of considerable value and in demand in this grade. In order to "reach" this grade a coin must be identifiable as to date and type and not be horribly damaged (such as containing holes). See "Professional Coin Grading Service (PCGS) Grades and Grading Terms."

POC

An abbreviation for "Pencil on Cover" regarding comics.

Polished Die

A die which has been basined to remove clash marks or other die injury.

Polypropylene
A type of plastic used in the manufacture of comic book bags.

Polyvinyl Chloride (PVC)
A chemical used in coin "Flips" to make them more pliable.

Pop Top
A coin which scores the maximum number of points on the PCGS Set Registry.

Popped Staple
A term used to describe a condition where the comic book cover has split at the staple and has become detached or "popped loose."

Porcelain
A hard, translucent, white ceramic material. Porcelain created a sensation when it was first imported from the Far East into 17th century Europe due in part to the mystery surrounding its creation. It started an intense competition among European factories searching for the formula.

Porous
A description indicating a rough or granular surface. A "Porous" quality on a coin is typically seen on copper coins minted before 1816.

Portrait Doll
Bisque dolls of the late 1800s and early 1900s which represented a person.

Post-Code
Describes comics published after February, 1955 and usually displaying the CCA "stamp" in the upper right-hand corner.

Post-Golden Age
Comic books published between 1945 and 1950.

Post-Silver Age
Comic books published after 1969.

Pottery
Refers to all ceramic wares with the exclusion of porcelain.

Pre-Code
Describes comics published before the Comics Code Authority (CCA) came into effect in March, 1955.

Pre-Golden Age
Comic books published prior to Action Comics #1 in June, 1938.

Premium Quality (PQ)
A term applied to coins which are the best examples within a particular grade.

Presentation Copy
A copy of a printed item which is inscribed and signed by the author or publisher, and is provided as a gift.

Presentation Striking
A coin, often a "Proof" or an exceptionally sharp business strike, which is struck specially and given to an important person or dignitary.

Presidential $1 Coin
One of the United States of America's official dollar coins. The "Presidential $1 Coin

Program" was enacted by an Act of the United States Congress in 2005 (Public Law 109-145, 119 Stat. 2664, 2665, 2666, 2667, 2668, 2669, 2670, 2671, 2672, 2673, 2674 and 2675, 31 U.S.C. 5112 -- Presidential $1 Coin Act of 2005) to honor each American President. For a president to be honored on the coin, he/she must have been deceased for no less than two years. The first Presidential dollar coin was minted in 2007. This coin, like all other dollar coins, carries a value of one dollar, or one hundred cents. Each Presidential $1 Coin is identical in color that's found in the "Sacagawea dollar coin." http://www.usmint.gov/mint_programs/$1coin/

Pre-War

Model and toy trains manufactured until approximately 1942.

Press

Any of the various coining machines used in the minting process.

Preview

The specified time frame which is available for individuals to view, examine, and critique items offered at an auction.

Price

The asking 'quotation' for a particular numismatic item.

Price Guide

(1) A document, in either paper or electronic form, which lists the values of a particular collectible. *(2)* A periodical listing approximate prices for coins and various other numismatic items.

Price Realized

The final selling price of a particular item at an auction.

Price Stickers

Adhesive backed stickers applied to comic covers to alter the cover price.

Print Through

The printing on the inside of the front cover which is visible to varying degrees if one were "looking through" the front cover of a comic. Also known as a "Transparent Cover."

Printers Smudge

Also known as "Ink Smudge."

Prism Foil Cover

A special reflective foil material with three-dimensional repeated designs and special effects.

Pristine

A term applied to coins in original and unimpaired condition which are graded at MS/PR-67 or higher.

Private Auction

A seller may choose this option for their eBay auctions as a way of protecting the soon-to-be bidder's identification from the other bidders and visitors to that seller's eBay auction site.

Professional Coin Grading Service (PCGS)

Established in 1985, this was the first third party grading service to grade, encapsulate, and guarantee the authenticity for coins and other numismatic material. The PCGS is based in Newport Beach, California. www.pcgs.com.

Professional Numismatists Guild (PNG)

A dealer organization established in 1955. Membership in the Professional Numismatists

Guild is restricted by financial and longevity requirements. www.pngdealers.com.

Progressive Rolled Spine
The spine roll is more pronounced on one end than the other.

Promo Cards
Trading cards which are distributed, typically in advance, by the manufacturer to enhance sales.

Prototype
A type of action figure designed never to make it to final production or manufacture.

Proof (PR)
A coin usually struck from a specially prepared coin die on a specially prepared planchet.

Proof Dies
Specially prepared dies, often sandblasted or acid picked, which are used to strike "Proof" coins.

Prooflike (PL)
Term to designate a coin which has mirror like surfaces. The term especially applicable to Morgan dollars.

Proof-Of-Purchase (POP)
The white area which displays the bar code for a retail item.

Proof Only Issue
A coin struck only in "Proof."

Proof Set
A coin set containing "Proof" issues from particular year.

Provenance
(1) The documentation of the history of ownership of an item. If provenance can be verified during the authentication process of an antique, signed document, or painting, then the value of the item will increase. (2) The place of origin or earliest known history of an item.

Proxy Bid
The auctioneers who accept and perform the bidding on behalf of buyers who are unable to attend an auction. Buyers will inform the auction house personnel what the maximum amount they will bid for a particular item is and the auctioneers will bid on behalf of the buyers incrementally, going up to, but not above the buyer's stated maximum bid.

Prunt
A piece of decorative glass fused and applied to a larger piece of glass.

Pull
To find a specific card or type of trading card in a pack or box of sports cards.

Pulp
A cheaply produced magazine made from low-grade newsprint.

Punch
A steel rod with a device, lettering, date, star, or some other symbol on the end which was sunk into a working die by hammering on the opposite end of the rod.

Put Together Roll
A roll of coins included in a roll which is not an "Original Roll."

Puzzle Filled In
A game or puzzle which has been written on, thus reducing the value of the comic.

PVC Damage

A thin film left on a coin after its storage in flips containing Polyvinyl Chloride (PVC).

PVC Flip

Any of the various soft coin flips which contain Polyvinyl Chloride (PVC).

Q

"Qualified"

A label used by the Certified Guaranteed Company (CGC) which designates those comic books with a significant defect that needs specific description.

Quarter

See "Washington Quarter."

Quarter Eagle

A two and one half dollar gold coin (with a face value of $2.50).

Quarterly

A comic that's published four times a year.

Questionable Toning

The term used to describe the color on a coin which may not be its original color.

Quinone

The substance in ink which promotes oxidation and discoloration and is associated with transfer stains.

R

R

An abbreviation for a "Reprint" of a comic.

Rack Pack(s)

Factory packs of unwrapped trading cards, designed for retail peg-hanger sales.

Racketeer Nickel

This nickel is a gold-plated, 1883 No "CENTS" Liberty Head five cent coin ("V" nickel).

Rain Check

A request form offered by stores for items carried by the store but not available in existing stock. Also known as a "waiting list."

Rainbow Toning

The term used for the non-original color seen on silver dollars which are stored in bags.

Rare

(1) Indicates a coin within a series which is very difficult to find. (2) Denotes a comic with very limited numbers in existence; approximately 10-20 copies.

Rarity

The number of specimens existing of any particular numismatic item. The state or quality of being "rare."

Rarity Scale

A term referring to a numerical rating system.

Raw

(1) A numismatic item, usually a coin, which has not been encased by a grading service.

(2) A trading card which has not been graded or sealed in any type of permanent holder.

RBC

An abbreviation for "Right Side or Edge of Back Cover" on a comic book.

Readers Crease

A defect in the spine of a comic book caused by someone folding back the pages.

Reading Copy

A comic which is in fair-to-good condition and is often used for research. Also known as a "Research Copy."

Recessed Staples

Occur when the staple lateral bar penetrates below the plane of the cover of a comic without breaking through.

Recut Date

Also known as "Repunched Date."

Red (RD)

A copper coin which still retains 95% or more of its original Mint bloom or color.

Red Back

A trading card with a red back. Most common with trading cards of 1951 from "Topps" called the "Topps Red Back Set."

Red Brown (RB)

A copper coin which has from five percent to 95% of its original minting color.

Redbook

A yearly price guide that has been called the "bible" of printed numismatic retail price guides. This price guide was first issued in 1947.

Redemption Cards

Special trading cards which are mailed back to the card's manufacturer for the return of a special card or some other gift.

Reeded Edge

Term for the grooved notches on the edge of some coins.

Reeding Mark(s)

A mark, or marks, caused when the "Reeded Edge" of one coin comes in contact with the surface of another coin.

Regional Set

A sports trading card set issued only in a specific geographic area.

Reglossing

A comic book repair technique whereby silicone or other clear sprays or varnishes are applied to comic book covers in an attempt to restore cover ink reflectivity.

Regular Issue

Coins which are struck and minted for commerce.

Regular One Sheet
When a "One Sheet" poster with credits follows the release of an "Advance One Sheet" or "Teaser One Sheet."

Regular Strike
Denotes coins struck with normal coining methods on ordinarily prepared planchets. Also referred to as "Business Strike."

Re-Issue
A manufacturing process of re-producing or re-casting an action figure or toy from an existing mold and re-distributing it to retailers.

Relief
The height of the devices of a particular coin design.

Re-listing
The process of listing an item again if it did not sell initially.

Remainders
Comic books which "remain" unsold at the newsstand.

Repaint
A type of manufacturing process regarding the casting or repainting, of an existing item in a different color plastic in order to create a "new" action figure or toy.

Replica
A copy, or reproduction, of a particular item. Also see "Fake."

Reprint Comics
Comic books which contain newspaper strip reprints.

Reprint Poster
A poster which has been exactly duplicated in image, color, etc. though it may vary slightly in size from the original.

Reproduction Poster
When very old movie posters are reprinted. Also known as a "Reprint Poster."

Repunched Date
When a date on a coin was punched into the die and then punched in again at a different position.

Research Copy
Also known as "Reading Copy."

Reserve
The minimum price that a seller is willing to accept for an item to be sold at auction. Also known as the "Reserve Price."

Reserve Auction
An auction where the seller reserves the right to establish and implement a "Reserve Price." The seller at a "Reserve Auction" may opt to accept or decline any and/or all bids, or to withdraw the item up for auction at any time prior to the announcement of the completion of the auction.

Reserve Price
The minimum price an item will sell for, which is set by seller and/or auction house prior

to the start of the auction. If auction bidding does not reach the seller's required minimum price, the item will not be sold.

Resin

A plastic material which allows for fine detailing in collectible sculptures.

Restoration

A treatment which returns a collectible to a known or assumed state through the addition of non-original material for aesthetic enhancement.

Restored Copy

A comic book which has had restoration work.

Restrike

A coin struck later than indicated by its date, often with different dies.

Retail Cards

Trading cards, packs, boxes, and cases sold to the public, typically via large retail stores, such as K-Mart, Target, and Wal-Mart.

Retired

A piece which the manufacturer has decided to stop making.

Retoned

A coin which has been dipped or cleaned and then reacquires color, whether naturally or artificially.

Retool

An action figure whose design recycles many parts from a previously-released item but represents a new character or version of a character.

Reverse

(1) The back side of a coin. (2) The back side of a card.

Revival

A comic book character that becomes active after a period of dormancy.

Rice Paper

A thin, transparent paper commonly used by restorers to repair tears and replace small pieces on covers and pages of comic books.

Riddler

A machine used by minting facilities which screens out planchets of the wrong size and shape. This procedure is completed prior to striking.

Rim

The raised area around the edges of the obverse and reverse of a coin.

Rim Nick

The term for a mark or indentation on the rim of a coin or other metallic numismatic item.

Ring Test

A test used to determine whether a coin is struck, is an electrotype, or is a cast copy.

Rip

A numismatic item purchased for an amount considerably below the price for which it can be resold.

Roll

A set number of coins "rolled up" in a coin wrapper.

Roll Friction

Minor displacement of metal, mainly on the high points, seen on coins stored in rolls.

Rolled Edge
Also known as a "Rim."

Rolled Edge Ten
Also known as the "Indian Head Eagle" coin, which was struck and minted as a regular issue coin with a mintage of only 31,550 units.

Rolled Spine
A condition where the left edge of a comic book curves toward the front or back. Also see "Progressive Rolled Spine."

Roller Marks
A term to describe the mostly parallel incuse lines seen on some coins after striking.

Roman Finish
An experimental "Proof" surface used mainly on United States gold coins between 1909 and 1910.

Rookie Card (RC)
The first sports trading card produced of a player or athlete which is a part of a nationally distributed, fully licensed sports card trading set.

Roosevelt Dime
The United States of America's official ten-cent coin picturing President Theodore Roosevelt. The Roosevelt dime was first minted in 1946 and carries a value of ten cents, or ten one-hundredths (10/100) of a dollar. Also known as a "Dime."

Rosette
A circular-shaped, floral ornament.

Rotisserie Restoration
When someone totally dissembles a car and the body is, then, taken off the vehicle's frame. The body of the vehicle is then placed on a rotisserie, which can be turned to show any area on the car.

Roundel
A circular ornament, which may or may not incorporate some applied or inlaid decorative moulding or carving.

RT
The abbreviation for "right."

Rub
The slight wear and tear on a coin.

Rust Migration
When rust stains have moved from the staples in a comic to the paper.

Rust Stain
(1) A red brown stain caused by a comic's proximity to a rusty object. (2) A stain associated with rusty staples.

Rusty Staples
Staples which have oxidized through over-exposure to moisture in the air.

S

"S" Mint
Refers to coins struck and minted at the San Francisco, California branch Mint. This Mint uses the "S" mintmark.

Sac
See "Sacagawea Dollar."

Sacagawea Dollar
One of the United States of America's official dollar coins picturing a Shoshone woman named Sacagawea. The Sacagawea dollar coin was first minted in 2000 and carries a value of one dollar, or one hundred cents. The Sacagawea dollar coin consists of a gold tone or color. Also called a "Sac."

Saint
A slang term used to describe the Saint Gaudens-inspired Double Eagle which was struck and minted between 1907 and 1933.

Saint Gaudens
Refers to the name of Augustus Saint Gaudens. The Saint Gaudens coin is also known as the "Liberty Head Double Eagle" or "Saint."

Satin Finish
An experimental "Proof" surface used on United States gold coins after 1907.

Satin Luster
A fine, silky luster seen on many business strike coins.

Satinwood
A pale yellowish West Indian wood with a satin finish that first gained popularity in Britain in the late 18th century, replacing mahogany for small scale furniture. Due to its rarity and cost it is typically reserved for veneer and inlays.

Scale
The size of a collectible, relative to its prototype.

Scraped Staple
A staple which has had rust or other discoloration removed by scraping the surface.

Screw Press
The first type of coining press used at the United States Mint.

Sea Salvage Coin
A coin which has been retrieved from the ocean, usually from a shipwreck.

Sealed Bid
An auction method where confidential bids are submitted, and are to be opened at a predetermined place and time.

Seated Coinage
A term commonly used for the Liberty Seated coinage.

Second Toning
Any toning which occurs after a coin is dipped or cleaned.

Second-Year Card
The card of a player for that player's second year in his or her professional sport.

Secondary Market
Collectibles, or items, sold by private collectors.

Seller
The person, business, or governmental entity which has legal ownership of any interests, benefits, or rights inherent to the real or personal property.

Semi-Exclusive
Collectibles similar to exclusives, but often offered to more than one store.

Semi-Mechanical Bank
A toy bank that performs a mechanical function, but is independent of coin activation.

Semi-Monthly
A comic which is published twice a month.

Semi-Numismatic
A term which indicates whether a coin has a significant bullion value or some other numismatic value.

Semi-Prooflike
A term used to describe a coin which has some mirror-like surface qualities, mixed with a satin or frosty luster.

Set
(1) A complete run of a given comic book title. (2) A grouping of comics for sale. (3) A collection of coins in a particular series.

Set Registry
The listing of registered Professional Coin Grading Service (PCGS) graded sets of coins.

Shallow Staple
A staple which has not penetrated all of the pages and is not visible at the centerfold. Also see "Deformed Staple."

Shield
The emblem used on certain issues which has horizontal and vertical lines in a shield shape.

Shield Nickel
The common name for the Shield five cent coin which was struck between 1866 and 1883.

Shilling
Auction bids made to artificially raise the price of an item by the seller or persons not intending to purchase the item.

Shiny Spots
The areas on Matte, Roman, and Satin Proof coins where the surface has been disturbed.

Short Print (SP)
A sports trading card which is printed in a smaller quantity than other cards in its set or subset.

Shortpack
An action figure included in a pack in limited quantities and there are less per case of this one item than the rest of its companions. Shortpacking causes "YDD Syndrome." Opposite of a "Heavypack."

Shotgun Rolls
(1) Rolls of coins which contain double the normal amount of coins in a roll. (2) Paper-wrapped rolls which are machine crimped.

Shoulder Head
A doll's head and shoulders molded together in one piece.

Shoulder Plate
A doll's shoulder portion of a "shoulder head."

Siamese Pages
A "Bindery Defect" in which pages are "trimmed long" and are not separated at right-hand corners or along the right edge. Also known as "Joined Pages" or "Bound Short."

"Sig" or "Sigs"
Short for "signature."

Sight Seen
A term to indicate when a buyer of a particular coin or numismatic item in a particular grade, wants to view the coin before he/she buys the item.

Sight Unseen
A term used to indicate when the buyer of a particular coin or numismatic item in a particular grade, will pay a certain price without examining the item.

Signature Duplicated
A rare "Bindery Defect" in which a group of comic book pages are inadvertently duplicated.

Signature Out Of Order
A rare "Bindery Defect" in which signatures of comic book pages are bound in the wrong sequence. For example; a 32-page comic book with this defect usually has pages in the following order: 9, 16, 1, 8, 25, 32, 17, and 24.

Signature Reversed
A rare "Bindery Defect" of comics in which the orientation of one of the signatures is reversed and appears upside down and backwards.

Signed Edition
A book which the author has personally signed.

Signed-In-The-Presence
An autograph that was signed in the presence of the seller or a representative of a third party authentication service.

Silver
A term to indicate coins struck mostly with silver metals. Silver coins usually consist of 90% silver.

Silver Age (S.A.)
(1) The period of time in comic book history between the late-1950s and early-1960s characterized by the re-birth of 1940s era comic book heroes. (2) September-October, 1956 (Showcase #4) through 1969. (3) 1955 through 1969.

Silver Commemoratives
A particular type of coin struck and minted between 1892 and 1954. "Commemorative Coins" are struck and minted to honor a person, place, or event, as well as to raise funds for activities related to a particular theme.

Silver Dollar

A coin with a face value of one dollar which has a silver and copper composition.

Silver Nickel

Also known as a "Wartime Nickel."

Silver Plug

On some early American coins, a silver plug was inserted into a hole in the center of the coin to add weight or value to the coin and to bring it into proper specifications for that time period.

Silver Proof

A black and white (B&W) actual size print on thick glossy paper hand painted by an artist to indicate colors to the engraver.

Single Signed Ball

Baseballs which have been autographed by only one player.

Sizing

The glaze applied to newsprint at the end of the manufacturing process.

Sketch Cards

Insert trading cards which feature near-one-of-a-kind artists' sketches.

Skirt Lines

The lines representing the folds on Miss Liberty's flowing gown on Walking Liberty half dollars.

Slab

Also known as the holder in which a coin is encased by a grading service.

Slabbed

The process of sending a coin to a third party grading service to have it authenticated, graded, and encased in a properly sealed holder.

Sleep Eyes

A doll's eyes that open when the doll is in an upright position and close when the doll is laid down.

Slick Cover

Any comic book cover made from a clay-coated paper stock.

Slider

A term used to describe an "AU" coin which can be sold as "Uncirculated."

Slug

A slang term used to describe the octagonal and round fifty dollar gold coins struck during the California gold rush.

Small Cent

Cents of a reduced size which replaced the "Large Cent" in 1857.

Small Date (SD)

The small size of the digits of the date on a coin.

Small Letters (SL)

The small size of the lettering of the date on a coin.

Small Motto (SM)

The common name for the particular variety of two cent coin of 1864 which included small letters in the "Motto."

Small Size
A term which refers to the particular diameter of a coin in a series.

Smoke Damage
A grey or black discoloration of a comic which is caused by smoke.

Sniperware
A computer program used to strategically outbid other auction participants at the last possible moment of an online auction so the individual using the sniperware program eventually becomes the auction winner.

Sniping
The practice of bidding at the very last moment before an online auction ends which results in the individual doing the sniping becoming the auction winner. Sniping can be done manually, or through the use of computer software programs called "Sniperware."

Soft Sleeve
A thin, transparent plastic holder used to protect a single sports trading card from smudges, spills, and anything which could damage the card.

Spare
A derogatory slang term used to describe any undesirable sports trading card, especially a "Rookie Card," memorabilia card, or autograph of an athlete who is not a top name in his/her sport.

Spark Erosion Die
A die of a coin made by an electrolytic deposition method.

Spark Erosion Strike
A coin made from spark erosion dies.

Specimen/Specimen Strike (SP)
The term used to indicate special coins struck at the Mint from between 1792 and 1816.

Spine
The left-hand edge of the comic which will not open.

Spine Chip
A small piece missing from the area of the spine of a comic book.

Spine Roll
A defect of a comic book caused by improper storage which results in uneven pages and the bowing of the spine.

Spine Split
An even separation at the spine fold of a comic, commonly above or below the staple. Also known as "Split Spine."

Spine Stress
A small fold on a comic book, usually less than a quarter-inch (1/4) in length. A "Spine Stress" is perpendicular to the spine of a comic.

Splash Panel
(1) The first panel of a comic book story, usually larger than other panels and usually containing the title of the story. (2) An oversized interior panel.

Splotchy Toning
The color of a coin which is uneven in both composition and shade.

Spoofing

The unethical act of sending an email which is sent to trick the email recipient into thinking the email is coming from a legitimate email address.

Standard Silver

The official composition of United States silver coinage which was set by the United States Mint Act of 1792.

Standing Liberty

A coin design with "Miss Liberty" in an upright, front facing position.

Standing Liberty Quarter

The common name of a quarter dollar struck and minted between 1917 and 1930.

Staple Extenders

(1) The portion of the staple on a comic book which actually penetrates the paper and can be seen at the centerfold. (2) The portion of the staple which is bent either upwards or downwards towards center of staple.

Staple Hole

A punched out area in cover and interior pages of a comic caused by staple extender.

Staple Lateral Bar

The portion of the staple which does not penetrate the comic book paper and lies on top of the cover parallel to the spine.

Staple Page

Used by early comic book collectors to describe the centerfold of a comic.

Staple Rust Migration

Rust stains which have moved from the staple to the paper of a comic book.

Staple Scratch

A specific line or mark on a coin which results from the improper removal from a 2 x 2-inch cardboard coin holder.

Staple Tear

Indicates paper separation where the staple resides in a comic.

Staple Popped

When a staple has "popped" loose from the cover of a comic.

Star

A term for the five pointed and six pointed symbols used on many United States coins.

State Quarters Program

Specific "Washington Quarters" struck with unique reverse designs for each state, issued in the order of admittance to the United States of America. All 50 State quarters were issued from 1999-2008.

Steel Cent

The common name for cents which were struck in steel and plated in Zinc. Steel cents were struck and issued in 1943 and 1944.

Steelies

A slang term used to describe 1943 steel cents.

Sterling

The term used to describe the standard metal mix in the United States and England which is 92.5% silver and 7.5% copper or another metal.

Sticker on Cover

A price sticker or other sticker attached to cover of a comic.

Still Bank

A toy bank with no moving parts.

Stock Edge

A counterfeit edge collar used for various dated fake coins.

Stoneware

A heavy, nonporous, opaque pottery that is fired at a high temperature. It originated in China and was exported to Europe in the 17th century where it was imitated by many factories in Germany, England and the Netherlands.

Store Stamp

The store name, store address, and store telephone number which is stamped in ink via rubber stamp and stamp pad on some comic books.

Stress Lines

Very light, tiny wrinkles occurring along, and projecting from, the spine of a comic.

Stretcher

A stabilizing rail that runs horizontally between furniture legs.

Striations

The term for the incuse polish lines on the die which result in raised lines on coins.

Strike

The act of minting a coin.

Strip

The flat metal, rolled to proper thickness, from which planchets are cut.

Struck

A term used to describe a coin produced from dies and a coining press.

Struck Copy

A replica of a particular coin made from dies not necessarily meant to deceive.

Struck Counterfeit

A fake coin produced from false dies.

Style Period

The furniture fashionable in a particular time period.

Subscription Center Crease

A large crease found down the center of a comic book which is caused by the folding of a comic book for mailing.

Subscription Copy

A comic which is sent through the mail direct from the publisher or publisher's agent.

Successful Bidder

The buyer of a particular lot from an auction.

Surface

Coating on the image of a baseball card, as well as, but to a lesser degree the printing on the back of the card.

Surface Preservation

The condition of the surface of a coin.

Surfaces
The entire obverse and reverse of a coin.

Susan B. Anthony Dollar
One of the United States of America's official dollar coins picturing woman's suffrage campaigner Susan B. Anthony. The Susan B. Anthony dollar coin was minted from 1979-1981 and once again in 1999. This coin carries a value of one dollar, or one hundred cents.

Swatch Cards
Insert trading cards which feature a mounted swatch of cloth, such as from a sports player's jersey or an actor's screen-used costume.

Sweating
A procedure in which coins are placed in a bag and shaken vigorously to dislodge or knock off small pieces of metal.

Swipe
New content borrowed from previously published material.

T

Tab Toning
The toning often seen on commemorative coins which were sold in cardboard holders with a round tab.

Tall Chest
A one-part case piece with five, six, or seven layers of drawers.

Tanning Line
A brownish stain line of tannin which occurs when wet comic paper dries.

Tape Residue
The adhesive substance from cellophane tape which has penetrated paper fibers.

Target Toning
Coins with circles of color, deeper colors on the periphery often fading to white or cream color at the center.

Tax Sale
The public sale of an individual's personal property at an auction initiated by governmental authority due to nonpayment of that person's property taxes.

Teaser One Sheet
Also known as an "Advance One Sheet" poster.

Tear Sealed
A tear which has been glued together.

Teddy's Coin
Also known as the "1907 Indian Head Double Eagle."

Telephone Auction Bids
Bids which are placed over the telephone, during a sale of coins.

Ten
A slang term used to describe an eagle or ten dollar gold coin.

Ten Indian

Also known as an "Indian Head Eagle."

Ten Lib

Also known as a "Liberty Head Eagle."

Tensor Light

A small, direct light source used by many numismatists to examine and grade coins.

Terms and Conditions

The printed rules of an auction house which are read and/or distributed to potential bidders prior to an auction.

Territorial Gold

Coins and bars privately struck during the various gold rushes.

Text Page

A comic page with no panels or drawings, text only.

Text Story

A story with a limited amount of illustrations. A text story may not include any illustrations.

The Numismatist

A monthly publication of the American Numismatic Association (ANA).

Three Cent Nickel

A nickel three cent coin with Liberty Head design. This coin was struck from 1865-1889.

Three Cent Silver

A three cent coin with a star design.

Thumbed

A coin which has been doctored in a specific way to cover coin flaws, marks, or hairlines.

Tie Bids

When two or more bidders bid exactly the same amount at the same time. When this occurs, the auctioneer must resolve the situation.

Tiffany Set

A high end set of cards issued by "Topps."

Tins

A factory metal can, typically filled with trading cards or packs, often with inserts.

Tintype

A photograph made by creating a direct positive on a sheet of iron metal that is blackened by painting, lacquering, or enameling. Tintype evolved from the ambrotype process, except that it was produced on iron rather than glass. The iron negatives were coated with black paint or lacquer. Tintypes were extremely popular during the Civil War Period and thousands were produced because they could be safely sent by mail. By the 1950s, tintypes were replaced by another instant photographic method, the Polaroid. Also see "Ambrotype."

Tissue Toning

Color, often vibrant, acquired by coins stored in original Mint paper.

Tobacco Card

Cards from the early-1900s which were issued with tobacco products.

TOBC

The abbreviation for "Top of Back Cover."

TOFC

The abbreviation for "Top of Front Cover."

Token

A replacement for a coin. For example, bus tokens and phone tokens can be used in place of actual coinage.

Toning

The color seen on many coins.

Tooling Mark

A small and fine line which is found on both authentic and counterfeit coins.

Top Loader

A plastic holder used to protect a single sports or trading card from bending, tearing, as well as from edge and corner damage.

Topps Company Inc.

One of the most famous of all sports and entertainment trading card manufacturers. Also known for their manufacturing of confections, stickers, and strategy games. Founded in 1938, Topps also manufactures the popular lollipop brands marketed as Ring Pops, Push Pops, Baby Bottle Pops, and other novelty candy and gum products. www.topps.com

TOS

(1) An abbreviation for "Tape on Spine." (2) An abbreviation for "Tales of Suspense."

Trade Dollar

A United States silver coin which is slightly heavier than the regular silver dollar. A "Trade Dollar" is specifically intended to promote trade in the Far East.

Transfer Die

A die created by relinquishing a coin for a model.

Transfer Stain

The ink from the first page of a comic which rubs off onto the inside front cover causing certain portions to appear to have a yellow color.

Transitional Issue

A coin struck after a specific coin series ends.

Transparent Cover

The printing on the inside front cover of a comic which is visible to varying degrees from the front cover. Also see "Print Through."

Treasure Coin

A coin which comes from a shipwreck, buried, or hidden source.

Trigate

A political item, such as a button or pin, which includes three images. A trigate pin may have the presidential and vice-presidential candidates, as well as the candidates party symbol or flags, pictured. Trigate images are also found on various forms of political campaign items such as postcards, pennants, and posters. Similar to a "Jugate" item.

Tri-Logo

Refers to the logo of a toy line which appears in three different languages on the toy's packaging.

Triple Struck

The condition which results when a coin is not ejected from the dies and is struck three times.

Troy Weight
A method of weighing gold and silver and the coins made from those metals.

Trustee's Sale
A sale at an auction held by a trustee.

Tudor
The "Style Period" in England from 1485-1600.

Twenty Lib
Also known as a "Liberty Head Double Eagle" or "twenty dollar gold coin."

Two and a Half
Also known as a "Quarter Eagle" or "two and one half dollar gold coin."

Two Cent Piece
Also known as a "Shield two cent coin."

Type One Gold Dollar
Also known as a "Liberty Head design gold dollar."

Type One Nickel
Also known as a "Jefferson Head five cent coin."

Type One Quarter
Also known as a "Standing Liberty quarter."

Type One Twenty
Also known as a "Liberty Head Double Eagle."

Type Three
Any coin from the third Type within a series.

Type Three Gold Dollar
Also known as a "Small Indian Head designed coin."

Type Three Twenty
Also known as a "Liberty Head double eagle."

Type Two
A coin from the second Type within a series.

Type Two Buffalo
Another name or term for an "Indian Head nickel with the reverse buffalo on level ground."

Type Two Gold Dollar
Also known as a "Large Indian Head design gold dollar."

Type Two Nickel
Also known as a "Jefferson Nickel."

Type Two Quarter
Also known as a "Standing Liberty quarter."

Type Two Twenty
Also known as a "Liberty Head Double Eagle."

U

ULBC
The abbreviation for "Upper Left Corner of Back Cover" on a comic.

ULFC
The abbreviation for a comic book's "Upper Left Corner of Front Cover."

Ultra High Relief
Another name or term for an "Extremely High Relief" design on a coin.

Ultra Rarity
A coin or other numismatic item which is represented by only a few examples.

Uncirculated (Unc)
(1) A coin or numismatic item which has never been in circulation. (2) A coin without wear.

Uncut Sheets
Sheets of uncut base, insert, promo, or other cards.

Underglaze
Any porcelain or china decoration which is applied under, rather than over, its glazed finish.

Unreleased Cards
Trading cards printed by the manufacturer, but not officially distributed for a variety of reasons.

Upholder
A term used to describe an upholsterer in the 18th century.

Upper Deck, The
A major sports trading card manufacturer, founded in 1989. The Upper Deck manufactures cards from each of the four major professional American sports: football, basketball, baseball, and hockey. www.upperdeck.com.

Upsetting Mill
The machine which raises the outer rim on a planchet prior to striking.

URBC
The abbreviation for a comic book's "Upper Right Corner of Back Cover."

URFC
The abbreviation for a comic book's "Upper Right Corner of Front Cover."

V

"V" nickel
Also known as a "Liberty Head five cent coin."

Variant Cover
Refers to instances when a different cover image is used on the same issue of a comic title.

Vending Box
A box of trading cards, usually in quantities of 500, which were originally issued by the manufacturer for use in vending machines.

Vendor
The person or company actually selling an item.

Veneer

A furniture making process in which a thin layer of a more beautiful or valuable wood is affixed to a more inferior wood base.

Verifier

A grader at PCGS whom looks at graded coins and makes the decision whether the grade indicated is the proper one.

Very Fine

The term corresponds to the grades of a coin rated "VF-20," "VF-25," "VF-30," and "VF-35" on the "Professional Coin Grading Service (PCGS) Grades and Grading Terms" scale. This has the broadest range of any circulated grade, with nearly full detail on some "VF-35" coins and less than half on some "VF-20" specimens. See "Professional Coin Grading Service (PCGS) Grades and Grading Terms."

Very Good

The term corresponding to the grades of a coin rated "VG-8" and "VG-10" on the "Professional Coin Grading Service (PCGS) Grades and Grading Terms" scale. In these grades, a coin has slightly more detail than in "Good" condition. See "Professional Coin Grading Service (PCGS) Grades and Grading Terms."

Very Rare

When only one to ten copies of a comic are estimated to be in existence.

Vexillologist

Someone who studies and collects flags.

VF-20

Refers to the "grade" or quality of a particular coin based on the "Professional Coin Grading Service (PCGS) Grades and Grading Terms" scale. This designation is for "Very Fine" (the grade) and "20" (the numerical designation of the grade). Wing feathers show most of their detail, lettering is readable but sometimes indistinct and some minor detail is sometimes separate but usually blended. See "Professional Coin Grading Service (PCGS) Grades and Grading Terms."

VF-25

Refers to the "grade" or quality of a particular coin based on the "Professional Coin Grading Service (PCGS) Grades and Grading Terms" scale. This designation is for "Very Fine" (the grade) and "25" (the numerical designation of the grade). In this grade about 60% of the original detail is evident, with the major devices being clear and distinct. See "Professional Coin Grading Service (PCGS) Grades and Grading Terms."

VF-30

Refers to the "grade" or quality of a particular coin based on the "Professional Coin Grading Service (PCGS) Grades and Grading Terms" scale. This designation is for "Very Fine" (the grade) and "30" (the numerical designation of the grade). The devices are sharp with only a small amount of blending. Up to 75% of the original detail is evident. See "Professional Coin Grading Service (PCGS) Grades and Grading Terms."

VF-35

Refers to the "grade" or quality of a particular coin based on the "Professional Coin Grading Service (PCGS) Grades and Grading Terms" scale. This designation is for "Very Fine" (the grade) and "35" (the numerical designation of the grade). This grade used to be called VF/EF (or VF/XF) before numerical grading was accepted throughout the hobby. Devices are sharp and clear and up to 80% of the detail is in evidence. See "Professional Coin Grading Service (PCGS) Grades and Grading Terms."

VG-8

Refers to the "grade" or quality of a particular coin based on the "Professional Coin Grading Service (PCGS) Grades and Grading Terms" scale. This designation is for "Very Good" (the grade) and "8" (the numerical designation of the grade). A slight amount of design detail is still showing on the coin, such as a couple of letters in the word "LIBERTY." See "Professional Coin Grading Service (PCGS) Grades and Grading Terms."

VG-10

Refers to the "grade" or quality of a particular coin based on the "Professional Coin Grading Service (PCGS) Grades and Grading Terms" scale. This designation is for "Very Good" (the grade) and "10" (the numerical designation of the grade). A higher grade (less worn) than the VG-8 coin. Design detail is still heavily worn but the major devices and lettering are clear. See "Professional Coin Grading Service (PCGS) Grades and Grading Terms."

VHTF

An abbreviation for "Very Hard to Find."

Video Game Authority (VGA)

Professional grading agency which verifies, authenticates, and certifies Atari 2600/5200/7800, Gameboy, Gameboy Advanced, Gameboy Color, Game Cube, N64, NES, PlayStation, PlayStation 2 (PS2), PlayStation 3 (PS3), Sega Genesis, Sega Master System, Sega Saturn, SNES, Virtual Boy, Wii, XBox, and XBox 360 games, systems, and accessories. Video games from other game systems may also be graded with the VGA. www.vggrader.com.

Vinegar Smell

The effect which occurs when the smell of acetic acid in newsprint starts deteriorating.

Vintage Cars

Cars manufactured between 1915 and 1942.

Vintage Cards

Cards issued prior to 1979. Most commonly between 1930 and 1973.

Voice Box

A mechanism used in a doll to make a doll "speak" or make sounds.

W

Walker

Also known as a "Walking Liberty half dollar."

Walking Liberty

Also known as a "Walking Liberty half dollar."

Walking Liberty Half Dollar

A particular type of half dollars which were struck between 1916 and 1947.

Watch-List

A list of auctions in which someone is interested.

Wartime Nickel

A specific type of five cent coin which was struck during World War II.

Washington Quarter

The United States of America's official twenty-five cent coin picturing President George Washington. The Washington quarter was first minted in 1932 and carries a value of twenty-five cents, or twenty-five one-hundredths (25/100) of a dollar. Also known as a "Quarter."

Watermark

A design which is embossed into an item, usually paper, during its production and is used for identification of the paper and papermaker. A watermark can be seen when the paper is held up directly to a light. Many times currency (paper money) will have a watermark embossed on each bill to prove that the item is authentic and not counterfeited.

Watery Look

A look seen on the surfaces of most close collar "Proof" coins.

Wax

A universal collecting term for factory-sealed packs or boxes.

Wax Pack

An unopened pack of cards, named for its traditional form of wax packaging.

Weak Edge Lettering

Indicates the edge lettering has a portion of a letter, star, or inscription missing.

Weak Strike

A coin which does not show intended detail because of improper striking pressure or improperly aligned dies.

White Label

A promotional vinyl record pressing with a completely blank label denoting it is only a promotional record. This type of record may also have unique black on white printed labels with only the artist and title information, or "A" and "B" symbols on the record.

White Pages

A term used to describe interior pages in the best state of preservation.

Whiteness or Whiteness Level

The whiteness of interior pages of a comic compared against a whiteness grading standard.

Whizzing

The term used to describe the process of mechanically moving the metal of a lightly circulated coin to simulate luster.

Wind-Ups

Describes clockwork and spring-driven toys.

Wire Edge

The thin, knife-like projection seen on some coin rims, created when metal flows between the collar and the dies.

Wire Edge Eagle

Refers to the 1907 Indian Head Eagle. Only 500 coins of this type were struck.

Wonder Coin

A slang term used to describe a coin that's condition is superb.

Working Die

A die prepared from a working hub used to strike coins.

Working Hub
A hub created from a master die used to create the many working dies required for coinage.

Worm Hole
The small holes eaten into comic paper caused by a variety of termites, insects, mites and worms.

Worn Die
The die of a coin which has lost detail from extended use.

Wrappers
The original trading card pack cover, often with collectible variations.

Wreath Cent
A slang term used to describe a second large cent "Type," coin which was struck in 1793.

X

X-Over
See "Crossover."

Xylonite
An early and rare form of plastic invented in 1868 which was created to simulate wood.

Y

Yankee Auction
An auction with multiple bids up for sale, in which the winner pays the actual price bid.

Yatate
A Japanese brush and ink holder which resembles an antique fountain pen.

Z

Zar
A unit of measurement used in carpet-making between one yard and one meter in length.

Zoëtrope
A large revolving cylinder which produces an illusion of action from a rapid succession of static pictures. Used in early animation.

Lisa M. Barnes & Associates Art Consultancy & Appraisal Service, LLC

4205 West Anthem Way, Ste. 109
Phoenix, AZ 85086
Bus........... (623) 582-4500
Fax........... (623) 582-4505
lisa@rareart.net www.rareart.net

Biography:

Lisa M. Barnes is a successful and innovative founder of a highly respected international art consultancy. Over the past twenty-two years she has appraised both personal property and fine art for private and public collections and government institutions. She has extensive experience in expert testimony and mediation. Ms. Barnes has planned, developed, appraised and curated art collections for numerous corporate and private collectors. She has in-depth education and training in all facets of art history, appraisals, conservation and framing installation.

Ms. Barnes' comprehensive education includes attending Harvard University; Oxford University; the Louvre, the Jeu de Paume in Paris; and the British Institute in Florence Italy. Ms. Barnes has diplomas from Sotheby's, Christie's, and the New Academy of Art – all in London. She has attended courses at NYU and the Smithsonian in appraisal studies.

Credentials:

- American Assoc. of Appraisers. ISA, ASA
- Personal property/fine art specialist, USPAP
- Member: National Association of Auctioneers
- Member: Women in the Arts, Washington, DC
- Graduate of Southeastern School of Auctioneers
- Appraisal consultant, umpire, expert witness
- Expert witness in Superior Court, Phoenix, AZ
- Member: Forensic Expert Witness Association
- Expert in art and antiques, memorabilia, photography
- Insurance and third party loss, damage
- Estate trust/ probate violations